Gendering Minorities

Gendering Minorities

Muslim Women and the Politics of Modernity

Sherin B. S.

With a Foreword by
Susie Tharu

Orient BlackSwan

GENDERING MINORITIES: MUSLIM WOMEN AND THE POLITICS OF MODERNITY

ORIENT BLACKSWAN PRIVATE LIMITED

Registered Office
3-6-752 Himayatnagar, Hyderabad 500 029, Telangana, India
e-mail: centraloffice@orientblackswan.com

Other Offices
Bengaluru, Chennai, Guwahati, Hyderabad, Kolkata,
Mumbai, New Delhi, Noida, Patna

© Orient Blackswan Pvt. Ltd 2021
First Published by Orient Blackswan Pvt. Ltd 2021
Reprinted 2021, 2022, 2023

ISBN 978-93-5287-669-3

Typeset in Minion Pro 11/13.6 by
Jojy Philip, New Delhi 110 015

Printed in India at
Thomson Press, New Delhi 110 020

Published by
Orient Blackswan Private Limited
3-6-752 Himayatnagar, Hyderabad 500 029, Telangana, India
e-mail: info@orientblackswan.com

To
My father, Ahamed Basheer, and his mother Fathima

Contents

List of Images

Abbreviations

AFSPA	Armed Forces (Special Powers) Act
AIDWA	All India Democratic Women's Association
AIMWPLB	All India Muslim Women's Personal Law Board
BMMA	Bharatiya Muslim Mahila Andolan
CPI	Communist Party of India
CPI(M)	Communist Party of India (Marxist)
GIO	Girls' Islamic Organisation
INC	Indian National Congress
MWPRDA	The Muslim Women (Protection of Rights on Divorce) Act
NGO	Non-governmental organisation
PIL	Public Interest Litigation
SNDP	Sree Narayana Dharma Paripalana Sangham
UCC	Uniform Civil Code

Acknowledgements

This book emerged from my Ph.D. dissertation submitted to the School of Letters, Mahatma Gandhi University, Kerala, in 2011. But in the years following my Ph.D., a lot of discussions and debates helped me to reorder my thoughts and edit the work, keeping in mind the changing political visibility of Muslims in India and the state of Kerala. Many people and institutions have contributed to the process. Discussions that I had with friends and colleagues at the English and Foreign Languages University and Anveshi Research Centre, Hyderabad, have shaped my thoughts and urged me to revisit and perfect many of my arguments. The conference 'Histories, Cultures, Politics: Islam and Muslims in South India' (2007), organised by Anveshi Research Centre, helped me to frame the primary concerns outside the normative religious/secular binary. The Fellowship, Study of United States Institutes for Scholars on Religious Freedom and Pluralism (2015), hosted by the University of California, Santa Barbara, aided me to rework the initial drafts of this book. Exposure to scholarly discussions with academics, activists, and spiritual practitioners on Islam's presence in public life during my travels in the United States as part of the programme funded by the Bureau of Educational and Cultural Affairs, United States Department of State, and the extensive use of the Main Library at the UC Santa Barbara, played important roles in the final version of this book. I wish to extend my heartfelt thanks to the late Professor Wade Roof Clark and Professor Kathleen M. Moore at the Department of Religious Studies, UC Santa Barbara.

I would like to especially thank Susie Tharu for her presence in this journey as teacher, friend, feminist inspiration, and much more. I owe her a debt of gratitude for helping reshape my research by incorporating my identity as a Muslim woman, and for asking the right questions at the right times. I am also grateful to Dr H. Kalpana of Pondicherry Central University for the introductory readings in feminist scholarship.

I am forever indebted to my supervisor, the late Professor V. C. Harris, for his guidance, friendship, and care. His absence has been constantly felt during this process. Professor K. M. Krishnan, then director of the School of Letters, and Professor P. P. Raveendran (School of Letters) are fondly remembered for their encouragement and support.

Research of this kind involved a lot of search for vernacular materials. Sincere thanks are due to the librarians and staff of the Arakkal Archives and History Museum, Kannur; Archives of District Tourism Promotion Council, Kannur; Farook College Library and Hira Centre Library, Calicut; Iqbal Library, Kochi; Kerala Council for Historical Research Library (KCHR), Thiruvananthapuram; Kerala History Association Library, Ernakulam; Kerala University Library, Thiruvananthapuram; Maharajas College Library, Ernakulam; Mahatma Gandhi University Library, Kottayam; Maulana Azad Socio-cultural Centre and Library, Kochi; St. Teresa's College Library, Ernakulam; State Central Archives, Thiruvanathapuram and Kochi; State Central Library, Thiruvananthapuram; Thunchan Smaraka Library, Tirur; Vakkom Maulavi Foundation Library, Thiruvananthapuram; and Varthamaanam Library, Calicut. I am vastly indebted to Abdul Rahman Mangad, K. P. Kunhi Moosa, Mujeeb Rahman Kinaloor, N. K. A. Latheef, and A. K. Mohammed Tahar (son of the late A. A. Kochunni Master, former Cochin mayor), for allowing me to use their personal collections of journals and books, and for guiding me towards different directions. In fact, they are the ones to have designed and guided the trajectory of this research.

Thanks are also due to the staff of Maunathul Islam Sabha, Ponnani, and the staff of the mosques in Beema Palli and

Puthu Ponnani for patiently explaining their spiritual database to a curious researcher. Discussions with Shamshad Hussain, G. Arunima, Meena T. Pillai, and A. K. Rama Krishnan, and observations by E. V. Ramakrishnan and M. T. Ansari, have given me clarity and guidance.

I extend my heartfelt thanks to the team at Orient BlackSwan, particularly Veenu Luthria and Roopa Sharma, for their commitment and patience. I also thank Proteeti Banerjee for her editing.

A personal note of thanks to friends in Hyderabad: Uma Maheswari Bhrugubanda, Ipshita Chanda, Madhava Prasad, K. Satyanarayana, Satish Poduval, Sowmya Dechamma, Deepa Srinivas, A. Suneetha, K. Lalitha, and R. Srivatsan, whose intellectual presence and exemplary work have always been motivating. I appreciate the friendship and camaraderie of my friends and colleagues Rahul Kamble, Madhumita Sinha, Asma Rasheed, Indranil Dutta, Shilpaa Anand, and Srivani, without which it would have been difficult to sail through the tough times. My students Sindhu Jose, Asif Ahmed, Tony Sebastian, Ajay Mathew Jose, and Shahla Suban are fondly remembered for their love and care.

Sujith K. G. was a constant companion on my travels related to this research. I owe him for the photographs included in this book, and for being there throughout. Lukmanul Hakeem has graciously shared his photographs of the protests related to Hadiya's house arrest. Dr Jeevan Kumar, Henry Baker College, Kerala, helped considerably in the initial days of the research with reading materials, and also in editing the earlier versions. Conversations with Varsha Basheer on women, Islam, and feminism in Kerala have been inspiring and refreshing.

I am not sure how to thank Nijas Jewel, Amaya, and Ryan for their presence in my life—for putting up with my endless absences, for the compromises, for the encouragement, for love, and for being there always.

Foreword

*F*or any new study of Muslim women, the perverse visibility this figure has acquired in public discourse over the past three or four decades is the initial challenge. Fierce polemics related to marriage and divorce, maintenance payments, coverture, and even romance have drawn on a 'national bank' of commonsense to portray Muslim women as victims of their religion and Muslim ways of life as backward—and therefore (this is always the crux) as unjustifiably protected by their constitutional rights as a minority to their religion and ways of life. And this in a lived context where (to cite Sherin), 'being a minority subject whose subjectivity is demarcated somewhere along the margins of the secular, democratic State, I am far too aware of the contradictions between my assured constitutional rights and the otherness of my actual existence that recurs in myriad forms at multiple levels of exclusion.'

The polemics have played out as legal battles in the highest court, and have been staged as national issues. As we know, law has its own way of telling stories, identifying wrongs, and configuring redress. Shah Bano, Imrana, Shayra Bano are women, wronged in easily recognisable ways, seeking justice from the modern State. Their experience, as recounted in modern India's courts of law and broadcast to the nation, has become the singular narrative of the lives of Muslim women.

Concern for women is clearly not the driving force of these national initiatives, which have left Muslims, both women and men, feeling battered and ill-used. Yet—and here is the rub—the issues highlighted, as well as the arguments extended in support of these women, draw from the critiques of patriarchy newly elaborated in feminism. The result? A story in which feminism and Muslim women, soul/cell mates in this account, are yoked together in an awkward logic. Does feminism feel as ill-used by this narrative as Muslims, both women and men, do? A difficult question, for which the answer is both yes and no. 'Yes', because on the whole feminists have been suspicious of these initiatives and have not supported them. 'No', because the rich arguments of thinkers like Flavia Agnes and Nivedita Menon notwithstanding, feminism remains uneasy/agnostic/confused by the Muslim women question. To cite this book: Muslim women remain 'daunting subjects' for feminism. This could be why I found especially illuminating the surgical precision of the analysis in this book of feminist espousals of the cause of Muslim women—in activism, history, literature, ethnography, cinema, or theology. Feminism's narrow focus on patriarchy comes in for particularly sharp criticism. The cause of Muslim women in India cannot be separated from that of Muslim men.

However, feminism is not the theme of the book. It is Muslim women; and in relation to its object of study, this book effects a valuable paradigm shift, and it does so through a number of careful conceptual and methodological moves.

One: The discussion is set in Kerala. This is a state with a sizeable Muslim population and a history as well as a geography markedly different from that of northern India (which is the setting assumed in national narratives). So the memories that live on here are not of the Mughal/Muslim invasion or, for that matter, of Partition. Kerala's coastline receives the monsoon winds that brought the dhows across the Indian Ocean, and the region's trading ties with the Arab world and with Africa precede the rise of Islam by a few centuries. Traders stayed on for several months to await the turn of wind that would carry them back with their merchandise. St Thomas, who is revered by the Christians in Kerala as the missionary who brought Christianity to this region, would have been part of this voyaging, which included the exchange of ideas and of knowledge. For the men—sailors, merchants—the yearly round was a way of life. Women who stayed back cared for the family and maintained connections with the community. Drawing on histories of the period,

Sherin argues that the relationships between voyaging traders and local women could have been a factor in the consolidation of the custom of polyandry as well as the matrilineal inheritance practices that are extant also among Muslims of the region.

In Kerala, Muslims are largely concentrated along the northern coastline and the adjacent Western Ghat region. They comprise over 25 per cent of the population of the state and were originally mostly mariners, merchants, and fisherfolk, and of course peasants. Unlike Muslims in the north, they speak the regional language—Malayalam—in which many words of Arabic origin are still in common use. Until the twentieth century, Malayalam was also written in a specially modified Arabic script known as Arabi Malayalam. Much has changed over the centuries. But much also remains alive and is growing with major remittances and ideological influences coming into the state from trade and employment in the West Asian countries.

A *second* methodological move shifts the discussion out of the courts and away from the field of law, which has its own investments in the ideas of nation, modernity, secularism, and the histories that trail along with these ideas, both in India and in Europe. In the theatres of the law, there is little possibility of an invested, contextual definition of these principles and formations, which can have different implications for different Indians.

Finally—and this is the joy of this book—in place of legal cases, we encounter here a surprising and unexpectedly productive set of cultural 'texts'—an archive, no less—for the exploration of what Sherin terms the 'feminist enterprise' of Muslim women. This is an enterprise that involves *exercising agency as women*, not in line with some abstract idea of women's freedom, but in settings crisscrossed by grounded pulls and pressures that importantly includes their religion, their social positioning, and the predicament of Muslim men. Among her 'texts' are histories of the region, Beevi worship in the southern coastal area, important early journals and educational initiatives run by Muslim women that have been totally overlooked by feminist research, accounts and practices related to Arakkal Beevi, a cherished Hindu queen in the royal Arakkal household, a well-received novel by a Muslim woman writer, and not least, examples from Sherin's own experiences, which are offered at different points to illuminate an argument. For Cultural Studies, too, this is an original and important work.

Are there not problems with the unified category of Muslim women? Can they be studied as a singular entity? Surely not. Both caste and class feature prominently in the discussion. Yet, differently situated though they may be by class, education, caste, region, and even political ideologies, there are reasons why such an entity has conceptual significance. To quote the study:

> [T]he gradual draining of the political and economic powers of the community in the post-independence political scenario, the continuous targeting of Muslims by the religious mainstream of late, the violence committed on Muslims in general, and Muslim women in particular, during such attacks, the constant framing of Islam as the antithetical Other to the progressive and development vocabularies of the State, the mainstream branding of Islam as the dangerous Other in a post-9/11 Islamophobic environment, and the wide use of Muslim women as a global index for profiling Islam as premodern, anti-feminist, and authoritarian in mainstream campaigns are some of the premises that *may usher in the unified conceptual subject of 'Muslim woman'*. (emphasis mine)

One last word about method. Faced with the difficulty of studying difference—say, in the experience different groups have of 'development' or medical care, of globalisation and even of popular cinema—social scientists have called for 'conjunctural analyses', 'fuller narratives', 'thick descriptions'. This study suggests that thickness or layering is useful, but is not enough. What might be needed is more like a scene change (the field shifts), a reframing (the focus shifts), a new framework altogether. In the arts and social sciences, the important breakthroughs are never simply conceptual; they are also political. Experience, insight, passion, and desire drive these breakthroughs. A century ago, Gramsci too had argued that significant new knowledge will only come from intellectuals who are organic to a historically important group.

Susie Tharu

Nationality is a social feeling. It is a feeling of a corporate sentiment of oneness which makes those who are charged with it feel that they are kith and kin. This national feeling is a double-edged feeling. It is at once a feeling of fellowship for one's own kith and kin and an anti-fellowship feeling for those who are not one's own kith and kin. It is a feeling of 'consciousness of kind' which on the one hand binds together those who have it, so strongly that it over-rides all differences arising out of economic conflicts or social gradations and, on the other, severs them from those who are not of their kind. It is a longing not to belong to any other group. This is the essence of what is called a nationality and national feeling.

B. R. Ambedkar, *Pakistan or the Partition of India* (1945)

INTRODUCTION

Messy Mediations

Feminist Politics and Muslim Identity in India

*I*n what ways do Muslim women inflect feminist histories? Why is it important to consider Muslim women a daunting subject in historicising feminist projects? Is it significant to consider Muslim women an entity similar to the way we consider Dalit, Afro-American, and other non-White categories of women outside the mainstream feminism? Are Sharia and Islamic jurisprudence positing a different destiny for women in Islam as legal subjects of non-Islamic countries, which differentiate their existence and plight from the categories of women mentioned above? Some of these questions become major concerns while discussing Muslim women in India, and there are no clandestine ways of addressing these issues. An engagement with these questions is embedded in the lived reality of a minority identity as it cuts across gender and class. In India, tracing the social history of Muslim women is not an easy task for a feminist historian. Regional variations in practising the religion of Islam, the nuances in the social status and political identity of Muslims in different geographic locations, and above all, caste, which clearly raises concerns for scholars of Islamic studies in India,[1] make it difficult to extend the label of

---

[1] Masood Alam Falahi's Urdu book, *Hindustan Mai Zat-Pat Aur Musalman* (*Casteism Among Muslims in India*), parts of which have been

Muslim feminism as a guide to address the politics of women in Islam in India.

For instance, the commonly used nomenclature 'Mappila', which is used to refer to Muslims in Kerala, represented for me an impasse as the term was associated more with northern Kerala or Malabar; in the southern regions, from where I hail, Mappila is not associated with Islam, but with Christianity. So I could never call myself a Mappila woman. Yet, being a minority subject whose subjectivity is demarcated somewhere along the margins of the secular, democratic State, I am far too aware of the contradictions between my assured constitutional rights and the otherness of my actual existence that recurs in myriad forms at multiple levels of exclusion. Engaging in debates and arguments related to what can be called a 'defence of reservation', I have personally experienced what Partha Chatterjee calls the wide gap between the ideal civil society and its demographically limited actual existence (2006b, 39); at the same time, in my urge to justify multiple policies of welfare and security measures by governmental agencies (ibid., 37), I have been in a way dealing with the strange necessity to be on the defensive for being a Muslim in India. Both appear as formidable parts of my existence on the margins of what could have been a 'Hindu State', were it not for the 'generosity' of a large majority of 'secular, democratic' souls. But in spite of my own complicated personal relationship with the identity of a 'Muslim woman', as a non-practising Muslim mostly located in academic

---

translated into English by Yoginder Sikkand, is a pioneering study of caste-based discrimination among the Indian Muslims and of the continued domination of 'high'-caste Muslims that parallels the Hindu caste system. Similarly, the *Pasmanda* discourse critiques the existing conditions of Islam in India as hierarchical, and a recurrent theme in *pasmanda* narratives is that minority politics has singularly failed to address the day-to-day struggles of the *pasmanda* Muslims, who constitute about 85 per cent of the Indian Muslim population. *Pasmanda*, a Persian term meaning 'those who have fallen behind', refers to Muslims belonging to the Shudra (backward) and *ati*-Shudra (Dalit) castes. It was adopted as an oppositional identity to that of the dominant *ashraf* Muslims (forward castes) in 1998 by the Pasmanda Muslim Mahaz, a group which mainly works in Bihar.

engagements in 'secular, progressive spaces', it is difficult for me, if not impossible, to engage with this identity as a singular and unified point of reference.

While it becomes necessary to address differences, the gradual draining of political and economic powers of the community in the post-independent political scenario, the continuous targeting of Muslims by the religious mainstream of late, the violence committed on Muslims in general, and Muslim women in particular, during such attacks, the constant framing of Islam as the antithetical Other to the progressive and development vocabularies of the State, the mainstream branding of Islam as the dangerous Other in a post-9/11 Islamophobic environment, and the wide use of Muslim women as a global index for profiling Islam as premodern, anti-feminist, and authoritarian in mainstream campaigns are some of the premises that may usher in the unified conceptual subject of 'Muslim woman'. Imagining this 'Muslim woman' within the Indian context leads to certain rigidly formed categories, vividly connected to the lived reality of Indian minorities in the postcolonial nation. Historically, if Islam and Muslims emerged as the 'Other' to the contextually defined colonial modernity along with nationalist movements, in a post-Partition nation it implied not only an erasure of the community's political power, but also a marked discontinuity in relation to the secular vocabulary of nation-building. The organisation of secularism and other liberal values during the process of nation-building have created a postcolonial dilemma in countries like India and Pakistan. While the colonial construction of identities along communitarian lines had implications for Partition and subsequent events in the postcolonial nation, the undercurrents of the nationalist formulation of identities based along caste and religious hierarchies have had a major impact on the way that marginalised people experience their lived realities. The experience of secularism in the postcolonial nation has never been the same for different communities. Pogroms, State-sponsored violence, the evident casteism, and mainstream discourses on Muslim and Dalit existential realities have always undermined liberal promises and the strict adherence to secularism.

THE UNIFORM CIVIL CODE DEBATE AND MUSLIM WOMEN AS 'OTHER'

Discussions on minority and Islamic identities have led to a chain of arguments on Sharia following the Parliament debates on the Uniform Civil Code (UCC) in the post-Shah Bano phase. A repeated engagement with Sharia and cries for a Uniform Civil Code have come up in the context of a few historic moves. One of these is the July 2014 Supreme Court ruling that Sharia courts and their *fatwa*s (a ruling in Islamic law) cannot be generalised. The Supreme Court, while rejecting the Public Interest Litigation (PIL) filed by lawyer Vishwa Lochan Madan in 2005 to abolish the Sharia courts established by the Muslim Personal Law Board on the ground that their verdicts were often anti-feminist, also issued guidelines to institutions like the Darul Quda and Darul Ifta regarding the discretions to be adopted while giving *fatwa*s. What is interesting is that the Court accepted the claim of the Darul Uloom Deoband and Muslim Personal Law Board that institutions like the Darul Ifta and Darul Quda are modes of resolving civil cases outside the judiciary within a stipulated time, without financially encumbering the complainants. At the same time, following the claim of the respondents, the Court asserted that the individual has the right to decide whether or not to abide by the *fatwa*. Most of the mainstream media reported this as the Court's overruling of *fatwa*s issued by Sharia courts. Naturally the discussions also pointed towards the necessity of the Uniform Civil Code, the longstanding demand of Right-wing Hindu nationalists.

Right from Shah Bano to Imrana (whose case was implied in the verdict on *fatwa*s), the discussion always switches back and forth between justification of Islamic jurisdiction and the cry for a Uniform Civil Code, at the centre of which gender plays a crucial role. In the case of Imrana, a Muslim woman raped by her father-in-law, the Muslim Panchayat ruled out the validity of her marriage and asked her to marry her father-in-law instead. Incidentally, Darul Uloom supported this through a *fatwa*. Interestingly, in this case it was a journalist who approached Darul Uloom for a decision on the issue, while neither Imrana nor her husband followed the *fatwa*. The accused was legally punished as per the criminal justice system of the country. Presenting this case as a point of reference, the Court opined that there is a choice before a Muslim when it comes to accepting a *fatwa*, and that Sharia institutions should be discreet about the implications and social consequences of the *fatwa*s they issue. Also, the right to issue a *fatwa* should be restricted to direct appeal from the affected individuals.

This situation was complicated further by the failure of both the secular media and the Muslim Personal Law Board to react responsibly to the issue. While the Muslim Personal Law Board celebrated the moment as a validation of the relevance of Sharia courts, the mainstream media and the secular public chose to read it as a critique of Sharia courts instead. Between these two extremities can be found the complexity of addressing gender in Islam in India. The mainstream readings of this case, and the immediate resolution granted to Imrana as the victim of Muslim jurisdiction, rise from prejudiced notions about Islam and women, and fall in line with the view of Muslim women as potential victims to be saved from the clutches of Islamic primitivism. There is a series of debates on the Uniform Civil Code, the Triple Talaq, polygamy in Islam, and the Supreme Court verdict on the Triple Talaq.[2] While discussing the interest that Western feminists have taken in Afghan women and being critical about the 'Save Afghan Women' campaign in the West, Lila Abu-Lughod, in 'Do Muslim Women Really Need Saving? Anthropological Reflections on Cultural Relativism and its Others' (2002), points to the Western interest in highlighting the cultural icon of Muslim women as the victims of Islam over messier political and historical realities. She is critical of both the rhetoric and the concept of liberation in feminist politics and urges feminists to be wary of taking a patronising position:

---

[2] Please see my articles at https://www.outlookindia.com/website/story/shortcomings-in-the-triple-talaq-debate/297366; and https://www.outlookindia.com/website/story/feminism-at-a-crossroad-triple-talaq-judgment-and-the-question-of-gender-justice/300801. See also Sherin (2018) for a detailed reading of the debate.

Suspicion about bedfellows is only a first step; it will not give us a way to think more positively about what to do or where to stand. For that, we need to confront two more big issues. First is the acceptance of the possibility of difference. Can we only free Afghan women to be like us or might we have to recognize that even after 'liberation' from the Taliban, they might want different things than we would want for them?…. Second, we need to be vigilant about the rhetoric of saving people because of what it implies about our attitudes. (Abu-Lughod 2002, 787)

The Indian media in general, and mainstream feminism to an extent, have used this patronising vocabulary vis-à-vis Muslim women without understanding the social relationships and structures pertaining to Muslim communities in India. The Shah Bano case and, later, the Imrana case have been used by the mainstream to generate a particular rhetoric on the plight of Muslim women. That there are multiple levels at which Muslims, and especially Muslim women, engage with Islamic jurisprudence is not mentioned anywhere as part of this discussion. The very fact that neither Imrana nor her husband followed the instructions of the Sharia court and chose to maintain their status as per their individual discretion in this regard shows how personal engagements differ, and in many cases move beyond a hegemonic practice or adherence to Sharia. Often, local practices of dowry, kinship structures, and adherence to local customs influence the ways in which individuals resolve civil issues in their lives.

Apart from the reading of Muslim women's plight as part of a universalised feminist liberation project, the modes of addressing the question of gender within the community also evoke interest while discussing Muslim feminism. The Supreme Court verdict warning third parties from obtaining *fatwa*s from Sharia courts without the interest or involvement of the actual complainant is not discussed much in Muslim circles. At the same time, Muslim women in different parts of the country engage with Islamic jurisprudence through modes that are not singular.

The All India Muslim Women's Personal Law Board (AIMWPLB) is an organisation constituted in 2005 to adopt strategies for the protection and continued applicability of the Muslim Personal Law in India, with a particular focus on women's issues, including marriage, divorce, and other legal rights. The AIMWPLB comprises of a thirty-member executive board. In March 2008, it released a twelve-page 'Sharia Nikahnama' which sought to offer India's Muslim women a religiously-sanctioned alternative to conventional Islamic marriage contracts. The Nikhahnama, according to the AIMWPLB, is applicable to Sunni and Shia Muslims, and would give equal rights to both Muslim men and women. A Muslim woman would be entitled to seek divorce if her husband was found to have an illicit relationship with another woman. The AIMWPLB functions as an alternate space for raising the concerns of Muslim women within the premise of the Sharia. They have also suggested various reforms for some Islamic practices which they felt have been oppressive to Muslim women. Likewise, there are organisations like the Bharatiya Muslim Mahila Andolan (BMMA) that claim to work towards understanding and ameliorating the marginalisation of the Muslim community in general and Muslim women in particular, empowering Muslim women, and taking steps to ensure their social, economic, political, civil, legal, and religious rights. So Muslim women have developed multiple modes of dealing with the question of gender in Islam and are divided in their position regarding their relationship with religion and the State. While BMMA assumes a more secular outlook, there are organisations that follow a strict adherence to Sharia. The formation of the AIMWPLB and many of the Muslim women non-governmental organisations (NGOs) represent efforts on the part of Muslim women in India to develop a dialogue amongst themselves, with the religion, with the community, and at a wider level, with society on issues related to women. While attempting to locate themselves within the community, these organisations address issues pertaining to the custody, guardianship, and adoption of children, women's rights in their marital homes, marriage and divorce, *mahr* (dower), etc. The all-India meeting of the Muslim Women's Rights Network held in 2005 in Lucknow discussed the role of the State in protecting women's rights, the impact of communal violence on Muslim women, and the challenges facing Muslim women's activism (Vatuk 2008, 500–01). These initiatives reflect the community's attempt to develop a politically vibrant dialogue with contemporary realities. At the same time, when women become prominent participants within the Muslim public sphere, they do not contest their identity as Muslims. But it may be a misreading and an appropriation to homogenise these organisations as platforms for women's liberation within the community. While the politics of gender is just one of the causes, they also engage with the contemporary realities of life in India as members of a minority community in an effort to address the internal discrepancies within the apparently secular framework of the nation.

Sylvia Vatuk, in her article 'Islamic Feminism in India: Indian Muslim Women Activists and the Reform of Muslim Personal Law' (2008), differentiates between Islamic feminist activists and Islamist women. Studying the discourse on women in contemporary Islamic reform movements, she finds that all share a preoccupation with the need for women to conform to 'islamically prescribed norms' (ibid., 501). While this may not be completely untrue, the perspective of Left organisations and feminist movements on women in Islam is always determined by preconceived notions. While they are happy to engage with visibly secular outfits like BMMA and consider them the spokespersons of Muslim women, they are sceptical about engaging with Islamist organisations or Muslim women's groups that adhere to religious practices. While consolidating Muslim women's voices on the UCC or Triple Talaq, excluding the majority of practising Muslim women leaves incomplete the debate on rights that they attempt to raise.

Islamic Feminism: Praxis and Theory

Islamic feminism, a comparatively new coinage, has entered academic discussions at a time when the increasing hostility towards Islam and orientalist assumptions of Muslim women as victims of a primitive and patriarchal culture have been ruling the scene. There are different schools of thought within the large body of writings under the heading 'Women and Islam'. The new school of Muslim women scholar-activists who critically study the foundational texts of Islam have been challenging canonical texts and conventional histories. Thinkers like Fatima Mernissi and Amina Wadud attempted to clarify the gender status of women in Islam through concepts of individualism. Casting doubt upon the authenticity and reliability of the '*hadiths*', Mernissi presented Islamic history from a woman's perspective. In her path-breaking discourse on women in Islam, Mernissi (1993b) showed how the mullahs, like the clergy in Christianity, interpreted the religion to project a patriarchal perspective. By accepting the mullahs' interpretation of the Quran and the words of the Prophet as sacrosanct religious doctrine, Islam took the false step from a secular and equality-oriented perspective to a more male-centric view.

Amina Wadud focuses on the Quran for her feminist interrogation by concentrating on anti-women Quranic exegeses that interpret the Quran on the basis of the social reality in Saudi Arabia (Wadud 1999). I believe her reading also involves an overt focus on the feminist methodology, especially that adopted by the second-wave feminist practitioners of the West—that of reading old texts from a feminist perspective. Wadud offers an alternative Quranic exegesis based on a female-centric perspective, which she claims is suitable for the 'modern woman':

> I have demonstrated the relevance of the Qur'an to the concerns of the modern woman…. On one hand, some limitations exist in the text—such as when it specifically addresses the social situation in Arabia at the time of revelation—on the other hand, most limitations are reflections of the interpreters who restrict the universality of the divine message to their individual perception…. I believe the Qur'an adapts to the context of the modern woman as smoothly as it adapted to the original Muslim community…. This adaptation can be demonstrated if the text is interpreted with her in mind, thus indicating [its] universality…. (ibid., 95)

It is to be noted that the Quran's ability to adapt to the needs of the 'modern woman' becomes an imperative for its universality.

While acknowledging the work of these thinkers who enable us to revise our perceptions of texts which have been strictly treated as androcentric so far, I feel that their strategy of revising or rewriting Islamic texts based on a Eurocentric feminist methodology highlights a flawed juxtaposition of a teleological sense of 'the modern' with the exegetic practices of premodern societies and cultures. Also, these readings locate the Quran and Islam in an ahistorical continuum, without acknowledging how women have adapted these to present-day requirements. The political reality of Islam and Muslim men escape these readings. The idea of validating the Quran for a proper feminist reading does not problematise the category of gender as it is undergoing constant revisions and negotiations. The discontinuities and rupture in the religious and cultural identities of Muslim women are not explored in this simplistic reading of Muslim women conditioned by the Quran and its exegesis. This stable, unchanging category of the Muslim woman conditioned by the Quran alone goes against feminist interests as it claims some authenticity and legitimacy through the religious text. How this undercuts the feminist ethos and the ontology of feminism is made clear in the Triple Talaq verdict, where the Supreme Court of India had to finally pronounce Triple Talaq illegal as it was unIslamic. It is also a bit disturbing to see if the authors succumb to the inevitability of proving Islam, too, as 'liberal', thus bringing forth the inner conflict arising out of a necessity to prove the liberal compatibility of the Islamic tradition.

The excessive interest in projecting Islam alone as anti-women when the modern secular State also asserts a male order of some kind shows a tendency to read religion in an ahistorical sense. Moreover, post-secularist thinkers have pointed out that rather than attempting to make Islam compatible with liberal democracy, liberal categories themselves need to be questioned (Asad 1993, 2003, 2008). Nawal El Saadawi, in 'Towards Women's Power, Nationally and Internationally' (1986), reflects upon how her conception of religion strictly adheres to her allegiance to modernity, and how she is inspired by the liberal spirit of modernity and its thrust towards the individual as against the collective premodern consciousness:

> Part of our strategy may be to use religion. I am not against religion itself. But I am against religion if it is going to be used against women. I want to live, and I want to enjoy life, and I want to give life my ideas, and to take from life. If religion is going to stop me, I am going to stop religion. This should be the character of women: to stand up and to rebel if we must. (ibid., 251)

The hegemony of liberalism in El Saadawi's discourse comes through in the prominence given to the ideals of individual freedom and autonomy. Discourses of these kinds often fail to recognise the problems inherent in a blind adherence to the tradition of individualism and equality, as evident in Western societies. By reproducing the liberal assumptions of Eurocentric feminism, the validity of an essentialist notion of an opposition between individual and society is established, while in the lived experience in even Western liberal societies, such an opposition hardly applies (Mahmood 2008a, 151). They are unable to see through the mere legal equality existing in these liberal societies, which is often contradicted by an uneven political and economic status. Likewise, relegating religion to a premodern consciousness often ignores the reforms and modernisation that take place within religion, for instance the mosque movements and Sharia revisions, in many of which women have had an active role. The 'modern-religious' is a category that never enters these discourses, while in reality religious communities exist in modern societies in quite conspicuous ways, engaging with apparatuses of modern jurisdiction and governmentality.

The interest of the international community in Taslima Nasrin of Bangladesh or Nawal El Saadawi of Egypt (two women known for their Islam-bashing) does not stem from genuine empathy with the plight of Third World women, but from a legitimisation of their prejudices against Islam as anti-modern and anti-women. In the West, the 'save Afghan women' campaign legitimised American intervention in Afghanistan. In such issues, the Muslim woman becomes a cultural icon, strategically placed to hide problematic political and historical narratives. Lila Abu-Lughod presents this Western tactic of 'saving' as a strategic move to enforce Western political interests in the region:

> … this notion of 'saving' Afghan women, [is] a notion that justifies American intervention … and that dampens criticism of feminist intervention by American and European feminists. It is easy to see through the hypocritical 'feminism' of a republican administration. More troubling for me are the attitudes of those who do genuinely care about women's status. The problem, of course, with ideas of 'saving' other women is that they depend on and reinforce superiority by Westerners. (Nermeen 2008b, 145)

Prejudices against Islam and Muslim Women

To show how discourses on women and Islam get diverted from their avowed interest in Muslim women towards a critique of Islam, I would like to point to the reading of Khadija Mumtas' work *Barsa* by a renowned Malayalam critic as well as Marxist enthusiast from Kerala, P. K. Pokker, in his article 'Sthree Mukhavaranam Neekkumbol' [When the Woman Unveils].[3] Arguing that women cannot even attain the status of a 'social animal'[4] without first challenging the traditions and practices maintained through patriarchal perspectives and value systems, he goes on to say:

> Both men and women should have the right to veil and similarly to discard it. But the woman who covers her head and extends her *hijaab* to her breasts, as instructed in the Quran, veils even her eyes. The assured safety of this woman is a fantasy. As long as her eyes and ears remain closed, she is a victim. (Pokker 2008, 17)

---

[3] This article is referred to in my discussion of *Barsa* in Chapter 3.

[4] 'Social animal' is given in parentheses in his account in Malayalam. All Malayalam references are my translations, unless otherwise stated.

The dramatic title that the author has chosen for the article should not go unnoticed. The title definitely implies a liberated woman, unlike the mute, passive victims of the community. While Pokker's genuine interest in Muslim women emerges clearly through this discussion, the discourse leads us to the hidden danger belying it, that is, a critique of Islam. Thus, while pointing out what the contemporary Muslim woman is capable of, Pokker in a way goes along with the modern view of feminism to say that only by challenging the rigid norms of Islam can Muslim women become active agents. He fails to see that as products of different histories and manifestations of differently structured desires, their primary ideal may not be freedom of a particular kind. The article even discards the possibility of freedom within a veiled existence. Since it claims a perspective that is empathetic to Muslim women's subjectivity specifically and to the Islamic tradition at large, I feel it poses a greater danger than the usual critique of Islam as anti-women levelled by agencies outside the domain of Islam.

To elaborate my argument, let me also recollect an instance from personal memory where prejudices formed the basis of the wider public's notion of what constitutes a Muslim woman. This was at an international conference in a college run by the Catholic management in Kerala, where teachers from various colleges and universities in Kerala comprised the majority of the audience. After successfully presenting my paper on the veil and Muslim women, I was engaged in a friendly conversation with fellow participants. Since my argument was that the veil has been associated with Islam as a derogatory term and that clothing becomes crucial in demonstrating feminist alliances, I tried to point out that freedom of choice regarding clothing may also be conceived of as a capitalist agenda in post-industrialist societies, where you can choose between different brands and patterns, in contrast to the situation prevailing in premodern communities. To my satisfaction, there was a vibrant discussion on the topic, and I felt I had been able to convey my point clearly. At this point, a well-known academic came to me and asked a very disturbing question in a rather condescending tone: 'Do you know the reason behind most of the young Muslim women in Kerala adopting *purdah* these days?' I tried to answer him politely, although I was disappointed because it looked as though he had not understood my argument at all. I tried to point out the post-Babri Masjid, post-9/11 context where religion and religious symbols reflect people's insecurity, and also the pan-Islamic revival that has been taking place in the Islamic world. I was disappointed that he, like many others, did not understand my argument regarding the irrationality of 'getting overtly concerned about the veil' when it comes to any discussion on the Muslim woman. To my dismay, he did not let me continue and said dismissively that it was not all that 'rubbish'; rather, it stemmed from the insecurity of the husbands of these young women who were away in the 'Gulf countries'. I was left disturbed and helpless at such a conclusion. Had he placed such an argument in public, there would have been a chance of disclosing the prejudices underlying such a statement. Apart from the implication that a woman would never adopt the veil willingly, he repeated the assumptions regarding the freedom of clothing being a symbol of emancipation. There had also been dangerous hints about how an insecure Muslim masculinity uses this religious symbol to control female sexuality. This emasculation of Muslim men highlights the larger political implications of the post-Babri Masjid India.

I was baffled by this 'interest' of the academic world in the increased use of the veil among Muslim women in Kerala. The adoption of the burqa (veil) as the uniform clothing of Muslim women is a response to the pan-Islamic movements and the vibrant Islamist wave sweeping the state of late. And in Kerala, historically, different religions have adopted different styles of clothing. Religions like Christianity, too, had seen clothing impositions at different times. Also, in the past, clothing had severe caste markers attached to them. For instance, the attire of Christian nuns has never been subject to as much debate as Muslim women's veil. The 'nun', as an extension of colonial modernity, fits into our cultural space as an ordinary phenomenon, while a Muslim woman in *purdah* becomes a spectacle, a matter for concern.[5]

FEMINIST DISCOURSE AND ITS DISCONTENTS IN INDIA

The concerns of a secular and liberal framework, which lacks an organic conception of political realities and the locus of identities, have problematised mainstream feminist discourses in post-independence India. It is important to acknowledge that liberal theories of feminism have failed to incorporate the overlapping of gender, caste and minority issues when it comes to discussing women's questions. Way back in the 1990s, Susie Tharu and Tejaswini Niranjana had pointed this out in 'Problems for a Contemporary Theory of Gender':

> In the late 1980s and the early 1990s—the Mandal/Mandir/Fund-Bank years—however, we face a whole new set of political questions. Entering into new alliances we have begun to elaborate new forms of politics. They have demanded engagement with issues of caste and religious affiliation/community and with new problems emerging from the 'liberalization' of economy, creating contexts in which the contradictions implicit in earlier initiatives have become increasingly apparent. (Tharu and Niranjana 1996, 234)

The contradictions that confront gender analysis of the time, and the impasses faced by notions such as women's freedom, self-determination, or their right to choose, are analogous to the contradictions faced by class analysis, caste initiatives, and democracy and secularism. Tharu and Niranjana conclude that

---

[5] *Rethinking Muslim Women and the Veil* by Katherine Bullock (2002) discusses in detail the Western antipathy to the veil and traces its origins in orientalist assumptions. I am not trying to bring in a parallel between nuns and Muslim women. But nuns and priests have permeated the public space of Kerala as symbols of aristocratic Christianity, and have gained acceptance in modern political and cultural domains.

the humanist subject at the centre of these analyses, including 'the subject of feminism', calls for a critique.

Subsequently, many feminists like Kalpana Kannabiran have further focused on the social relations of caste and gender to say that both are based on the exercise of power through the use of force, or structural violence through customs and rituals (Kannabiran and Kannabiran 1991). However, the question of women in Islam or in Dalit communities evokes so much conflict and confusion in feminist politics that redefining feminism becomes necessary in the context of these identities in India. Likewise, feminism's uncritical relationship to its own power needs to be addressed more severely, as discussed in works like *Split Decisions: How and Why to Take a Break from Feminism* (Halley 2008). The patronising position that many feminist discourses assume with respect to women's issues from marginalised locations have always been problematic. This has also resulted in a wide discontent amidst the presence of various identity movements, which has led to scepticism about feminist cultures and practices in India.

In the context of the brutal rape and subsequent murder of a 23-year-old physiotherapy student in New Delhi in December 2012, who was dubbed 'Nirbhaya', the fearless one, in the media, feminist discourses took different positions in terms of punishment, legal security for women, the role and involvement of the State as a law-enforcing body, etc. But the predominant concern that many raised was the folly of addressing the crime as an entity in itself without considering the locus of the criminal. The issue of an impartial response to rape, irrespective of the social status of the criminal, was dealt with in many debates surrounding the Nirbhaya case. The question was asked: Why do all rape cases not receive the same agitated response from the public? While acknowledging the brutal nature of the crime committed and the necessity of addressing patriarchal violence, the inevitable need to address the triggers to one's own response to a crime committed on women was a concern. Arundhati Roy's response to Channel 4, a British media house, generated much criticism for what many considered a shocking indifference to the violence involved in the crime, but sadly reveals the prejudices, partisanship, predilections, and predispositions that underlie feminist responses in the country:

> We are having an unexceptional reaction to an event that isn't exceptional. It is really very sad, because you know it is a terrible thing to say to such a tragic event.... But the problem is that, why is this crime creating such a lot of outrage? It is because it plays in to the idea of the criminal poor ... you know ... the vegetable vendor, the gym instructor, the bus driver actually assaulting a middle class girl.... (Roy 2012)

The event that led to many candlelight marches and calls for a feminist revival all over the country was also critiqued for the modes of protest it evoked, and the inability of many women to identify with the caste and class evoked at the venues of these protests. While the academic and intellectual platforms were marked by a sophistication that many could not access, in some other contexts the extreme Right-wing perspectives alienated a sizeable number of women from the protest venues. There was strong opposition to what was seen as a strictly middle-class elite feminism.[6] The shocking gang-rape of two sisters from the Maurya caste (a backward caste), whose bodies were later found hanging from a tree in Badaun, Uttar Pradesh, in May 2014, led to a major critique of mainstream feminist apathy. This moment was used

---

[6] For instance, in Hyderabad, when a candlelight march was conducted with wide publicity as a midnight march, *Dalit Camera* representatives interviewed women who swept the streets at night on their notion of safety. This was meant to counter what they considered the 'mainstream feminist march' (*Dalit Camera*, 'We Were Never Part of Dalit and Women's Movement', Part 1/Part 2; available at https://www.youtube.com/watch?v=PWOiTXPq6_s). Women who responded to the questions expressed total ignorance about the march being held at Indira Park. They also remarked that their need for survival outweighed their concerns for safety. This march took place through what could be seen as a sophisticated and elite route, excluding the spaces taken up by women sweepers, sex workers, and many other women who work at night, distanced from the normative ethics of 'night-work'.

as an indicator to test the feminist concerns of the academia and the media, and the biased political positions in the demand for gender justice. Comparisons with the earlier response to the Delhi gang-rape led to the prevailing feminist sensibility in the country being branded as elite and biased towards the upper class/caste. Kannabiran points to the politics of understanding this crime, the politics of caste that forces one to view the crime beyond a sexual assault:

> My raging grief is about the loss, the deaths of these children, both girls; but there are accounts of a boy killed here as well not so long ago after being brutalised; it is about the unspeakable torture they were subjected to, of which sexual assault was a part; it is about our collective inability as people committed to the annihilation of caste, to make any difference in a context where caste atrocity is at best a spectacle for consumption and speculation; where images of children who have been brutally assaulted and murdered are traded by the media in unthinkable ways and their experience negated by the rogue state. Where does one begin to roll this back? (Kannabiran 2014, 13)

She adds:

> Although the writing on the Budaun violence has opened out several discussions—from eliminating open defecation to increasing helplines to castigating the Government of Uttar Pradesh—I think this is an issue that goes far beyond the sexual politics of the Samajwadi Party (SP), or the tasks before the toilet ambassadors of the Ministry of Rural Development. Can we forget that Mathura was sexually assaulted in the toilet of a police station? While unarguably women need access to secure basic facilities, this issue is quite separate from their vulnerability to sexual assault. (ibid.)

She raises the pertinent question: Why did the country not come to a standstill after the Khairlanji massacre, which was far graver in terms of the numbers assaulted and killed? The alienation of the Bhotmange family in Khairlanji reflects the inequality of protests, as highlighted by Dalit Bahujan groups and anti-caste intellectuals.[7] The Delhi victim's suffering led to the immediate constitution of a committee, legislations in her name, and trial and convictions at the speed of light. Despite the Bhotmange family's suffering, aggravated sexual assault as part of targeted caste violence was not included in the new, expanded definition of sexual assault, and justice continued to elude the sole survivor. Kannabiran's conclusion that all are not equal, neither in public perception nor in the criminal justice system in India, also leaves room for revising feminist concerns, not along the lines of women as a universal conceptual subject, but as subjects with different political destinies and in different locales. In fact, there are strands of feminist thought that tried to point towards women's lack of basic amenities in this context, and Kannabiran highlights the futility of such attempts.

It is important to address these critiques as well as see the crisis facing feminism in India. Feminism needs to address the locus of identities as much as the political existence of such identities while speaking of issues pertaining to women. Feminism should extend its discursive frame beyond the essentialist notions of patriarchy, men and women, to address the complex formulations of power produced and contained within its own operational space. While advocating the cause of women as citizen-subjects empowered with their own rights as the liberal ideal, the extent to which Indian feminism has produced a sustained discourse on the interlocking of caste, class, religion, and sexuality, along with gender, is still debatable. Although feminism in India includes minorities, Dalit, and backward-caste women, there has been a consistent failure to produce a

---

[7] The Khairlanji massacre refers to the 2006 murders of four members of the Bhotmange family, members of the Scheduled Caste, in a small village called Khairlanji in Maharashtra. The murders stemmed from a land dispute between the Bhotmange family and upper-caste villagers, and sparked off protests across various parts of Maharashtra. In 2008, six people were found guilty and awarded the death penalty for the crime; however, in 2010, the Nagpur Bench commuted the death penalty to a jail sentence of twenty-five years.

sustained engagement with the diverse political trajectories and lifeworlds of women. This is a critique that deserves immediate attention. However, the consideration of patriarchy as a binding oppositional force for all women is still unilaterally used on many feminist platforms. Feminism, while addressing women as citizen-subjects, somehow fails to incorporate the multiple points of identification and inclusive/exclusive frameworks that apply to different citizens. It has failed to address women in terms of their political power as citizens of the nation. A question that has not been explored to any great extent in feminist discourses is: Where do women from Dalit and minority communities stand vis-à-vis the State? While addressing women as a group in essentialist terms, this locus is often overlooked by mainstream feminism. Social conventions and liberal rights often come into conflict with each other while discussing women. This is not just in terms of the conflict between gender and religion; even in terms of nuanced community concerns, feminism at times fails to address or incorporate issues raised by women from these groups. Dalit feminism, through constant engagement with the politics of identity, has successfully emerged as a category in itself, challenging unilateral mainstream views on the essential identity of women. Indian feminism has learnt quite a lot from Dalit feminists. While discussing women from marginalised communities, there needs to be legitimate engagement with the notion that along with patriarchy, the State itself can turn out to be oppressive.

There have been extensive studies on caste and gender in India since the 1980s (Rao 2005; Rege 2006, 2013). Likewise, there have also been many recent attempts to study or incorporate Muslim feminism within the fold of feminist movements in India. Apart from the work of scholars like Gail Minault, Zoya Hassan, Ritu Menon, and Barbara Metcalf, women and Islam in India has been studied as part of different projects and through multiple funding agencies. Despite such immense engagement, why are the repeated charges of appropriation, patronising, and exclusion often raised by Muslim, backward-class, and Dalit activists?

While feminists have engaged with the multiple ways in which Muslim and Dalit women counter and engage with internal patriarchies in their respective communities, what is absent in many such discourse is the troubled relationship of many of these women with the nation in general, and in terms of secular democracy in particular. The banality of the struggles and violence that mark the daily existence of these women at the margins of the nation escape feminist analysis, mostly because of the mainstream feminist inability to identify with, and, more crucially, underwrite one's own centrality in these discourses as a subject of dominance. Dark episodes in the history of the nation, which are discussed as external to the frames of the everyday experience of sexism and oppression, situate these women outside the normal everyday reality of the nation. If the violence inflicted on women during Partition was a major theme in literatures discussing gender and conflict, there have since then been instances from Kunan Poshpora,[8] violence on women in the Northeast,[9] in Gujarat,

---

[8] The Kunan Poshspora event remains a black day in Indian history. On 23 February 1991, units of the Indian army launched a search and interrogation operation in the remote village of Kunan Poshpora in Kashmir. At least fifty-three girls and women, ranging from the ages of eleven to eighty-one, were allegedly gang-raped by soldiers that night. Human rights organisations have reported that the number of women raped could be as high as 100. Amnesty International's documentary highlights terrible violations of citizenship rights committed on these women. Although the Indian government's investigations into the incident rejected these allegations as 'baseless', international human rights organisations have expressed serious doubts about the integrity of these investigations and the manner in which they were conducted. *Do You Remember Kunan Poshpora*, the book published on the twenty-fifth anniversary of the event (Batool, et al. 2016), narrates the victims' terrible experiences and urges the Indian legal system to extend justice to them.

[9] During protests against the 2012 Delhi gang-rape, there were clamours to remove the Armed Forces (Special Powers) Act (AFSPA), which, as per the accounts of victims from the Northeast of India, has given the army enormous power, which is often abused to rape women. Massive protests have taken place in the area, alleging the Indian Army of being composed of rapists.

Muzaffarnagar,[10] and Thankamani[11] in Kerala, where massive violence from the state apparatus questions these women's sense of belonging to the nation.

The way the media and academic work in India construct and propagate identities needs major revision and research. Often, concerns about internal patriarchies raised by the mainstream overlook the specific political identities of individual groups. While there are ethical implications of these demands, the consequences of such political campaigns often push the already alienated Dalit and Muslim men further towards the margins. While invoking justice[12] for Muslim and Dalit women, mainstream feminism's reading of these projects assumes a vantage point that places Muslim and Dalit men at the receiving end of a highly sophisticated and structured critique, obtained from the perspective of their own privileged locations. Therefore, the novel *Barsa,* discussed elsewhere in this book, fails to see themselves as part of the nationalist project that adds to the alienation and emasculation of men from marginalised communities. I am not undermining the importance of the resistance mounted by women through various local movements, like the Women's Jamaat movement in Tamil Nadu, against the oppressive practices of patriarchy, religion, and the State. Instead, I would say that the mainstream representations of these movements are often hurried and appropriating, mostly ignoring the political awareness that activists in these groups exhibit when placing the community's concerns in an equally prominent position with questions of patriarchal violence. Dowry deaths

---

[10] There was massive and inhuman violence committed on Muslim women in both cases and State interventions to protect the perpetrators. Women were targeted as markers of a community's honour, and as a mode through which to annihilate and emasculate its men.

[11] In 1986, in village Thankamani of Kerala, as part of a search programme, police attacked tribal households and beat up the men and raped women. Although the media and political parties in the opposition raised the issue, none of the accused was punished.

[12] This term is borrowed from Deepa Danraj's documentary on women Jamaats in Tamil Nadu (WMM 2011).

and domestic violence are also addressed in women's Jamaats and similar platforms as part of local customs and cultures, rather than as purely feminist critiques of Islam. Mainstream representations of these movements unfortunately position Muslim/Dalit women against the men of their own communities.

ISLAM AND REFORMISM IN CONTEMPORARY TIMES

Religious piety together with reformism is a modern phenomenon in most South Asian religions, and Islam in South Asia has been going through a phase of dynamic transformation. Salafism and Wahhabist movements have influenced South Asian Islam, and all Muslim communities in India have experienced a great deal of political activism and reformism. Increased migrations to the Gulf countries have resulted in the religious modernisation taking place in those regions being copied. But the growing insecurity amongst Muslims in India in relation to the mounting Hindutva agenda and fissures in our practices of secularism have given rise to political mobilisation among Muslim communities too. In this revived piety and politics, Muslim women have participated actively.

While feminism is an inherently modern politics committed to rights, emancipation, and agency, women have developed multiple modalities of engaging with identities, communities, and religion in a modern space. Inherently flawed in feminist representations of women's activism in marginalised communities is the adoption of certain common denominators to engage with women's aspirations and desires. It may not always be a discourse on rights that motivates women in Jamaat or piety movements. Or even if there is a discourse on rights, it cannot be essentialised across communities that experience different political realities and destinies in the country. Mainstream feminist engagement with the judiciary for women-friendly laws and an anti-rape culture cannot be juxtaposed with Muslim women's engagement with Islamic jurisprudence. As Sharmila Rege has rightly pointed out:

> ... recognizing differences, power and connections of class, caste and community means transforming subjectivities, politics and pedagogies. At the level of practice, for those of us who have been complicit in the power and privileges of caste, one of our first realizations is about the little knowledge of the cultures that have been violently marginalized. A large part of the feminist discourse of experience has been an autobiography of the upper caste woman, her conflict with tradition and desire to be modern. (2006, 63)

At times, Indian feminism makes irresponsible interventions in the lifeworlds of Muslim women, without engaging with the questions of State and citizenship, under the pretext of women's rights. Anupama Rao, in her Introduction to *Gender and Caste: Issues in Contemporary Feminism* (2005), warns of feminism's self-assumed right to intervene in the histories of women: 'Perhaps Indian feminism too is guilty of holding a set of un-interrogated assumptions about whom it speaks for, who forms its constituency, and the life-worlds and situations it assumes as normative while developing strategies for feminist intervention' (ibid., 29).

Rao is apprehensive about the prejudiced vantage points that Indian feminism assumes while engaging with the lives of women from different communities. My intention is also to go beyond the normative strategies of feminist intervention and focus on the complex relationship that women from various communities share with the nation. This problematic relationship not only makes normative feminist interventions impossible, but also makes them politically and ethically flawed. The point of departure for Dalit and Muslim feminists is this realisation of a political existence outside the privileged sections of women in the nation or, in Partha Chatterjee's words, a point of exit from 'the nation and its women' (2008b, 117). Feminism calls for alliances across differences through an intersectionality of experiences. However, bonds formed through women's voices, conjoined in terms of their exclusion from the centre of the nation, will have the strength to sustain differences while forming constructive associations. The centrality of upper-caste/middle-class women's experiences in feminism when it comes to defining rights often hinders such intersectional associations. In the 'postnational' phase, as Mary John (2009) points out, the crumbling of the alibi of the nation becomes the prime necessity that enables one to view one's own location, rather than normative commonalities. She further argues, in the context of rethinking the questions of nation in terms of globalisation from different vantage points, that ruptures and disorientations give feminists an opportunity to look back from different subaltern locations towards the making of India (ibid., 49).

While Mary John stresses on the troubled position of the nation in the history of the women's movement in the country, I would like to stretch the argument further to see how discourses on rights from liberal vantage points also focus on the individual's relationship with the State. The histories of the life worlds of Muslim and Dalit women are situated outside the premises of the nation inasmuch as they are construed as outsiders in the discourses of nationalism. So in order to incorporate Muslim/ Dalit women within the feminist fold, feminist projects may initiate concerns regarding their different political realities and social status. In fact, the crisis facing Indian feminism today is the functional impediments it experiences in terms of being a movement based on modern political rights. This strict adherence to a political modernity may not be viable to accommodating the everyday lives of women from heterogenous communities. An exploration of the life worlds of women across communities, feminist rights, and individual autonomy cannot be juxtaposed against the fraught relations that secular citizenships have with minority identities. Feminist politics is currently in turmoil, with gender entangled with community and national identities; often, mainstream feminism is unequivocally juxtaposed with hegemonic narratives of nationalism, experienced through the privileges and promises of secular citizenships in the postcolonial nation. The contradictory effects of Dalit/minority identities on women participants are often outside the frames of these feminist analyses, leaving one to wonder whether we should rethink the contours of Indian feminism.

This book studies Muslim women from Kerala, historicising them within Kerala's cultural and political landscape. While it is important to conceptualise identities using a common cultural identity of a shared historical past, one cannot escape the discontinuities beyond this singular formation.

Feminism is going through a problematic restructuring and rearticulation of its political positions. Different ideological frameworks of feminism face strong interventions from the propositions set forth by identity politics. The emancipatory politics of resistance and liberation seem inadequate to the task of registering the predicament of women in religious communities, given that they fail to characterise women's relationship with national and religious practices. Instead of viewing religion as a viable tool of female agency, the secularist model for women's liberation views it as a monolithic tool of oppression. The demand for analyses of the contradictory effects of religion on women invariably expands the borders of feminism. This involves the re-conceptualising of feminist agency in keeping with the negotiations women undertake in indigenous communities to claim political rights within their own societies.

A critical engagement with the lives of Muslim women challenges the secular-liberal assumptions of feminism, especially in a time of increased hostility against, and intensified focus on, Islam. The challenges that Islam poses to normative conceptions of feminist agency through a liberal-secular focus on individualism and individual freedom form the rubric under which the theoretical propositions of this book can be articulated. Contesting the notion of Muslim women as victims of a misogynist religion, I focus on variables like ethnicity, class, sexuality, and historical contexts that shape women's agency. Drawing on Saba Mahmood's attempt to rethink feminist agency in terms of the socio-religious heterogeneities that formulate the subject, I have engaged with the 'feminist enterprises' that Muslim women from Kerala were involved in at various historical junctures through their complex negotiations with their religious and cultural identities, yet without violating or opposing the 'normative structures' of religion. I have extended my argument to analyse the dynamics of exclusion and homogenous categorisation that ignored or were hesitant to register them as active political agents, complete with self-realisation and self-representation. Thus, I argue that this limitation is not only a result of reading Muslim women through the emancipatory politics of feminist ideology and the notions of modernity it is anchored to, but that it also deals with larger issues pertaining to the limitations of the modern secular State and its paradoxical existence in terms of 'collective national conscience' and 'moral heterogeneity'. These exclusions are made manifest in the inevitable violence that liberal democracy resorts to in depicting what can be called a monolithic composite of secular history, reflecting the fissures in the process of nation-formation.

In order to undertake such an investigation, I have constituted an archive consisting of the cultural and political engagements of Muslim women in Kerala in the process of self-realisation and representation within the structure of religion. While my vantage point does not exclude the one that revises and re-reads Islam from a modern feminist perspective, I have considered the lived experience of Muslim women in an attempt to explore the possibility of agency within the structure of religion, which liberal perspectives often consider a 'confined existence'. It follows, then, that the ways in which these women perceive or embrace Islam cannot be homogenous, but is a historically contextualised matrix that responds to class, caste, and ethnic categories. Historical contextualising is significant to this examination as Muslim women have responded to several key concerns in the history of Kerala.

The archive that I use cuts across different disciplines and periods in history. I have discussed literature, journal entries, historical narratives, and oral narratives that reflect an articulation, participation, defiance, and sense of community vis-à-vis the contexts from which they originate. I also explore the representation of Muslim women in literature while studying Muslim female subjectivity in Kerala. This is an effort to knit together various instances where Muslim women have been powerful agents of their own action and not merely subject to the norms of their religion, as a counter-narrative to both feminist misreading and ideological distortions. 'Muslim woman' is not a signifier that negates class and caste, or geographical contexts in my study. I am far too aware of the class differences in terms of economy and social status that make impossible a unilateral conclusion or even analysis. In my discussion on women and Islam in Kerala, I look into how subjectivity has been perceived and defined in various discourses on Muslim women. My argument is that Muslim women could develop 'a capacity for action within the systems of religion, and that this is invariably not a well-defined system of domination', and I critically engage with the construction of the identity of Muslim women which exaggerates her as a victim of religion in the contexts of colonial modernity, nationalist movements, and post-Independence progressive dialogues.

Chapter 1 explores the identity of Muslim women in Kerala and how this subjectivity has been influenced by multiple categories within Kerala society, ranging from geographical variations to caste and class denominations. The locus of this study on women and Islam has been consciously and carefully chosen: it is Kerala, and not the wider context of a universal Islam. I have assessed Muslim women's position in oral and written historical narratives across a range of loci varying from religion to rule, from teaching to cooking, and from oral historians to Sufi saints, teachers, and artisans. Through these varying modes of participation, these women developed concrete engagements with their respective historical contexts within the determined space of religion, which differed from the universal umbrella of a misogynist Islam.

Chapter 2 focuses on the participation of Muslim women in early twentieth-century reform movements in Kerala, and how their contribution went unacknowledged in the discussions on reform movements. I begin with a reading of the reform movements from a disturbing vantage point to reveal the inherent contradictions in the formation of a secular civil society in Kerala, and then explore how Muslims in Kerala responded to the call for reform, and how nationalist historians dealt with this resurgence in the Muslim community. I highlight the tactical incorporation of the reform movements of other communities within the nationalist movement, and the conscious negligence towards Muslim reform movements. This predilection, I feel, is subjected to two aspects: *first*, the prejudiced notion of Islam as an anti-women and anti-modern community that cannot respond to the call of modernity; *second*, the precarious position of Islam in the history of the subcontinent, which sentimentally, and even nostalgically, retains the memories of wars and conquests, and invasions and violations of the past.

Chapter 3 offers a critical reading of the novel *Barsa* by Khadija Mumtas in the background of contemporary discourses on Muslim women in Kerala. The representation of the Muslim woman in *Barsa* is in accordance with that in literature and popular media, and has therefore been widely accepted by mainstream Malayali discourses on Islam. The chapter reads *Barsa* along with feminist interpretations of the Quran and Islamic history, and finds the monolithic construction of the 'Muslim woman' as solely subject to Islam in these texts problematic. Besides, *Barsa* shares most of the common prejudices against Islam in general and Muslim men and women in particular. Reading Muslim women in contemporary times thus necessitates a reconstitution of our strategies of reading and understanding the feminist enterprise, and a revising of Eurocentric liberal categories.

Thus, my engagement with women and Islam in Kerala presents Muslim women as subjects of differently conceived notions of the religion, shaped by different factors of time, region, class, ethnicity, etc. In my attempt to conceive of the Muslim woman of Kerala at specific moments in Kerala's history, I have presented her as a heterogeneous subject whose agency has not been determined by a singular political formation. In her negotiations with religion and the larger society, she enacts her political concerns through modes of expression that may be termed religious conformism by liberal secularism. As much as I explore the possibility of feminism within the category 'Muslim', I also reconnoitre the obvious omissions and distortions in conventional historiography in order to project a particular vision of the nation. In this context, it is also important to mention my take on the differences in the political agency of Muslims in Islamist organisations and the large group of Sunni Muslims who do not necessarily identify themselves as part of the new-wave reform movements in Islam. While it is important to admit these diverse formations, my approach is to think about Muslim women's identity as being othered and marginalised by discourses on nationalism and a strong liberal thrust towards individualism. So internal differences in practice have not been much of a concern for this book. Further, Muslim women as targets of a violent and virulent Hindutva nationalism require an empathetic and politically appropriate conceptualisation in feminist spaces, which accommodates both men and women of the community.

1

Islam in Kerala

History and the Underpinnings of Women's Agency

The Muslim woman, as a political subject of the secular nation, often invites paradoxical propositions involving her minority status and the stereotyped gender constructions drawn from her Muslim identity. While the rudimentary definition of 'multiple jeopardy of existence' was used to define the intersectional identities of women in feminist discourses in the past, it seems too narrow to include these contesting categories. Being a minority subject within a 'secular' nation, together with the added complexity of gender inequalities, makes for a layered existence, denoting the politics of inclusion and exclusion at various levels. Modern interpretations of the Muslim woman as the victim of her religion without considering ethnic, cultural, and geographical heterogeneities do not add to an understanding of the inherent complexity of her identity. Islam is not a monolithic structure, nor do Muslim women make a homogenous group. Even within the peninsula, the way Islam has been conceived, imbibed, and followed differs drastically according to geographic and cultural variations. In this chapter, I trace the history of Islam in Kerala, focusing on Muslim women's agency in the rise and dissemination of the religion in the erstwhile territories of Travancore, Kochi, and Malabar. Exploring the history of premodern Kerala brings out a complex array of cultures and religiosities. Various aspects, such as the rigid caste system, the welcome accorded to foreign religions in its territory, the status of women in Kerala society of the time, and the effect of colonial invasion in the religious and gender equations of the state have exerted a great influence on the way Muslim women's identity has been formulated and appropriated.

The Arabs in Premodern Kerala

Trade relations between Arabia and Kerala date back to the second and third centuries, much before the advent of Islam in Arabia. Since the coastal areas of present-day Kerala had trade links with Arabia, it can be concluded that Islam came to Kerala through the Arab traders around the time of its formation in Arabia itself. Unlike northern India, Islam did not come to Kerala as part of conquests and territorial invasions. Therefore, Islam's role in the political society of Kerala, the ramifications of Muslim identity, as well as religious tensions between various groups are different from that in the rest of India.[1] In variously narrated histories, hagiographies, and oral literature, we come across different versions of Islam's arrival and dissemination in premodern Kerala, but rarely do we encounter frictions between Muslims and other native communities. The widely accepted Islamic tradition in Kerala is that of Malik Ibn Habeeb and Malik Dinar, although

---

[1] For instance, north India has always had a long history of centuries of invasions, and stories and references to past crimes to which the current tension between religious communities has been attributed. These keep recurring in the collective memory, and are wilfully ignited during times of riot and political issues. The genocides in Gujarat in 2002, the anti-Mandal Commission protests of 1990, and the demolition of the Babri Masjid in December 1992 are examples of such moments. Shahid Amin (2005) discusses the irrational slogan, *'Badla lenge Babur ki santanon se'*, in the context of fabricated pasts to show that even though Muslims of India in no way resemble their so-called exotic Arab, Central Asian, and Irani lineages, these imagined pasts continue to clutter the minds of the subcontinent, both Hindu and Muslim alike.

this has also been debated. Arabic signatures in Tarissappally copper plates[2] vouch for the presence of Arabs in Kollam during this time. Many Islamic travellers and traders refer to Kerala in their narratives. Sulaiman, Abu Sayyed, Masoodi, and Abul Fida in the ninth and tenth centuries, and Al Idireeni, Dimishqi, Qazneeni, and Ibn Bathutha between the twelfth and fourteenth centuries describe Kerala as a land of spices and mysteries. It can be concluded that Kerala had a full-fledged Islamic community by the fourteenth century.

The Cheraman Perumal Myth

The oft-quoted story of Cheraman Perumal's conversion[3] is the first reference to a strong Islamic presence in the oral history of Kerala. The reliability of the story is debated even now, yet no one can rule out the truth of this great conversion in the collective memory of this population. However, P. K. Balakrishnan, in his *Jaathi Vyavasthayum Kerala Charithravum*, rules out even the existence of a second Chera empire.[4] In widely differing arguments, Balakrishnan, Sreedhara Menon, and K. N. Ganesh

[2] Tarissappally *Tamra Saasana* was issued during the reign of the Chera emperor Sthanu Ravi (AD 844–55) by the Venad chieftain Ayyanadikal in AD 849. According to this, Christian traders were extended several concessions and privileges. The Arabic signatures in the copper plates testify to the high status that Arabs enjoyed in the society of the time, and to their involvement in the administrative functions of the kingdom. See Balakrishnan (1987, 61, 297, 298); Kareem (1997, 95–96).

[3] In different versions of the story, it has been stated that Cheraman Perumal, the last Chera king, went to Mecca to convert to Islam and died there. Both A. Sreedhara Menon (1987) and K. N. Ganesh (1997) refer to the story of this conversion. While Ganesh accepts the story based on the records of the construction of the first Muslim mosque, Sreedhara Menon refers to the story to show the impact of Islam on Kerala society of the time.

[4] P. K. Balakrishnan (1987) tries to trace the trajectory of the caste system in Kerala and demystify the claims of upper-class Kshatriyas and Nambutiris. He traces the origin of these mystified pasts in the late seventeenth and early eighteenth centuries.

study the history of Kerala from different angles. Locating the trajectory of this myth may be difficult, but the historicity of the myth—the way it was constructed and circulated in a society of religious plurality—is interesting. In Shaykh Zainuddin's *Tuhfat al-Mujahidin*, written in the sixteenth century, the conversion of the king marks the beginning of Islam in Malabar. Section two of the 2006 edition of the book begins with the arrival of the Jews and Christians and, a few years later, the Muslims:

> … there arrived at Kodungallur a party of Muslims, who were poor, with a Shaykh. They were on their way to visit the footprint of our father Adam in Ceylon. When the King heard about their arrival, he sent for them …. The leader of the group, the Shaykh, informed about Prophet Muhammad and the religion of Islam …. Allah, glory be to him and exalted be He, caused to enter in his mind the truth of the prophet's mission. He heartily acknowledged him and his love for the prophet took possession of his heart. He asked the Shaykh and his companions to call on him on their return journey … for the reason he might go with them.
>
> Thus, on their return journey … they called the king. The king asked the Shaykh to arrange, without any one's knowledge, the ship and other things necessary for his journey with him. (2006, 29–30)

The work goes on to say that the king divided his provinces amongst several of his ministers and family members and set off for his conversion. It is stated that his kingdom covered the entire territory of Malabar, from Kanyakumari in the south to Kasargode in the north. K. P. Padmanabha Menon, in *The History of Kerala*, Vol. 1 (2001, 451–52), refers to *Keralolpathi* (*The Origin of Kerala*) and supports this version of Perumal's conversion. The author of *Tuhfat al-Mujahidin*, Shaykh Zainuddin, goes on to describe the death of the king at Shuhr (2006, 29-31),[5] where he entrusted a group of Muslim travellers with the task of constructing mosques in different parts of Kerala. This group, which included Malik bin Dinar, later built mosques in various parts of Kerala, starting with

---

[5] Rolland Miller also sticks to Shaykh Zainuddin's version (1976, 48).

Kodungallur. Historians have different versions of this conversion and its historicity, but attempts have been made to trace the tomb of Cheraman Perumal in Arabia (Bahauddin 1992, 21; Kareem 1997, 110–11; Miller 1976, 48; Sreedhara Menon 1987, 34). As mentioned earlier, the socio-political relevance of this conversion in the history of Islam in Kerala lies in locating Islam in our cultural past. Mystified stories about collective pasts are in no way new to Indian history. In Kerala, too, every community has added to the collective memory, glorifying their origins in Brahmin and Kshatriya lineages. The Catholics of Kerala cling to the myth of the great conversion of Nambutiris under the auspices of St Thomas in order to prove their aristocracy. Collective responses to and circulation of myths on conversions were prototypical of premodern religious societies. Over centuries, these myths assumed different roles, and were assimilated into the cultural past of communities, but not as recurrent archetypes. Rather, the 'conversion stories' impacted the cultural existence of these communities as intercessions in historical moments, reshaping the everyday experience of religious reality vis-à-vis syncretic practices.

The Untold Muslim History of Kerala

In *History of Kerala and Muslims* (1997), C. K. Kareem discusses Islam in premodern Kerala. Referring to the Tarissappally copper plates and their Arab witnesses, he claims that Muslims must have been a well-respected community of the time to stand as witnesses to a royal order. And his critique of prominent historians of Kerala as communal in their outlook cannot be overlooked, as conspicuous in their histories is the absence of the Muslim existence. Kareem delineates the development of the Mappila community in Kerala from the *Mu'ta*[6] marriages between

---

[6] *Mu'ta* marriages are marriages of convenience permitted by Islamic law; however, these existed in pre-Islamic Arabian society as well. As per this custom, a man was permitted to enter into a contract of marriage for

the Arab traders who stayed here for about three months during their journey in search of spices and the native women in Kerala, stating that the matrilineal system that existed in Kerala society of the time was conducive to such marriages. According to Kareem, the fact that such a matrilineal system existed in Arabia as well facilitated such alliances.[7]

To return to the conversion of Cheraman Perumal: Kareem turns to a widely circulated legend of Cheraman Perumal and the marking of his journey as the beginning of Kolla Varsham,[8] as the country was then divided into various regions amongst the relatives and allies of Perumal. He compiles the available documents to conclude that Bana Perumal, the last Chera King, took his nephew with him to Arabia; the latter returned after the king's death to establish the Arakkal royal family in Kerala. It is interesting to examine Cheraman Perumal's conversion in the history of Islam in Kerala as a recurrent myth in formulating the identity of Muslims in premodern Kerala, and how later interpolations in the story deflected the originary versions. Colonial historians like Logan (2004, Vol. 1, 196) and Barbosa (Kareem 1997, 41) refer to the story of Perumal's conversion. But the twentieth-century historians no longer wish to accept this tradition; rather, they insistently refute it and point out the irrationality of the tradition.

---

a stipulated period with a woman and stay in her household. During the latter half of the twentieth century, the system came under social scrutiny for exploiting girls from poor families of Malabar, which was locally termed '*Arabikkalyanam*' (marriage to the Arab). Stereotyped portrayals of such exploited Muslim girls formed the sub-plot of many popular Malayalam movies of the time.

[7] Among pre-Islamic Arabs, a bride price called *mahr* was an essential condition for a legal marriage. The *mahr* was given to the guardian of the bride. Islam made *mahr* a wife's property. Arab women definitely had the upper hand in material transactions related to the marriage.

[8] Kolla Varsham is the Malayalam calendar. There are various stories about its origin. Many historians accept that Perumal's journey to Mecca and the resulting division of Kerala into different territories mark the beginning of Kolla Varsham. At the same time, historians like Ilamkulam Kunjan Pillai (1971) and M. G. S. Narayanan (1973) contest this argument.

Perumal's conversion, and the way it permeates the premodern history of Kerala, provide glimpses of the status of Muslims in premodern Kerala society. In public life and society of the time, Muslims were viewed with undisputable recognition. Moreover, the myth was in a way facilitating increasing conversions to the community, and that too, promoted by the upper castes and the rulers. In *Kerala Samskaaram*, Sreedhara Menon refers to an order by the Samutiri (Zamorin) of Calicut, encouraging conversions to Islam (1987, 34–35). According to this order, it was mandatory for at least one person from every Hindu fishing family of Calicut to convert to Islam. These attempts to proselytise, which took place at a strategic level, are often referred to as examples of the Samutiri's religious tolerance. The converted Muslims were taken into the Samutiri's naval force. The fact that the captain of the Samutiri's navy was Kunjali Marakkar also adds to the regard that rulers of Kerala had for the community. The vast maritime experience and exposure of the Arabs who reached Kerala for trade may have motivated the Samutiri's decision to retain the Muslims as allies. And this accounts for the wealthy status of the Samutiri compared to other provincial rulers of Kerala.[9] Given the absence of luxury and wealth in Kerala's past, wealth obviously constituted one aspect of the charm of Arab intervention. Marriages between Arabs and Muslims were promoted for this reason. Kerala's only revenue was accentuated through trade, and the early marriages between Arabs and the women of Kerala might not have been attempts to escape caste through conversion. Given the circumstances, the mass conversions to Islam as part of an anti-caste movement would have taken place much later, during the colonial intervention. Cheraman Perumal's conversion was kept alive in society to maintain legitimacy for the Muslim folk of premodern Kerala, and also to justify the extreme patronage extended by the then rulers

---

[9] P. K. Balakrishnan talks about the penurious existence of the rulers and the absence of luxury in the palaces or royal lifestyles in the princely states of Kerala, pointing to the absence of architectural splendours, for example, when compared to the neighbouring states of Tamil Nadu and Karnataka (1987, 96–101).

to the Muslims, which was strategically motivated to regulate socio-economic equations. Moreover, the rulers of Calicut were obligated to the Arabs and Muslims for their expertise in naval strategies and exposure to the sea. The forcible promotion of religion was never encouraged and conversions never disturbed the social order or communal harmony.

Conversions and Tensions

Religious conversion in India has always been caught in 'moments of dialogue and religious interchange', instead of being viewed through the prism of 'insider and outsider religions' (Robinson and Clarke 2007, 14). In premodern Kerala, the history of Christianity was not the same as that of Islam. And the responses to Islam in premodern Kerala society and colonial Kerala stand apart in different spatial and temporal contexts through their distinct cultural implications, which can in no way be mapped along a singular formation. In their Introduction to *Religious Conversion in India: Modes, Motivations and Meanings*, Rowena Robinson and Sathianathan Clarke state:

> The popular imagination overtaxes itself by considerations of coercive conversions to Islam or Christianity but the material shows that in many areas where Islam has spread among vast numbers of people it has done so through trade links, through the influence of Sufis or through other processes that have little to do with political oppression. (ibid.)

Ibn Battuta's evidence has been considered by Stephen F. Dale, who recorded the size, character, and institutions of the Muslim community in Kerala. Dale states that in general, Muslims of Kerala shared the Arabic-Islamic culture scattered over different regions across the Indian Ocean (2007, 54–77). Battuta described the wealth and high social status enjoyed by Muslims of the time. Two major historians of the sixteenth century, Barbosa and Shaykh Zainuddin, provide different dimensions of the realities of the time. While both Zainuddin and Barbosa talk about conversions to Islam, Barbosa studies class among the Muslim population of Kerala. The Portuguese traveller depicts the Mappilas as converts from the lower castes and the upper-class Muslims as traders from Arabia, who stayed in Kerala for only a few months and were known as *Pardesis* (outsiders to the native community). These foreign Muslims gradually stopped coming after the Portuguese took control of the sea route and trade in the Indian Ocean. Both Barbosa and Zainuddin describe the warm welcome extended to the converts in society, which triggered mass conversions in the sixteenth century, perhaps with a view to escaping caste. We can make the following inferences from these historians' work: (*i*) since the sixteenth century, Islam as a community in Kerala has no longer been an economically homogenous group as it used to be in earlier centuries; and (*ii*) the lower castes were able to escape caste through conversions. But in the legends on conversion, the only significant references are those that reiterate the illustrious conversions of Nambutiris and Kshatriya kings, thereby camouflaging the heterogenous trajectories. From the sixteenth century onwards, the legendary conversions took on a different meaning vis-à-vis the poor economic and social status of the Mappilas. The legends also enabled the converts to look back upon a glorified, homogenised past that erased all traces of caste oppression from their collective memories. The disentangling of legend from history requires a revision of the spatial and temporal contexts where they have been reproduced and internalised.

From being the sole proprietors of trade and commerce in the Indian Ocean, the Muslims were slowly reduced to a population that confined themselves to agriculture (as documented in colonial records[10]), and religious proselytising became a spiritual and political engagement. The rising insecurity amongst Muslims in the presence of Christian missionaries patronised by the European

---

[10] Logan refers to Barbosa to describe the early Muslim population of Kerala (Logan, Vol. 1, 2004, 193–98). Dale, too, refers to Barbosa (2007, 58–59).

invaders would have been one reason for this (Zainuddin 2006, 5–7). In Kerala, missionary activities of Christians and Muslims followed different paths. Muslim conversions were by and large encouraged by the rulers of Kerala, while conversions to Christianity were not patronised by the State in premodern Kerala history. However, this changed during the colonial period as the Europeans patronised mass conversions to Christianity. The status of Muslims in the social hierarchy also declined with European invasions. Parallel to the legend of Perumal's conversion is upper-caste Christian communities' own legend of St. Thomas converting 500 Nambutiri families to invigorate the Aryan lineage of the Roman Catholics in Kerala. The validity of this claim has been contested, but the legend serves the purpose of allowing early converts to maintain an aristocracy vis-à-vis the mass conversion of lower castes to Christianity during the nineteenth and early twentieth century. Shaykh Zainuddin gives a detailed description of the atrocities committed by the Portuguese on the Muslims:

> The Portuguese invaded the Muslim abodes and subjected them to all kinds of oppressions. The abominable atrocities and cruelties the Portuguese openly unleashed on the Muslims were countless. This Portuguese reign lasted for more than eighty years. By that time the condition of the Muslims had become extremely pathetic. They had become impoverished, weak and powerless. They could not find a way to get out of this wretched hole. (2006, 5)

Under such humiliation, the Perumal story served as a reminder of the ancient glory of the Muslims, especially when the relationship between the rulers and the Muslims worsened due to the intervention of colonial invaders. Thus, the legend has, over time, deviated from its originary function and acquired an altogether different role. Historicising the conversions in premodern Kerala as 'a political rather than a spiritual activity' (Viswanathan 2001, xxvii) also reflects the shift in the concerns of premodern princely states in their transition to colonial modernity. Let us look back on the formation of various minor territories in Kerala in place of one unified kingdom. The origin of the matrilineal communities in Kerala and the trajectory of the participation of women in the dynamic social network of conversions and assimilation are the two aspects that I focus on here. In the following section, I will be looking at premodern Kerala as an interface of dialogue and assimilation between cultures and civilisations. I feel that women had a major role to play in this realm of cultural exchange and mutual interchange of ideas. This was in accordance with the matrilineal system that existed in Kerala at the time, but it was having Arab traders as males of their households that made it necessary for the women to take charge. In the absence of men who had to return to Arabia after their three-month stay in Kerala, women were left in total control of their families, the sole agents of the entire household.

MATRILINY, ISLAM, AND CONVERSIONS

Dealing with the question of conversion in premodern Kerala entails studying the dynamic exchange of identities between matrilineal communities and Arab culture. It is Gauri Viswanathan who points out how conversion resists 'positivist ways of conceptualizing difference through ... essentializing markers as race, religion, colour, ethnicity and nationality' (2001, xv). In spite of the spiritual claims made in *Tuhfat al-Mujahidin*,[11] I will be focusing on the relationships of convenience between the Arab men and Hindu women of premodern Kerala which challenge essentialist categories of race, gender, and religion. Viswanathan elaborates on this aspect of conversion:

> In destabilizing the determinants of race, religion, gender, and so on, conversion unsettles the understanding of difference through purely essentialist categories. As a knowledge-producing activity, it shifts the focus away from visible markers of difference (such as race or gender)

[11] In the Introduction and first chapter of *Tuhfat al-Mujahidin*, Zainuddin quotes the spiritual intentions of Muslim pilgrims. The first chapter is dedicated to a discussion of *jihad* (Viswanathan 2006, 3–25).

to the distance in viewpoints emerging from the pragmatics of communication. Such gaps in communication are the starting point for conversion's reconstructive role in initiating movement between opposing viewpoints. (2001, xv)

The dialogue between Islam and the Kerala community began with marriage. These short-term marriages, legitimised by Islam through *Mu'ta* marriages in their multiple manifestations, provided the foundation for Islamic communities in Kerala. In his *History of Kerala and Muslims*, Kareem describes the possibility of relationships between Arab men and the women of Kerala:

Due to the fall of the Roman Empire after the fourth century AD the trade between India and the west was stagnant for a while. This gap of absence of Greek and Roman commerce was soon filled by adventurous Arabs. From then onwards till the sixteenth century they maintained their authority over the Indian Ocean. (1997, 91–92)

This phase clearly saw a continuous exchange of culture, values, and linguistic development, which cannot be confined to the term 'hybridity'. Viswanathan rejects 'hybridity', viewing it as a term too debilitating to engage with the dynamics of reciprocal movements in a conversion:

While terms like hybridity are offered as an alternative to essentializing identities, it does not capture the dynamism of movement signified by conversion, which regards crossovers of identity not merely as items of exchange or even fusion but as remaking of the categories that define identity. Nor is syncretism a satisfactory term to describe the overlapping of identities, since, as its etymology and historical usage indicate, it constitutes a blurring rather than a negotiation of differences. Moreover, syncretism is as much a construct as are terms like 'tradition' and 'modernity'. (2001, xv)[12]

---

[12] Talal Asad (2003) discusses the construct of tradition versus modernity in terms of the European Enlightenment, which forms the site of all discourses on non-Western histories.

The new community of Islam that evolved in Kerala was thus not a spiritual hybrid of Islam and Hinduism, but a more dynamic movement that restructured categories. Therefore, the claims for a universal Islam that recurs in stereotypical narratives of Muslim experiences of the past as well as the present prove irrational. When rethinking this cultural exchange in terms of fluidity, it is possible to arrive at a negotiation of differences. Leaning towards Viswanathan's notion of 'movement from one world view to another, with the regularity of border crossing' (ibid., xv), the precolonial period of interaction between the Arabs and Muslims in Kerala can be viewed as a period of cultural mediation.

Kareem describes this interface of cultural dynamics as a mutually productive process that benefits both groups and is at the same time deeply rooted in material realities rather than the spiritual. In his narration, the Arabs who left their homeland around July–August returned only in about eight months. This period of abstinence encouraged their sexual intimacies with the women of foreign lands, and the early associations between Arabs and the natives would have been led by such demands. Studying the social system of premodern Kerala, Kareem concludes that the climate was conducive for both Arabs and Muslims to enter into such relationships. According to him, there existed in Arabia the system of *Mu'ta* marriages based on polyandry. The family and children were under the care of women, and even strangers were warmly welcomed by the women into their households. The children born out of these alliances remained the responsibility of women.[13] The man lived with the woman's family for a stipulated period and paid an amount as *mahr*.[14] This, in Kareem's version, was important to maintain the moral stability of the society. These

[13] Islamic moralists often posit the pre-Islamic Arabian community as a loose community. They defend the reformative practices of the Prophet, who wanted to correct the morally deviant Arabs through strict measures, especially in terms of controlling women's sexuality.

[14] In Islam, *mahr* or *mehr* is a mandatory payment in the form of money or possessions, paid by the groom to the bride at the time of marriage. This legally becomes the property of the woman.

Mu'ta marriages were common in every port city that the Arabs visited, and were called Bi'na marriages in Ceylon. Robertson Smith highlights three characteristics of these Arab marriages: (*i*) the woman had the right to choose the husband; (*ii*) she could stay in her family after the marriage; and (*iii*) she could leave the alliance whenever she wanted (1907, 77–79). The Bi'na marriages were similar to the polyandry that existed amongst Nair women of premodern Kerala. It has been observed that the rigidity of Islam is due to many such 'loose' practices that existed in pre-Islamic Arabian society. *Mu'ta* marriages are practised even now among the Arab Muslims.

It can be presumed that Kerala was a major centre for foreign trade in India right from the Roman age. In the absence of documented history, travelogues and assumptions design the history of the time. The Aryanisation of Kerala took place only around the ninth century AD, in Bahauddin's opinion (1992, 74). He observes that the entry of Nambutiris dated between the ninth and eleventh centuries, and by the fifteenth century they had consolidated their position. In order to establish a Brahmin-centred, caste-based land system, appropriate legends, such as that of Parasurama,[15] were propagated. He also points out how the Brahmins manipulated the absence of concepts of territory and property ownership in the inlands to become landowners and enslave the natives (ibid.). However, it should be noted that even prior to Aryanisation, the coastal areas had the dynamism peculiar to a society in transit due to the constant presence of foreign traders. These aspects are discussed further in Balakrishnan's *Jaathivyavasthayum Kerala Samoohavum* (*The Caste System and Kerala Society*), where he claims that till

---

[15] A widely circulating legend on the origins of Kerala says that Parasurama created Kerala by throwing his axe into the sea, whereupon the sea gave way up to the point where his axe had fallen. Historians like Balakrishnan (1987) argue that the Brahmin community of Kerala constructed appropriate legends to assert their supremacy. Balakrishnan also studies the construction of the Nambutiris as a privileged clan even among the Brahmins, with their consciously distinct customs.

the beginning of the eighth century, Kerala society was entirely 'barbaric' with no concept of family, property or agriculture. Into this terrain the Brahmins had a smooth entry (Balakrishnan 1987, 261).[16] If the Aryans eyed the inlands, it was because the coastal areas, being centres of foreign trade, were beyond their capacity to contest for power. The constant presence of foreigners along the coasts would gradually have led to the evolution of a matrilineal system in Malabar through the institutionalised relationships between native women and foreign traders. Furthermore, the Roman and later, the Arab, traders were used to various forms of such institutionalised practices in their homelands as well. If institutionalised marriages were an imposition upon the natives by the Brahmins, these practices would have placed no moral burden upon the society. Thus, even before the Nambutiris, the foreign traders would have been instrumental in founding the system of polyandry. Once this was institutionalised through constant practice, the Arab *Mu'ta* marriages and various modes of the concubine system provided the base for the unique matrilineal system in Malabar. Families became women-centric, with the woman and her children from many relationships living in her own house, with all bringing wealth and respect to the family. The 'sambandhams'[17] of the Nambutiris were a later modification of this practice.

Thus, the growing Muslim community in Kerala had a woman-centric family structure, with the woman standing at the interface

[16] While differing with Balakrishnan's projection of pre-Brahmin Kerala society as barbaric, I draw upon his time-frame to discuss premodern Kerala society.

[17] *Sambandhams* are institutionalised sexual relationships between Nair women and Nambutiri men. The colonial historian views this from the perspective of Christian morality. It has been recorded that Tipu Sultan also had a negative impression of this practice (Kareem 1997, 280). Padmanabha Menon discusses the Malabar Marriage Commission Report and British responses to matriliny (2001, Vol. 3, 302–05). Alternate readings are available in Arunima's *There Comes Papa* (2003) and Anitha Devasia's 'Critical Introduction' to her doctoral thesis, 'A Translation of O. Chandumenon's *Indulekha*' (1999).

and as the link between two cultures and communities. Material exchanges in the realm of trade were not replicated exactly in the domain of religion, as pre-Islamic Arab society was not inclined towards spiritual or religious communication. Even in the Islamic period, religion was not the priority in the context of trade. Therefore, the native Muslim in general and native women in particular had the right to adhere to their cultural practices and customs. Apparently, most rituals of the Sunni Muslims of Kerala are rooted in Kerala's cultural practices. But during the process of Aryanisation, it would have become necessary to establish their identity and status in a dynamic society, which had suddenly turned into a melting pot of cultures and spiritualities. Subsequently, religious identities, which may have kept a low profile in social life until then, would have gained momentum, allowing legends on conversion to proliferate.[18]

Historicising the Muslim experience often begins with the statement that relations between Kerala and Arabia existed prior to Islam. It then shifts to the conversion of Perumal,[19] leaving a huge gap between the two historical contexts. After this, we see a direct leap to the *Tuhfat al-Mujahidin* of the sixteenth century. These gaps lead us to several less-known crucial junctures in the development of the religion in Kerala, and we ought to grapple with the 'multiple genealogies of religious freedom', as Viswanathan puts it (2001, xv), which allows us to study conversion in terms other than assimilation or forcible change. Instrumental as they are for the shifting paradigms of culture and the overlapping of identities, it is within these gaps that I place woman's agency as an active determinant of the political existence of the Muslim community in Kerala. Contrary to the widely circulated assumption that

[18] Kareem (1997, 108) even states that Sankara's monotheistic propaganda must have sprung from the wide circulation of Islam, which he considered a threat to the Aryans.

[19] Some argue that two Perumals must have existed, owing to the difference in opinion regarding Cheraman Perumal's conversion and that of Bana Perumal. Muslim historians like Kareem accept this version (1997, 105–15).

matriliny in Malabar was extended to the Muslim families of Malabar, it can be assumed that this matrilineal system also evolved from the alliances between the Arabs and native women, which were later institutionalised by the Aryans (the Nambutiris) as *sambandhams*. The Aryans had arrived at a much later phase in the history of Kerala, compared to the Arabs.[20] To arrive at such a conclusion, I rely upon the similarity between *Mu'ta* marriages and *sambandhams*, as well as the fact that the Arabs had arrived much before the Aryans.[21] Balakrishnan's observation of the caste system in Kerala and his discussion on the roots of Nambutiri Brahmins reveal them to be a group of Brahmins who migrated from territories north of Kerala, for instance, present-day Andhra Pradesh and Karnataka. He discusses the peculiar customs that Nambutiri Brahmins developed, which are different from those of any other Brahmin community in India. He concludes that this group would have consciously formulated a code of rules different from other Brahmin communities to demarcate themselves as a distinct group, and to put forward claims of being higher in the hierarchy than other Brahmins. Balakrishnan also points out the irrationality of the argument that Sankaracharya had codified the set of moral and religious norms for the Nambutiris (1987, 328–30).

So, prior to the arrival of Brahmins in Kerala, what existed there was a society that practised various forms of polyandry—fraternal polyandry in some communities, polygamy in others. In spite of the Brahmins and their concept of morality, this system continued undisturbed till the nineteenth century. The Brahmins accepted the system with minor modifications; while maintaining the purity of their women through rigid customs, they simultaneously enjoyed

---

[20] Balakrishnan (1987) claims that Malayalam became a distinct language from ninth century AD, and that this development was chiefly initiated by the sudden influence of Sanskrit brought by the Nambutiris. From this, he concludes that the Aryan invasion of Kerala took place around the ninth century AD, and was established by the eleventh century.

[21] If Sankara's period is estimated between AD 788 and 820, Kareem refers to many scholars who have opined that the *adwaita* had been influenced by the monotheism of Islam (1997, 108).

the fruits of this system through practices like *sambandhams*. They did not question or compete with the status of the Arabs, nor did they tamper with the Arab presence and the native associations with these traders. Rather, they moved strategically to the inlands and developed a caste system that allowed them to be the authority over land, taking workers from the lower castes to till the land. *The Book of Barbosa* (fifteenth century) and *The Voyage of Francis Pyrad de Laval* (sixteenth century) reflect a society based on matrilineal values and sexual morality that were similar to the practices of polyandry and polygamy of ancient tribes and clans. Pre-Islamic Arabian society also followed such practices. While shifting to the caste system enforced by the Nambutiris, the tribe that later came to be known as the Nair community retained its sexual practices but shifted to the transfer of property through women, once the concept of property had evolved (Balakrishnan 1987, 357–59). Taking advantage of the peculiar situation, the Nambutiris continued with existing practices. Once again, accepting Balakrishnan's view, Nambutiri debauchery had been the real reason for their insistence on intra-caste marriage only for the elder son, and Nair *sambandhams* for the rest (ibid., 363).

While discussing the roots of matriliny as it existed in Kerala, I have inferred that women who were drawn into polyandry were instrumental in the institutionalisation of matriliny. In the discussions above, it has been argued that female sexuality becomes the binding force that decides the moral values and practices of a society. In the transition from a clan to a caste-oriented political society, Kerala retained most of its ancient practices and adapted them to changing situations. The absence of men in the family (considering that most men were into trade) entrusted women of the early Muslim community with the responsibility for both the family and the community. We read about instances of Muslim missionary activities for the first time in Kerala history in Zainuddin's *Tuhfat al-Mujahidin*:

A party of foreign Muslims entered some ... seaports of Malabar and settled there. In course of time, the inhabitants of these towns began to embrace Islam …. Before long, Islam spread all over the region at great pace and the Muslim population began to grow, and soon in the cities of Malabar heralded the settlement of Muslims in big numbers. In those days, they did not face any kind of opposition or oppression from the non-Muslim rulers who were then in power. As for these rulers, they continued to live adhering fully to their own ancient religion and its rites. (2007, 4)

This proliferation of the Muslim community in Kerala, as described in *Tuhfat al-Mujahidin*, lacks temporal markers. The narrative starts with the arrival of Islam, followed by the conversion of Perumal, and leading on to the arrival of the Portuguese. In the intermittent period, Islam gradually spread through a social system that was itself in transition from a fluid tribal value system to a hierarchically structured political society imposed by the Aryans. In Arabia, Islam had come up as a harsh monitoring system against the 'loose' Arabian tribes, and therefore this transition in Kerala was in a way helpful for the advent of Islam there. There had also been some exposure to other Semitic cultures like Judaism and Christianity, all of which demanded a transition to a structured family system. So matriliny was the only possible outcome if the existing value system in Kerala had to fit within the social transformation taking place.

The reliability of the Perumal story in the history of Kerala has been debated, with Muslim historians citing different historical evidence. The archetype of this conversion recurs in various instances in Kerala's history. For instance, during his coronation, the Samutiri takes an oath to keep the sword until his ancestor, who has gone to Mecca, returns (Bahauddin 1992, 23). In northern Kerala, the cultural performance of *Madai Theyyam* invokes the event of Perumal's conversion. Bahauddin writes:

According to Hindu religious songs associated with the *Theyyam* festival, Cheraman Perumal sailed from Kodungallur secretly and on reaching Dharmapattanam the next day, he entrusted the *Kovilakam*[22]

---

[22] The abode of the king.

to Samutiri. His followers also sailed from Kodungallur. Prophet Mohammed was staying in Jeddah. Perumal went there, embraced Islam and took the name Tajuddin. (ibid.)

THE ARAKKAL ROYAL FAMILY AND MATRILINY

The transformation of a tribal culture into organised princely states included the evolution and circulation of legends related to historical events. Thus, the Muslim royal family of Arakkal finds itself attached to the Perumal legends in many ways. Although Balakrishnan and other historians deny the existence of a unified Kerala prior to the evolution of the princely states, they all agree on the existence of the Arakkal royal family. Arakkal Ali Rajas minted silver coins dated Hijra 122 and 163, which shows that the family had been in power before that time.[23] The Arakkal Dutch record mentions Hijra 56 as the entry of Malik bin Dinar. Therefore, Balakrishnan's argument that there had been no organised rule in Kerala till the eleventh century cannot be considered. While his conclusions about the natives and inlands appear relevant, the coastal areas at this time had witnessed a dynamic cultural exchange. The Aryan invasion, the formation of Malayalam, and the spread of Islam should be seen as simultaneous, intertwined processes.

It has been stated that Perumal took Kohinoor, the son of his sister Sree Devi (of Dharmadam), with him to Arabia, and that the prince returned as Muhammad Ali. This is the legend widely in circulation regarding the formation of the Arakkal dynasty. I believe that most legends about Kerala's origin, conversions, and establishment of kingdoms developed around the same time, based on the fact that all such legends have served similar political purposes of establishing each community in premodern Kerala society. The Parasurama legend, Perumal's conversion, the Arakkal legend, and even the St Thomas episode have helped in consolidating the respective community's prospects in society. Apart from historical evidence that supports the factual data, the

---

[23] Kareem (1997) talks about coins dated Hijra 31, 35, and 161.

legends, and variations thereof, led to the intermeshing of the real with the surreal, the physical with the metaphysical, the natural with the supernatural, and the spiritual with the superstitious. Every community has its repository of myths, which constantly engage historiography with questions of accuracy and legitimacy. These legends serve a historical purpose and attain multiple levels of signification in the collective memory at various historical contexts. I intend to look into instances of female agency made viable through the spread of Islam in Kerala in the form of a strategic coalition of legends and history. The archives that I focus on are from different periods in the history of Kerala. Spatially and temporally, they may denote different sites, but while examining the Muslim woman's agency, I emphasise how these myths, as they are appropriated into history, contribute in shaping not only the Muslim community and its ethos, but also the structure and nature of the social systems in this land.

Arakkal Beevi: Muslim Women Rulers

The connection between matriliny, Muslims, and the Malabar coast has been discussed earlier. The Arakkal dynasty and stories related to its formation constitute a major episode in the history of this state, although it is not often treated with the regard it deserves. As a practice, matriliny evolved in Kerala out of convenience, through the coast's constant interactions with foreign traders, especially the Arabs during the pre-European phase. Later, the Aryans would have established this as a social system. The formation of the Arakkal dynasty reflects the impact of matriliny amongst the Mappilas of Kerala; religion was not a basis for social customs in premodern Kerala. Kareem states that the formation of the Arakkal dynasty played a major role in the spread of Islam in Kerala. In his opinion, Bana Perumal's sister Sree Devi's son returned from Mecca as Saifuddhin Mohammed Ali, and settled down in Dharmadam (1997, 129). The rest is incorporated into vernacular history in the form of various legends. One version says that as a convert, he hesitated to return to his mother's palace and settled in Dharmadam with his fellow men, after buying some land from a local launderer. He converted to Islam, changing his name from Appu to Mahin. Arakkal was their family name; slowly, his mother and other relatives were also attracted to Islam, leading to the evolution of the Arakkal dynasty. The kingdom was more interested in Muslim missionary activities than in explanding its territory (Kareem 1997, 129). Once, while travelling across a river, Mohammed Ali happened to save a woman from drowning who was apparently naked. He offered the woman his cloak. The woman was the princess of Chirakkal palace and she pleaded with her father to let her marry the man who had saved her life. Now the only choice before the king was to expel the woman because of her encounter with an outcast, or give her in marriage to this Muslim. The king took recourse to the second option and gifted the newly-weds more land near Arakkal, thereby expanding the Arakkal kingdom (ibid., 130).

Padmanabha Menon tells a different version of the story. In his narrative, Arayankulangara Nair, a minister of a Kolathiri Raja, converted to Islam as Mohammed Ali and married a princess from the Kolathiri dynasty, thus laying the foundations of this kingdom (2001, Vol. 1, 333). Sreedhara Menon agrees, and declares that this took place in the twelfth or thirteenth century AD (2007, 265–66). A wide range of versions is available for this story. Logan's *Malabar Manual* also reflects the story in *Keralolpathi* regarding the evolution of the Muslim dynasty:

> Cheraman Perumal, the text goes on to say, encouraged merchants, and invited Jonaka Mappilas (Mohemmadan) to the country. In particular he invited a Mohemmadan and his wife to come from his native land of Aryapuram and installed them at Kannur (Cannanore). The Mohemmadan was called Ali Raja, that is, lord of the deep, or of the sea. (2004, Vol. 1, 236)

All these historians believe that Arakkal followed the matrilineal line of succession. Unlike in other royal families, the eldest member, even if that was a woman, would become the ruler. The kings were called Adi Raja and the queens Adi Raja Beevi. The succession chart displayed at the Arakkal Archives names nine female rulers in its history. The Archives have kept copies of treaties signed by the Beevis of Arakkal and letters addressed to the Beevis from foreign rulers. British historians who argued that Arakkal was actually ruled over by the husbands while the Beevis were merely figureheads ignore the Arakkal records that clearly state that all orders and proclamations require the visible consent of the queen. The following is an extract (translated from the Arabic original) from a letter dated Shaivall 1194 (the Hijra Era) from the Emperor of Constantinople to the Queen Beebe of Cannanore.

> We commence this, our condescending letter with royal compliments showing kindness and courtesy towards one who has covered herself with the sheet of modesty, who is adorned with the ornaments of truth and justice, venerated in pedigree, viz. Bebee Sultan the Queen of Malabar. May God preserve her in her country to defend the pillars of faith and Islam. (Kurup 2002, 108)[24]

The Archives also contain documents on the discussion of Dominigo Rodrigues with Arakkal Beevi (Beevi of Cannnanore), submitted to Stephen Law, the Chief of the Council Board of Tellicherry, as well as manuscripts pertaining to the surrender of Dharmapatanam signed by the Beevi. Arakkal has always been haunted by the intermeshing of legend and history, and there have been various assumptions and conclusions related to this dynasty. All legends related to Arakkal connect the kingdom to the Perumal conversion, and there is a web of intertwined legends that are repeated at regular intervals. Kareem considers the version of the Chirakkal princess getting married to Ali relevant, as he believes that the dynasties were not merely tied by friendship. He even recalls a recent interview of Mahaprabha Thampuratty of Chirakkal, where she apparently narrates nostalgic memories of their relationship with Arakkal (Kareem 1997, 131).[25] It is

---

[24] The letter is preserved in the Arakkal Archives.

[25] The interview took place between *Thampuratty* and the journalist Kamal Ram Sajeev.

interesting that while all the other matrilineal kingdoms had a preponderance of male rulers, Arakkal maintained provisions for female rulers. Even so, the first female ruler of the dynasty is recorded to be the nineteenth in the succession list, during Hijra 903–07 (AD 1728–32).

Image 1.1: Photo of Arakkal Aysha Beevi, Ruler of the Arakkal Kingdom (1921–31), at Arakkal Museum

Source: Sujith K. G.

While connecting the Arakkal legend to the Chirakkal kingdom, it is said that when the Chirakkal princess left for Arakkal, her mother sent a lantern with her, asking her to keep it lit forever. A lamp named the *Thampuratti Vilakk* is kept at Arakkal Palace even today. This legend revises the repeated motif of conversion to Islam embedded in the history of the Muslims of Kerala. In the previous section, I had argued that the matrilineal tradition in Malabar could be a kinship structure formed on the basis of existing arrangements in society that allowed women to have short-term relationships with men, whether foreign traders or native superiors. This practice later developed into an institutionalised matrilineal system and *sambandhams* for Nair women. The legend of the Chirakkal *Thampuratty* (princess) moving to Arakkal reflects the same practice, with the lamp signifying the Hindu tradition that was retained in the lineage even after the conversion. The photos exhibited at Arakkal show its Beevis without veils. The same was the case with the whole of Malabar, to the surprise of many European historians (Barbosa, in Dale 1980, 24; Logan, 2004, Vol. I, 198). The Arakkal dynasty and its tradition of female rulers has a recurring motif of conversions to the Muslim community, enabled by alliances between Muslim men and Hindu women. Here, the princess retains her Hindu ritual traditions in the form of the lighted lamp, while embracing Islam as a historical necessity. It should be noted that the legend reflects no romantic illusions, but dwells upon the inevitability of the situation.

It took about 850 years for the kingdom to have a female ruler, and this occurred during the colonial invasion. If Arakkal records are to be trusted, the first female ruler was Harrabichee Kadavoobi Adi Rajah Bebee of 903–07 Hijra Era, that is, AD 1728–32. Almost around the same time, from 1678–98, in the southern-most part of Kerala in the Attingal Swaroopam, a woman named Aswathy Thirunnal Thampuratty, who later came to be known as Umayamma Rani, was the ruler. While confronting the European invasion and missionary activities, there seems to have been a resurgence in the matrilineal tradition, rather than a move towards European models.

COLONIAL DISTORTIONS OF ORATURES

Every society has its repertoire of collective memory that shapes and structures its existence. The tradition, rituals, kinship structures, social system, and even beliefs revolve around these archetypes. The Muslims of Kerala trace their origins back to the alliances between native Hindu women and Arab men. It is not just an instrumental presence that these women exhibit; rather, they shoulder the responsibility of mediating between two cultures and spiritualities. The entanglement of history and legend serves this purpose. This archetype of conversion—a Hindu woman walking over with her tradition to a foreign spirituality—dwells in the memory of the society, to be reworked and resurrected at regular intervals. Pierre Nora writes about the phenomenon of memory in historiography, albeit in a different context:

> Memory and history, far from being synonymous, appear now … in fundamental opposition. Memory is life, borne by living societies founded in its name. It remains in permanent evolution, open to the dialectic of remembering and forgetting, unconscious of its successive deformations, vulnerable to manipulation and appropriation, susceptible to being long dormant and periodically revived. History, on the other hand, is the reconstruction, always problematic and incomplete, of what is no longer. Memory, insofar as it is affective and magical, *only accommodates those facts that suit it … * memory is blind to all but to the group it binds. (2006, 285–86; emphasis mine)

Fabricated memories often serve to consolidate distorted images of marginalised communities. Here, memories are consciously created to manipulate history and invent new pasts, so as to meet the needs of the mainstream. Indian history is often flooded with such distorted images of Muslims (Amin 2005, 1–35). The legends in circulation in Kerala, in the context of conversions to various religions, are unique because of the absence of hostility in their treatment of foreign religions. This results in popularising legends of conversion to Islam as memories of splendour and esteem in Kerala. These popular legends have presented Muslims as an indigenous community, and justified the natives' association with the foreigners. In this assimilation of a cross-cultural and multi-ethnic population, women, as the link between the two communities, had a major role to play. The distortions occurred only during European colonisation, when the invaders tried to historicise their hostility towards the Muslims who, unlike them, were very much a part of the land. Thus, the European historian found it necessary to estrange the Muslim. A memorandum prepared by Adrienne Moens in 1781, titled 'Adi Rajah: The Chief of Moors', viewed the Arakkal family history from a different perspective:

> To speak about this person, one should know about his status, wealth and the relationship with the company. He is from the Kolathiri lineage. A princess of this dynasty had some unfortunate encounter with a lower caste due to which she had to lose her aristocracy and become an outcaste. In order to escape this, she was married off to a wealthy Arabian Moor and he was given the title of the Adi Rajah. This signifies him as the first king of the moors, that is, Mappilas of that country [specifically, Azhi Raja, that is, the King of Sea]. (Kurup, n.d.)

Apart from the hostile portrayal of the Muslim king in this document, the twist to the legend behind the formation of Arakkal also needs to be taken into account. By referring to the princess being married off to the Moor, the European historian is trying to link this to the *Smartha Vicharam*,[26] which existed in the Nambutiri communities of his time in Kerala. At the end of *Smartha Vicharam*, the excommunicated woman had the choice to go with a Mappila or a Christian.

The reworking of the Chirakkal princess' conversion recurs in Kerala literature as a favourite motif. More urgently, this conversion figures in our imagination of Muslim women who retain their native custom, while at the same time extending a link between

---

[26] *Smartha Vicharam* refers to the trial of a Nambutiri woman and fellow men who were accused of illegitimate sexual relations. If the accused woman was found guilty, she and the men involved with her were excommunicated from the caste (*Bhrastu*). This took place with the permission of the king and a council of elders, called *smartha*, who claimed expertise in the *Vedas* and *Puranas*. The most sensational *Smartha Vicharam* was the one in 1905 that involved Kuriyedath Thathri, married off at an early age to the 60-year-old Raman Nambutiri.

the native and the foreigner. The legend serves to institutionalise the native practice of willingly giving their women to the Muslims, and also internalising a foreign religion through its women. This, I find, is contrary to the relationship between Islam and the rest of India. The conscious effort of the Hindutva agenda to present Hindu women as the chaste model for Indian womanhood also does not function in this context. The split between the aristocratic Hindu and the lower-class Mappila occurs only in the colonial phase, mainly because of the European monopoly over the spice trade, previously a Muslim domain. The relationship between the Mappilas and the mainstream was complicated during this phase, and this was precisely when the 'othering' of the Muslim woman was imposed, mainly by a colonial hierarchy.

Thus, in the collective memory of Kerala society's conception of Islam, the legend of the Arakkal Beevi is embedded on two levels. On one level, it relates to the ancient past of native womanhood as linking the foreign and the native, where the woman's role is to mediate between the reception of the foreign and the retention of the native. The second relates to a more recent past, where the Muslim male is redefined as 'other', without any remnant of his past glory, and a relationship between him and the Hindu woman becomes a matter of disdain.[27] Here, society invents symbols to demarcate the Muslim woman. In the context of the colonial invasion, representative clothing began to evolve for various communities. Apparent differences began to arise between the Muslim and the Hindu woman.[28] This notion of the Muslim woman reappears at multiple instances in our history. A contemporary example is the conversion of Kamala Das to Islam, which evoked much controversy, but at the same time was appropriated by

---

[27] Even here, it is more a class issue than a religious one.

[28] Bindu Malieckal refers to Abu Zaid (AD 1916), who commented on the unveiled Hindu and Mappila women whom he met on the Malabar coast. He was surprised to find the kings allowing their women to be seen by men (Malieckal 2005, 305). Stephen Dale refers to Barbosa's report stating that Mappilas spoke Malayalam, dressed like Nairs, and adopted the matrilineal inheritance (1980, 24).

many within the Arakkal framework.[29] But again, the responses it evoked were two-fold: there was a nostalgic recapitulation of the princess being married to the Muslim, but the undercurrents of the twentieth-century progressive, liberal, secular image of Kerala were too complex to accept this conversion completely.

KAMALA SURAYYA: THE CONTROVERSIAL CONVERSION

Kamala Surayya's high-profile conversion to Islam has not been viewed kindly by Hindu fundamentalists. Announced at a critical juncture when the nation was discussing conversions in the context of the murders of Australian missionary Graham Staines and his two children, the Wadhwa Commission Report,[30] and then Prime Minister Atal Bihari Vajpayee's call for a national debate on conversions, it evoked a violent reaction from Right-wing Hindutva segments. The same Sangh Parivar that had applauded Kamala Das when she celebrated the Pokhran blast turned against her. When Surayya was honoured with the Ezhuthachan Award in 2002, in a caustic statement soon after the announcement, Bharatiya Vichara Kendra director P. Parameswaran questioned the propriety of giving the award to Kamala Surayya, stating that the awardee should have some similarity in her life, values,

---

[29] It was hinted that Kamala Das would marry a Muslim after her conversion, and the media portrayed it as a romantic picture of religious syncretism.

[30] Graham Staines, an Australian missionary, and his two young sons were burnt to death by a Hindu fundamentalist group in 1999 in Odisha. Staines had been working in Odisha since 1965 as part of an evangelical missionary organisation, caring for people with leprosy and the extremely poor tribal people in the area. Right-wing activist Dara Singh was convicted in 2003 for leading the group that carried out the brutal killing. Staines was alleged to have been forcefully converting the tribal poor to Christianity. The Wadhwa Commission, which looked into the murder, stated that there was no evidence of forced conversions, although some tribals had been baptised. However, in its judgment, the Supreme Court of India included strong remarks against religious conversions. These were later withdrawn after severe criticism from the media and the public.

activities, and contributions with the one in whose name the award had been instituted. A similar statement was issued by P. Narayana Kurup, president of 'Tapasya'. They argued that Ezhuthachan was not only a poet but also the father of the modern Malayalam language, as well as the proponent of the Bhakti Movement in Kerala. Therefore, presenting the Ezhuthachan Award to Kamala Surayya was as incongruous as giving an award in the name of a pre-eminent proponent of Islam to Salman Rushdie or Taslima Nasreen. The newspaper *Janmabhoomi* criticised the decision in an article titled 'Pativrata Puraskaram Vasavadattakko?' ('Chastity Award to Vasavadatta?', 7 November 2001).[31] The article, carried on the front page, described the decision as 'an effort to appease the Muslim community, which had been instigated by (People's Democratic Party leader) Abdul Nassar Ma'dani and other Muslim fundamentalists to rise in protest against the government.' It continued:

> It is a short cut to appease Muslim fundamentalists and communalists who are using Kamala Das, who converted to Islam and became 'Kamala Surrayya', as a weapon to implement their own agenda. They are trying to use Ezhuthachhan and the former Madhavikkutty as a cover to escape the wrath of Ma'dani. (2001, 1).[32]

These violent reactions were of course directed against Kamala Surayya for having given up Hinduism in favour of Islam.

[31] Vasavadatta, the courtesan in Upagupta's tale, stands for mortal beauty and the epitome of carnal desire. She had sent invitations to Buddha's disciple Upagupta, who disregarded them. Later, upon her fall, she was saved by Upagupta on her deathbed and was guided to righteousness and eternal bliss. Vasadatta is referred to as an archetype of passion and wantonness. The Vasavadatta reference not only implies the inappropriateness of conferring the award on Kamala Das, but indirectly also implies the possible character assassination of any woman who leaves Hinduism.

[32] *Janmabhoomi* is known for its RSS lineage. Abdul Nassar Ma'dani refigures in all discussions on secularism in Kerala, and both he and the political party he supports, the People's Democratic Party, were construed as fundamentalist by the media in opposition to the 'mild and secular' Indian Union Muslim League.

The agitated response and reactions to Kamala Das' conversion stems from a hostility rooted in contemporary Hindutva politics that treats conversion to Islam as a betrayal of Hinduism. However, discussions on conversion continued to dwell upon the Arakkal legend. At the time of conversion, Kamala Das was also questioned on marriage, particularly, on marrying a Muslim. She provided contradictory answers, at times hinting at a Muslim lover whom she hoped to marry. The question is: Why does love/marriage become a compulsion in such situations? Is conversion to a 'minority' religion mystified under the garb of love and marriage? Is that the only possible rationalisation the Hindu nation will accept before incorporating conversions within its narrative? Strangely enough, the Arakkal legend does not dwell upon such a romanticised notion of love. Rather, it presents the event in terms of a strategic arrangement conducive to both parties. It was this strategic assimilation that Kamala Das attempted to rework through her conversion, but failed to do so due to the changed contours of the Muslim community in contemporary Kerala. Her attempts to mediate and negotiate between the two identities were evident in her declaration that she planned to take Krishna along with her to Islam (Das 1999). The rigidity of current boundaries and the impossibility of starting a conversation were reflected not only in the hostile responses to her conversion, but also in her inability to cope with her new identity. Also, unlike the legend, the conversion was not a negotiation or a mediation of identities, but a transfer between two rigid categories, whose burden proved rather taxing for the writer.

Viswanathan's (2001) discussion on Pandita Ramabhai's conversion to Christianity is relevant here. She treats conversion as a knowledge-producing activity rather than as a marker of difference. The failure to view Kamala Das' conversion in these terms arises from the associations that conversion has with 'violence and erasure rather than mobility and communication'. Viswanathan analyses Pandita Ramabai's conversion thus:

> The fact that neither origin nor destination is finite and determinate allows converts like Pandita Ramabai ... to be critical of the religion

to which she converts, even as she seeks to reform the religion she has repudiated. This sense of critical distance and fluidity gives conversion its peculiar power—the power to destabilize, which belongs to the individual who moves incessantly between disparate viewpoints. (ibid., xv–xvi)

The contemporary meanings of Muslim and Hindu have changed over centuries and the pressure brought about by the conflation of conversion with violence rules our vision of conversion. Thus, in contemporary society, Kamala Das' conversion moves away from its original vision of mediation between identities towards violence against rigid religious borders. The transformation of femininity, burdened with the task of guarding the purity and chastity of the Hindutva nation, which took place with the colonial invasion, is universalised in the portrayal of the Hindu woman, a portrayal that Kerala too is party to. The same undercurrents are at play in the debates on 'love-*jihad*', an unusual term coined by the opponents of conversion, signifying the exploitation of Hindu girls by Muslim men, who coax them into marriage with the intention of converting them to Islam.[33] The transformation from a matrilineal framework, where the woman was entrusted with the task of mediating between cultures, to the realm of political iconography where female sexuality is symbolised and mythologised in accordance with the rising demands of a Hindu national identity, uproots both the precolonial context of conversion and the role of women within it. The consciously

---

[33] Here, conversion closes all possibilities of communication between categories, with some even saying that Kamala Das was a victim of 'love-*jihad*'. The oxymoronic term was coined by the critics of love-marriages between Muslim boys and Hindu girls (this is discussed in detail in Chapter 3). Several Muslim men were accused of this, and courts were taken recourse to against such 'traps'. The term '*jihad*' has become fashionable in the critique of Muslim engagements in Kerala. Recently, another coinage, 'the intellectual *jihad*', argues that intellectuals propagate Islamic fundamentalism in the guise of identity politics (Chendamangallur 2010, 8–19).

constructed nationalist discourses identifying the Hindu woman with the virtues of ideal womanhood also transformed the female body into the site of tradition and culture (Devika 2007; Gupta 2008; Katrak 1992; Sangari 1999). In all these discourses and debates surrounding the fall of the Hindu woman, 'the Muslim' attains the role of infiltrator, burdened with the sin of contamination. 'Syncretic worship' and 'eclectic mixtures' of religion have been rejected in the process of 'extracting the pure' from the contaminated matrix of cultures.[34]

In this changed scenario, the culture-specific customs of Hindus and Muslims become the arena for religious contest. Newly created discourses aimed at 'rebuilding the past' and dehistoricised images of the ideal woman easily repressed the legacy of a collective past. Shared practices and joint rituals were rejected. The warm relationship between natives and Arabs during the pre-Aryan era slowly shifted to an institutionalised proselytising. Historians point to the suffering of the lower castes at the hands of caste Hindus as a reason for mass conversions. But this would have occurred at the same time as the arrival of the Europeans. Hussain Randathani refers to Barbosa's description of the rising power of Muslims in the Malabar region:

> ... and if this governor finds any youth or young men, who are vagrant and have no employ, nor father nor mother, nor master with whom they dwell, those are forfeit to him and he sells them as slaves to the moors or to any other person whatsoever, who is willing to purchase them at a very low price from three to five cruzados each whether men or women. (2007, 15)

This would be the second phase of Islam on the Malabar coast. During this phase of mass conversions, a large number of the lower castes converted to Islam. Bindu Malieckal (2005) has discussed Malabar at the time of the European invasion, and tried to draw

---

[34] This is clearly evident in Hadiya's conversion and the related controversy. The Hadiya case will be referred to later in the book.

a parallel between *A Midsummer Night's Dream* and European encounters with the Mappilas of Malabar in terms of matriliny, focusing on the contentious element of gender:[35]

> Europeans were surprised to find that the Mappilas were matrilineal and … possessed no harem system …. This situation created some tension for European traders in Malabar. Although Elizabethan merchants were subservient to an English Queen, they were not so accepting of other female monarchs, especially if the ladies were Muslims. Europeans were disdainful of the many Malabari women who dominated social hierarchies. Thus, while many references to Indians in early modern English literature are descriptions of Mughals and Hindus … there are also allusions to Indians who were Mappila Muslims, both men and women, and Mappila's practice of … the perverse system of matriliny. (ibid., 297)

In her argument, Malieckal points out that it was the Egyptian named Hippolus who had harnessed the monsoon winds to quickly cut across the Arabian Sea and reach India. Rolland Miller holds the same view; and Malieckal further argues that soon after this, the oceanic highway to and from Malabar was full of ships from Hijaz, Uman, Bahrain, Yemen, Hadramaut, Basra, Kufa, Damascus, and other places. Even pre-Islamic Arab poetry has references to Malabar. Mohamed Koya's *Mappilas of Malabar* discusses an Arab custom of the early medieval period of a husband moving to the wife's family after marriage, making him the subject of his wife's milieu (1983, 17). Malieckal also quotes Francois Pyrard de Laval, a Frenchman who travelled in Kerala sometime between 1607 and 1610, on the regional flavour of Islam and how matriliny became a part of the Mappila Muslims:

---

[35] This article discusses the complicated relationship between Mappilas and the Europeans, which is reflected in the literature of the time. Malieckal finds the European reaction to the matrilineal Mappila community reflected in *A Midsummer Night's Dream*. According to her, the work presents an anthropology of the Mappilas, especially their matriliny, rendered through Oberon and Titania's quarrel over the Indian boy (Malieckal 2005, 312).

… fathers are not succeeded by their children, but by their nephews, the sons of their sisters, this being a more certain line. Mappila women have a little light jacket of cotton down to the waist, and another silk or cotton cloth which reaches from the waist down to the feet. They go barefooted, and are very fair in complexion …. The women are pretty, and addicted to *licentious practices* like the other Indian women, but not to the same extent as in other places …. Their women are dressed like the other natives, and wear nothing upon their hair. (2005, 306; emphasis mine)

The 'licentious practices' referred to here would be those of polyandry and matriliny. The reference obviously indicates the native customs of the Muslim community and also denotes the local history of the religion, which has been dehistoricised in contemporary contexts into a trans-historical version of the religion.

Bhakti, Sufism, and Islam in Kerala

Mass conversions to Islam took place in Kerala mostly near the coastal areas. One reason for this could be the strong presence of Muslim traders near the ports since ancient times. The coastal regions of Kerala also had a sizeable population of fishermen who belonged to the lower castes. That most later converts to Islam in these regions happened to come from the fishermen clan speaks to the fact that these conversions were intended to escape caste and the oppression they faced from upper-caste Hindus. Logan provides a detailed description of this phenomenon, quoting from many available records:

The race is rapidly progressing in numbers, to some extent from natural causes, though they are apparently not so prolific as Hindus, and to a large extent from conversions from the lower (the servile) classes of Hindus—a practice which was not only permitted but in some instances enjoined under the Zamorin Rajas of Calicut, who, in order to man their navies, directed that one or more male members of the families of Hindu fishermen should be brought up as Mohemmadan, and this practice has continued down to modern times.[36] (2004, Vol. I, 197)

While discussing conversions to Islam in Kerala, we cannot ignore the fact that the role of Sufi saints in these conversions was minimal, compared to elsewhere in India. As discussed earlier, the conversions were more in the nature of cultural mediations and strategic alliances rather than spiritual engagements. *Tuhfat al-Mujahidin*, the sixteenth-century historical epic, may have been the first attempt to create a spiritual foundation for the Muslim community in Kerala. But even here, the author describes the context in which he wrote the book as less spiritually inclined and more historically specific. In the Introduction, the uniqueness of Islam in Malabar is highlighted: the native population embraced the religion willingly. He was aware that this was not the case everywhere, and that in many places, conversions were forced. While writing the history of Islam in Kerala, he intended to record the atrocities that the Portuguese unleashed on the Muslims. Thus, the book became more of an anti-colonial resistance, and Muslim historians view it as a source of European colonial history. In its mundane engagements with Kerala history, I see European colonial invasion as the primary instance that raised the demand for a spiritual locus for Islam in Kerala. This was also the moment when historiography, as the notion of authentic history, stepped in. In the mid-nineteenth century, Guntert attempted to historicise the legends regarding the origin of Kerala through a compilation of these in the *Keralolpathi*. Multiple versions of *Keralolpathi* were available with different princely states in Kerala, and through its publication, Guntert legitimised the legends.[37]

This moment of fabricating and refashioning the past is in a continuum with the accelerated revisions and legitimising

[36] Logan also compares the increase in the Muslim population from the census of 1871 with that of 1881, and points out the fall in the Cherumar percentage. He concluded that they had converted to Islam.

[37] Some historians argue for the existence of multiple versions of *Keralolpathi*, with each royal family owning a copy of its own *Keralolpathi*. See Scaria Zacharia's 'Introduction' to *Keralolpathi* (1992, xiii–xvii).

processes that countered the colonial invasion of native culture. Hagiographies, myths, and anecdotes began to proliferate, shaping the present through retrieving—or, rather, constructing—a past. Personal remembrances and individual events were transformed into documented history as oral history gave way to the written. In this context, the Perumal conversion gained a new momentum as the St. Thomas episode or the Parasurama legend. It is precisely during this moment that stories of Sufis began to enter the locus of Islam in Kerala. *Mohiyuddhin Maala* and the genre of *maala* literature[38] praising the Sufi saints entered the scene, asserting the spiritual base of the religion and competing with the *Bhakti* tradition initiated by Cherussery and continued by Ezhuthachan. My interest lies in the new avenues of inclusion that opened up for Muslim women in the changed religious discourses. In the reframed context of religiosity accentuated by the European coloniser, the woman who mediated between two amicable cultures and religions found a new role. In this redefined environment, where mass conversions from the lower castes become a necessity as well as a system on its own, women's agency gets relocated as the facilitator of such conversions. I will specifically explore the religious conversions that took place near the coastal areas of present-day Thiruvananthapuram, concentrating on the Sufi saint Beema Beevi. I aim to look into how the discourse of Islam in Kerala has been built around women, extending the tradition from the matriliny of the land. In the more recent past, conscious efforts have been made to fabricate a patriarchal version of the religion, focusing on institutionalised religion and developing Ponnani as the centre of Islamic studies and proselytising in Kerala.

BEEMA PALLI AND BEEMA BEEVI: GENDERING FAITH

Beema Palli (the mosque of Beema) is located in the suburbs of Thiruvananthapuram, the capital city of Kerala state, in Poonthura

---

[38] *Maala* are hagiographies of saints and warriors sung by the Mappila community. There are different songs pertaining to different contexts.

village. The locality is itself known by the name of the mosque. Historians estimate that the mosque had been built some 400 years ago. The oral tradition in the region treats Beema Beevi and her son as Sufis who came there to promote religion. It is stated that the mother and son were killed in encounters with the king's forces as they refused to pay the tax. In varied narratives, it has also been claimed that this encounter was with the British. Some sources specifically mention Marthanda Varma as the then ruler of Travancore. There are gaps in logic and coherence in these narratives as the period specified in most is Hijra 850 (AD 1429). Marthanda Varma was not the ruler during that time, and the British encounter too becomes suspect. The written history with its adherence to authenticity and factual data need not be replaced by oral narratives. But the intertwining narratives of oral histories constantly restructure the official history. While the religious songs available at Beema Palli[39] try to place her son at the centre, there is no question regarding her authority. In his M.Phil. dissertation, S. Siddique[40] tackles this dual centrality of worship in Beema Palli (2008). In the oral tradition, that is, in the stories popularised by the local population living around the mosque, the mother is at the centre of belief. But in official modes of worship, hymns, and songs, the son replaces the mother. There is an obvious imposition of a patriarchal Islam here, which took place in the nineteenth and twentieth centuries.

Putting aside debates around oral versus written history, where oral history problematises the written, or how women reconstruct their pasts through oral history, I would rather look into certain aspects of oral history, inspired by a reading of Joan Sangster (1998, 88–90). Sangster tries to connect class, race, and ethnicity and the way people recollect their pasts. The need

---

[39] The songs are called *Mauluds* and *Munajaaths*. The patriarchal ways of narration attempt to centralise the role of Mahin, her son, in and around the region.

[40] Siddique provides a cultural analysis of the rituals and legends associated with Beema Palli. He records the way the woman's role is underplayed in the official history of the mosque.

Image 1.2: Beema Beevi's Mosque, Known as Beema Palli,
Thiruvananthapuram

Source: Sujith K. G.

to create a collective history is also illuminated through oral renderings. In the case of Beema Palli, the need for a woman Sufi saint itself denotes the role of a matriarch who commands the converted fisherfolk of this coastal area. The practice of treating the sea as goddess is quite common among the fishermen of Kerala. This deification of nature in no way correlates to the aristocratic feminine goddesses of the Brahmanical imagination. The gendered ideal of the woman as goddess in upper-caste Hindu versions finds no parallel with this subaltern engagement with women and deification. The matriarch controls the community, its system, beliefs, and ways of living. Laws are created and defied based on this omnipresent deity, known commonly by the name *Kadalamma* (the mother of the sea). The Muslim community of fishermen looks up to Beema Beevi as an incarnation of this deity, rather than as a preacher and promoter of Islam. Memory is constructed on the basis of this assimilation of Beema Beevi into their tradition. The political context in which these conversions take place also draws upon the construction and circulation of these myths.

There was no elaborate missionary agency on the western coast to promote Islam, the task being entrusted to the local agencies of Muslims instead. Qadir Husain Khan considers the conversions of the lower castes a blessing for them. He notes that these converts are called *Putiya Islam* (New Islam), shortened to *Pu'islam* in the local dialect. However, converting to Islam does not divorce them from their Hindu pasts, and the communities continue to retain their rituals and customs. Towards the southern coastal areas are the *Marakkayars*, who have converted from the fishermen community (Khan 1910, 43).

The oral tradition popular in and around Beema Palli valorises the Beevi and considers her the sole protector of the entire region. The term Jonakan, repeatedly used in these songs to refer to the Muslims, harks back to the eighteenth and nineteenth centuries, since in most colonial narratives, Jonaka Mappila is the term used to refer to the Muslims of Kerala (Innes 1997; Logan, 2004, Vol. 1). Here, I would like to address two questions related to the dissemination of Islam in Kerala: *first*, the intervention of the Sufi lineage in Kerala, which took place at a later stage compared to north India. This should definitely be seen as a resistance to colonial intervention, demanding a strengthening of the religion's roots in Kerala.

As a tradition, Sufism does not have much of a presence in Kerala except for the popular hymns and hagiographies promoted during the seventeenth and eighteenth centuries. This period also saw the rise of the Bhakti cult and the use of pure Malayalam in literature, and Sufism in Kerala should be viewed more as a response to these phenomena than as a link with the northern tradition of Sufis.[41] The popularisation of Beema Beevi's miracles and her proselytising mission was thus a direct outcome of efforts on the part of Hindus and Muslims to resist the Christian missionary

---

[41] This will be discussed later while re-locating the reform movements as an extension of the *Bhakti* movement.

activities promoted by the Europeans. At the same time, it also carved a space for the Muslim community in the socio-political design of Kerala society, where caste and religious equations have been redefined in the context of the colonial invasion.

Apart from its role in the proselytising mission, Beema Beevi's story extends to another aspect of Kerala's religious tradition. A thread of matrilineal beliefs and rituals runs parallel to the emergence of a patriarchal version of Islam in Kerala. In my research, I have come across several tombs of Muslim women who claimed miraculous powers spread across Kerala, alongside the institutionalised version of official Islam. These places of local worship may not be as famous as the Beema Palli mosque, but are deeply rooted in the local histories of the respective places to which they belong. In Edappally near Kochi, there is a tomb attributed to Sherifa Beevi, who is portrayed as a victim of conspiracies of the enemies of the religion. Elderly people from some old Muslim families of the region narrated the story of Beevi, within the context of a battle between the rulers of Kochi and Calicut and the deaths of hundreds of Muslim soldiers. The reference must be to the war between Samutiri and the King of Kochi, when the then Kochi Maharaja plotted with the Dutch to fight the Muslim soldiers of Samutiri. Local myths place the story of Beevi within this realm of hatred for Islam. In many versions, Beevi, who was engaged to a Muslim trader, was coaxed into an affair with a *Kaffir* (non-Muslim) by the enemies of Islam when her brother was away on trade. The tarnished Beevi faced a jury of elders, who ordered that she be flogged to death. Soon after her burial, her tomb showed signs of miracles, which led her to be raised to the status of deity.[42] Beema Beevi was presented as an Arabian woman who came to Poonthura with her son to promote religion.[43] Beevi was killed during the proselytising mission. Both

---

[42] In Kannur district, there is another tomb of a Muslim woman called Moonnupettumma Jaaram (the tomb of the mother of three children).

[43] The mosque at Beema Palli, according to historians, is around 400 years old.

mother and son are buried along the coast, and the tomb is an important Muslim pilgrim centre in south India. Frequented by people of all religions, the rituals followed there are far removed from the Islamic tradition that strongly rejects such tomb worship.

Image 1.3: The *Dargah* or Tomb of Beema Beevi

Source: Sujith K. G.

An interesting thing to note here is how the religion is conceived at multiple levels in Beema Palli. The locals and visitors to the mosque consider it strictly the tomb of a matriarch with divine power, who could heal and perform miracles. The local population refers to her as *umma*, the term used by Muslims of Kerala to address one's mother. But in the institutionalised versions of the legend of Beema Beevi, there is a conscious effort on the part of proprietors to authenticate the son as the missionary, with the mother being given a supporting role. This disparity is evident in the oral and written histories of Beema Palli. Oral history places the mother at the centre and provides multiple versions, which state that Beema Beevi and her son had come from Mecca. It also said that they were members of the Prophet's family, had fought against the British and the landlords, were engaged in spiritual healing, and performed miracles. These stories develop into heterogeneous plots in the oral version. Interestingly, in the *Munajaats* (songs praising Mahin, the son of Beema Beevi, promoted by authorities of the mosque), the son gains in importance and the mother performs a secondary function. The son's war against the authorities was apparently in defence of his mother's honour (Siddique 2008, 34). *Marakkars*, the Muslim population surrounding Beema Palli, look upon Beema Beevi as a goddess who attends to all their emergencies on sea, much like any other fishing community would venerate their goddess. *Munajaats* and official versions of the legend are a more contemporary phenomenon,[44] catering to the demands of a patriarchal religion. Interestingly, though, even after such attempts, at the performance level, Beema Palli is experienced by the devotees and natives on a totally different realm.

The prominence accorded to the son in the written version is visible in the pamphlets circulated in the mosque premises. A booklet titled *Beema Palli Charithram* (1996), written by K. P. Ahammed Musliar, is another attempt at institutionalising a patriarchal version of the legend. Modernity demands a historicising and legitimising of legends, making it convenient to project a male-centric version. In contrast, from its name to local practices, the mosque in its spatial and temporal reality projects a female deity.

Beema Palli in the Political Map of Kerala

Beema Palli and its premises are important in the political map of Kerala for many reasons. Tension between religious groups is frequent here, especially between the Christian and Muslim fishermen clans, both converts during a later phase of proselytising. The region has also sent meagrely educated immigrants to Gulf countries, who form a source of cheap labour. The locality sells

---

[44] In his thesis, Siddique claims that *Munajaat* was written in 1966.

goods smuggled in from the Gulf countries and is popular across Kerala as a cheap source of foreign goods. The products range from electronic appliances, to clothes and perfumes, to pirated copies of the latest foreign and Indian movies. The business centres around the mosque, and the rules and regulations of the state seldom enter this region except during emergencies, when one sees a forced entry of the state machinery. A parallel system of governance, too, centres around the mosque, dictated by the locals and mosque authorities. A counter-culture that simultaneously broadens and limits the prospects of the citizens permeates the day-to-day existence of people. Major decisions are often taken by the mosque committee. The reign of the mosque and its dictates are, however, unlike the control of other Jamaats in different parts of Kerala. The uninterrupted continuity of a matrilineal tradition of norms and values permeates every aspect of existence here, resulting in a counter-culture that resists and defies the intrusion of the state apparatus. Here, the mosque redefines citizenship; this citizenship, limited to a particular region and strengthened by the legend of a woman missionary, creates an alternative space, distanced from the state. The legend is as political as it is spiritual. Beema Beevi thus functions as the agency that builds up a subaltern counter-culture that resists both caste and class, while equally challenging the governmentality of the secular State. The failure of the modern secular State to generate equality and a neutral secularism results in this counter-rule, where the rule of the law seldom enters. The mosque and Beema Beevi are thus not a reflection of an abstract spiritual existence for the converted masses, relating them to a Hindu past, but form an organic agency that resists the governmentality of the State while providing a counter-terrain to the State's power.[45]

[45] It is precisely for this reason that Beema Palli is a threatening space for the State. The police firing on Beema Palli in 2009 indicates the State's attempt to exert its power over the Muslims in the region. On 17 May 2009, between 2.30 and 3 PM, the police shot and killed six Muslim fishermen, and injured fifty-two others. While police records claim that the firing was a response to communal violence and mob attacks on a nearby Latin Catholic

Image 1.4: Beema Palli Street:
The Commercial Street Surrounding the Mosque

Source: Sujith K. G.

The Subaltern Mosque at Ponnani

A late twentieth-century version of such a parallel attempt to construct another vision of religion, replacing the governmentality of a region with its supporting institutionalised religions, can be seen at Ponnani. Ponnani is the centre of Islamic studies in Kerala and the seat of the most reverend heads of Islam in Kerala. It is also the seat of the Makhdhum family, where the tomb of Shaykh Zainuddin Makhdum exists. However, despite the many tombs of great men and the existence of aristocratic Muslim families,

---

church, fact-finding committees led by independent agencies question this. It was the second largest police shooting incident in the history of Kerala since 1957. However, compared to the importance given to other such political events in the history of the state, the Beemapalli police firing is seldom commemorated in official histories and is often written off as communal violence, both by the media and the state.

Ponnani is not a pilgrim centre; rather, it serves as the centre of institutionalised Islam and Islamic studies for Sunni Muslims. It is also a legitimate centre for conversions to Islam. Ponnani legitimises the history of Islam in Kerala through its written tradition, which dominates multiple versions of oral histories. Ironically, the institutional organisation of the premodern religion is concretised through a modernity that asserts written forms and modes of learning and interpretations. In contrast, about 15 kilometres from this centre, near the coastal area of Ponnani, a mosque dedicated to Ibrahima Beevi is evolving into a pilgrim centre. In spite of the resistance put forth by the aristocratic Sunni[46] centre at Ponnani, this tomb has developed into a sphere of political mobilisation and counter-resistance to the aristocratic religion. Once again, as in Beema Palli, the converted lower-caste fishermen continue to hold on to their matrilineal traditions and rituals.

A great deal of political mobilisation takes place here in terms of bargaining for electoral votes, but at the same time, a parallel governance has slowly arisen as well. The revenues of the mosque have increased exponentially, mainly through offerings from devotees, and with every year, its performative progress can be witnessed in the increased ritualisation and institutionalisation of practices. However, the official version of Islam at Ponnani does not recognise the miracles of Beevi, and openly denies any divinity attached to the place. During my visit to Ponnani, the office staff and the secretary of the Ponnani Centre told me that these miracles were mere gimmicks, and that the tomb was just the burial place of an orphaned female. The history of this mosque is available for scrutiny, as the miraculous event that led to the mosque's origin took place only in 1986. It is true that the corpse of an anonymous female was washed ashore on the Ponnani coast, and the fishermen's attempts to cast it back into the sea were not successful. Finally, after repeated efforts, they decided to bury

---

[46] The elite Sunni Muslims who follow the tradition of Ponnani Thangal with a claim to aristocracy and religious authority.

Image 1.5: The Site of Beema Palli Police Firing

Source: Sujith K. G.

the body on the coast. According to the local version, on the third day they heard prayers issuing from the tomb. Even here, this history of a fairly recent past is legitimised through various popular narratives. Plenty of stories about the miracles of Beevi are available amongst the fishermen of the region.

The mosque of Ibrahima Beevi can claim neither the history nor the legacy of Beema Palli. But the place where the mosque is situated has been renamed Puthu Ponnani, and is the centre of a subaltern version of the religion that counters the mainstream version centred at Ponnani. The deification that took place here and in Beema Palli is not the patriarchal deification of women, aimed to control and limit female agency. Multiple levels of resistance operate here, countering the mainstream beliefs and practices. This resistance is made possible through extending to women a politically viable agency, which represents the larger interests of a people on the margins of society. Shamshad Hussain, in *Nyuna Pakshathinum Linga Padhavikkumidayil* (*Between Minority and Gender*, 2009) views this deification from a different perspective:

Image 1.6: The Mosque of Munambam Beevi at Ponnani, Northern Kerala

Source: Sujith K. G.

There are tombs of women known as Beevis who were said to have possessed divine power. They practised medicine and also suggested solutions to the grievances of people. At one point this has been opposed in terms of superstitions and belief in god men. But perhaps these women would have failed to see the market value of what they had been practising in a premodern society and therefore would have been worshipped by the local people. (ibid., 15)

While accepting Hussian's speculation, I would like to look into how these movements offer a resistance to institutionalised patterns of Islam that move away from local histories towards pan-Islamism. Such efforts have been countered through these local agencies, both at Ponnani and Beema Palli. The cultural past of a matrilineal tradition is reflected in the worship of women as Beevis. In local histories, women as powerful agents mediated religion to a converted populace. During the nineteenth century, in many predominantly Muslim areas, women served as instructors of the Arabic language and religion in general. These

Image 1.7: The Mosque of Munambam Beevi

Source: Sujith K. G.

Image 1.8: The Tomb of Munambam Beevi

Source: Sujith K. G.

were not institutionalised practices, and the women were forced to withdraw during the reform movements in the light of colonial modernity. In northern Kerala, they were also known as Beevis. In the south, a Muslim teacher who taught the Quran was called *labba*, which in the local dialect became '*elappa*', and women who taught Arabic were called '*elappachi*'. The most prominent Muslim families had women staying with them, teaching their children Arabic. After the advent of institutionalised forms of religious teaching through the modern *madrassas* (religious schools), this practice slowly came to an end. The change occurred when colonial modernity led to a redefinition in gender roles, forcing women into domesticity. Matriliny itself was challenged by colonial morality.

Muslim women claiming divine power and practising traditional medicine and spiritual healing are a common phenomenon in rural areas of predominantly Muslim centres like Ponnani, Kodungallur, and the coastal areas of Thiruvananthapuram. These women, addressed as Beevis, wield a sovereign power over the local population. They even control the electoral votes of a region, and in Ponnani, I came across a Beevi who could manipulate votes by supporting a political party for election to the local bodies.[47]

Whether it is the saintly presence of Beema Beevi and Ibrahima Beevi or local spiritual heads, mainstream Islam does not hold these practices in reverence. It has to be noted that this resistance comes not from a monotheistic version of religion that defies tomb worship and godmen.[48] Rather, the resistance is to the presence of women leaders, and to the subaltern counter-resistance with

---

[47] It was reported to me that a day's campaign by Beevi drew about 1,000 votes from the opposition camp.

[48] The Islamist and reformist political schools of Islam in Kerala focusing on Salafism and pan-Islamic practices, which include the Jamaat-e-Islami and Kerala Nadvathul Mujahideen, are against human deification. But Ahl al-Sunna (the Sunni Muslims), who constitute the majority of the Muslim population in Kerala, do not seem to have much against saints or tomb worship, or against performative rituals like *Mualuds* and *rathibs*.

these women as their spiritual heads. The Islamic study centre at Ponnani does not acknowledge the divinity of Ibrahima Beevi, and Beema Palli has seen organised efforts to establish the prominence of the son over the mother. In modernised versions of the religion, female agency has been underplayed by historicising the religious experiences of Muslims through a male-centred perspective. I see this as a response to the call for modernity invoked by the colonial invader, and later taken up by the nationalists. The transformation from a matrilineal community to a modern society was the direct outcome of a morality imposed by the Western invader, and later adopted by reform movements in Kerala. These movements, intended to reform religion and caste from within, viewed women as objects, with the potential to be reformed. The thrust of modernity—educating women, turning them into ideal mothers and responsible homemakers—left women with no choice but to take up the 'refined tasks' imposed upon them. Muslim women were no exception. Rewriting legends, denying oral history, and closing up all avenues to a cultural past promoted and circulated by women became a necessity for the rising religious society. Modern religious institutions refined 'archaic' ways of learning and 'immoral' customs. With matriliny being treated increasingly as an immoral practice by Muslim preachers and rulers,[49] the subject position of women also declined gradually. The tug-of-war between reminiscences of a cultural past where women were at the centre and modern patriarchal religious institutions is reflected in all attempts to trace the local histories of Islam in Kerala. However, in places where mass conversions had taken place, especially in the coastal areas that witnessed cultural exchanges between Islam and the local populace, the collective memory preserves images

---

[49] It was colonial historians who first expressed their unease with the matrilineal practice and then branded polyandry immoral, viewing it through the lens of colonial morality (Barbosa, in Dale 1980, 24). Tipu Sultan, during his address to the people of Malabar, also called this practice immoral, and commented on the immorality of the Nair community (Padmanabha Menon, 2001, Vol. 2, 232).

of female spiritual heads and healers. Not only do they maintain this past through oral narratives, but new narratives are also created in contemporary times, such as in Ponnani, to counter the homogenised version of a male-centric religion.

2

Muslim Women and the Reform Movements in Kerala

The renowned Nambutiri reformer from Kerala, V. T. Bhattathiripad, writes about a Nambutiri woman in his autobiographical account, *Uma Ethathe Annam*, which roughly translates to 'Uma, Here's Your Food', in the context of the twentieth-century reform movements. Here, as the harbinger of modernity in the Nambutiri community, he talks about Uma as a Nambutiri woman who falls into 'immoral ways of life' being a victim of the evil traditions in the Nambutiri community. Uma later marries a Muslim and converts to Islam. Her husband, according to V. T.'s narrative, was only after her wealth. She is rescued from his clutches and sent to the Arya Samaj in Lahore, where she converts back to Hinduism and marries a Punjabi Brahmin. There is an encounter between V. T. and Uma's Muslim husband, witnessed by a crowd of Mappila onlookers, which he describes thus:

'Well, how is Uma Antharjanam? That's what I should ask, isn't it?' I touched upon the nerve.

'She is doing fine. Such silken behaviour. No problems or complaints. We would go on like it is Onam. I understood everything about Nambudiri women. I prepare kalan and olan for her. I tried out every Nambudiri dish. Whatever vegetarian dish she prepared was excellent. But however much I try that ass would never learn how to prepare a good dish of meat or fish.'

The moment I heard the word 'ass,' my whole body burned. 'Pha!' I swore at his face. I was burning and exploding all over. We never saw each other again. (Bhattathiripad 2005, 62)

This problematic portrayal of the Muslim in the reform context indicates the resolutions that Kerala society arrived at during the reform movements. In subsequent passages, V. T. also laments the plight of poor Umaben, the orphan, who was hunted down and driven to Ponnani by the Muslim, converted to the Islamic faith in the presence of invited mullahs (Muslim religious leaders), and made a 'concubine' through *nikah* (Muslim marriage). Here, V. T. emphatically uses the term 'concubine', whereas, while referring to polygamy in the Nambutiri community in the same account, he takes care to use the term *sapatni* (co-wife in polygamous marriages). This chapter addresses the problematic portrayal of the Muslim community as unrefined and ignorant of the progressive nature of women's empowerment highlighted in the narratives of reform movements, and therefore alienated from the domain of Kerala modernity. I attempt this through a systematic representation of Muslim modernity and women's movement in the community.

Renaissance/Modernity in Kerala

In the early twentieth century, Kerala witnessed revival and reform in religious practices. Like in the Bengal reform movements, the Hindu public sphere was restructured and practices like untouchability and, to an extent, issues such as women's condition in families were challenged. Thrust was given to education and reform. This was an all-India phenomenon that had begun in Bengal in the early nineteenth century and then spread to different parts of the country. The reformist wave was felt in all communities. Although reformism was the binding force behind this wave, caste and caste atrocities played a big role in the assertions made by the lower strata of Hindu caste society. Leaders of the reform movement hit out against the superstitious practices in Hinduism and demanded a categorical entry for all into the Hindu fold. The climate was largely conducive to religious reform, although the leaders also preached equality, right to education, women's liberation, and freedom of thought.

Premodern Kerala society was notorious for its evil practices of untouchability and intricate caste systems. Occupations defined by caste identity, denial of public spaces and landowning rights to the lower castes, and many other evils constituted the society of the time. Colonial interventions, missionary schools started by the Europeans, as well as a major mobilisation among the educated youth impacted the drive towards social change.

My contention is that while assessing caste as a social reality embedded in the hierarchical structure of Hinduism, the reform leaders demanded a place for their community in the political space of the nation. Thus, each caste group reorganised from within to emerge as a powerful political category. This is particularly true in the case of the Ezhava community. Under the spiritual guidance of Sree Narayana Guru, a major reform leader from Kerala, the different, scattered sub-castes among the Ezhavas[1] were bound within a unified community with a common set of customs and rituals. Subsequently, the Sree Narayana Dharma Paripalana Sangham (SNDP) categorically demanded the entry of Ezhavas into the Hindu fold. The reform movements are too intricate and diverse to be included in a linear narrative. It can be argued that the lower-caste reform movements thus revised the contours of communities once divided from within into more structured and unified caste groups. T. M. Yesudasan considers this overt focus on religion and caste a distinctive feature of reform movements in India, unlike those of European modernity (2010, 69).

Given the complex caste system and notions of untouchability in premodern Kerala society, the public sphere, under its garb of secular modernity, reflects a fundamental discrepancy in the constitution of Kerala's political society. Although the terrain of

---

[1] Ezhavas are one caste group on the lower rungs of the Hindu community. They are higher than the Dalits in the caste hierarchy.

reform movements is rooted in religion and caste, with every reformist leader presenting critiques of the superstitious practices within religion and demanding a reformulation of religious values and ethics based on higher ideals of equality, freedom of thought, and the right to education, it is the presumed secular motives of modernity that have shaped these movements in mainstream history. The predetermined structure of European modernity designs and ordains the trajectory of reform movements in such representations. Besides, the evolution of communist movements in early twentieth-century Kerala as a strong presence in the public sphere, and the loyalty with which Kerala's polity has adhered to the Communist Party of India (CPI) and its allies ever since (except for occasional violations), have contributed to this conception. Consequently, any discussion on identity and community rights in Kerala has been weighed against the legacy of this 'pseudo-secular' *modus operandi* that political and cultural societies assume in Kerala. The imbrication of religious reform movements of the late nineteenth and early twentieth centuries with the cultural renaissance of the early twentieth century highlight the enlightenment ideals of individual freedom, liberty, secularism, and progress as the foundation of Kerala's public sphere. Moreover, the contradictions between these mutually challenging categories have been appropriated within the legacy of the nationalist movement so as to claim a common past.

In this chapter, I look into how the Muslims of Kerala have engaged with the reform movements, and how women's agency has functioned in the contexts of Muslim reform movements. I am also concerned about how the history of reform movements has been constructed by the mainstream, and the conspicuous absence of Muslim reform movements in general and Muslim women's participation in particular in these histories. My focus is also on the overlap between these movements and religious reform movements in other parts of the country, and the interesting mediations and shifts they resorted to in order to accommodate each other. The absence of Muslim reform movements and Muslim women's agency in mainstream discourses has been structured by the politics of a Muslim existence in 'secular' Kerala, which in turn structured the discourses on Muslims and Muslim women. In the process of translating the reform movements into a monolithic narrative of secularism, a densely problematic field of discourses by Muslims, women, Dalits, and other marginal voices are erased.

THE REFORM MOVEMENTS

While the nation as a reality emerged from nationalist discourses, nationalists had attempted to hold on to the notion of a nation as an already existing category. The history of this nation was constructed along Hindu lines, with the reform movements contributing to such a formulation. The yearnings of different marginalised sections of Kerala society were incorporated into the national fold, and their aspirations towards asserting their identity coopted within the larger nationalist struggle. The caste-based movements of different communities, for instance, those of the Ezhava, Pulaya, or Nambutiri communities, were encapsulated within the nationalist discourse through the tools of conventional historiography. But in Kerala's history, running parallel to the nationalist movement led by the Indian National Congress (INC) was the strong communist movement, which was equally an expression of the society's engagement with modernity. If the freedom struggle had bound society with the thread of the nation, the communist movements highlighted the enlightenment ideals of freedom of self, liberation of the individual, and liberty of expression. The secular ideals of modernity were upheld in the communist movement, which efficiently translated the anti-caste vibrations into a class issue through the strategic manipulation of anti-feudal sentiments. At the same time, they mobilised a potential human resource that has since then remained loyal to the Communist Party. Thus, along with the nationalist history, the Marxist history of Kerala also appropriated the reform movements within its own context.

Although the reform movements in India stimulated further reform and dialogue, the early twentieth-century reform movements in Kerala had been influenced by Kerala's social and historical past. Reformism aimed to retrieve cultural specifications while correcting and asserting customs and rituals, establishing communal identities that led to the political bargaining of communities in electoral politics. The Nair Service Society and SNDP played crucial roles in promoting Nairs and Ezhavas as consolidated political groups. Kerala has always been projected as a community of secular values on behalf of the cultural renaissance brought about through the religious reform movements. It is even more complex, considering the social milieu that reflects the wide religious and caste demarcations behind the progressive image of the state. It is interesting to note how the values of reformation ('*navodhana moolyangal*' in Malayalam) appear as a nostalgic vantage point for all future discourses on Kerala's political and cultural choices. It is easy to conclude that the reform movements attempted to eradicate caste from society, or for that matter, that the values these movements espoused attempted to resist oppression based on caste. The reform movements were also conflicted: the lower castes' diverse responses to mass conversions disturbed upper-caste Hindu sensibilities, leading them to resist all such conversions, redesignating each caste group in conformity with the *chathurvarna* (four-fold division of the caste system) system through a restructuring of the sub-castes. Thus, aspirations towards Western modernity and the creation of the universal human were made available to the restructured caste groups through such a stabilising of community identity, albeit in a hierarchical fashion. The Sudra groups were consolidated under the Nair label and Ezhava became a community identity, and these reinforced a hidden hierarchy in the emerging modern public sphere, with the Nambutiri, Nair, and Ezhavas occupying the upper rungs. Even land reforms seldom went beyond the Ezhava to the large masses of the untouchable population, represented by the Pulayas and Parayas.

Cultural Renaissance or Religious Reform?

While *navodhaanam* (renaissance) is one umbrella term that historians use to record this period, the reform movements that transformed the public sphere in Kerala had divergent ethos and aspirations. The Nair community mobilised to demand their share in the political and bureaucratic space of governance, starting with the Malayali Memorial in 1891. The Malayali Memorial was a memorandum submitted by the people of Kerala to Maharaja Sree Moolam Thirunal, signed by more than 10,000 people that included Hindus, Muslims, and Christians (although Nairs predominated), and requesting Sri Moolam Thirunal to secure jobs for educated Kerala citizens in the Travancore civil service. At that time, most jobs were in the hands of Tamil Brahmins. Malayali Memorial was a major landmark in the struggle of the backward classes to gain legitimate rights in government jobs. In 1896, the Ezhava caste groups submitted another memorandum, known as the Ezhava Memorial. Although these caste mobilisations had the specific purpose of demanding a share in the modern political space, it would be incorrect to include them within a secular narrative of modernity.

I contend that the secular motives of modernity and the vision of a casteless society in the political and cultural spheres of the nation were promoted by mainstream historiography in order to accommodate the reform movements within the nationalist fold. While Kerala society of the early twentieth century accepted the reality of caste and tried to assert caste identities, nationalist historians tend to read such assertions as being part of the nationalist uprisings. In *Kerala Navodhanam*, Vol. 2 (*Kerala Renaissance*, Vol. 2), Marxist historian P. Govindapilla views reform movements as 'people's resistance against the hierarchical systems of priesthood, landlord, power structure and knowledge dissemination' (2009: 10). If the assertion of religious identities and demanding an equal share in the social structure had been the true motive of reformation, we need to explore the repercussions of such attempts. The national leaders incorporated the history of the reform movements into the nationalist discourse, and structured reformation along the conventional binaries of religious versus secular and tradition versus modernity.

Movements within caste were glossed over as secular within the nationalist discourse, which highlighted the 'higher' ideals of equality, eradication of untouchability, claims for social justice, and so on.[2] Pradeepan Pampirikunnu talks about this appropriation of caste movements in different frameworks, and emphasises the grounded, regional development that ran parallel to Western modernity in the efforts of Ayyankali and Sree Narayana Guru (2011, 560). The specific expressions of regional modernity in Narayana Guru's installation of the Ezhava Shiva, or Ayyankali's entry into Sree Moolam Praja Sabha, were appropriated by national modernity as examples of aspirations towards universal citizenship.[3]

Muslim Reform Movements

Muslims were denied entry into the category of universal citizen, making their inclusion in the cultural renaissance of Kerala problematic. The reform movements within the Muslim community could not be included in this history of cultural renaissance through a universalisation of modern ideals. The

[2] Movements like the Vaikkom Sathyagraha or Channar Lahala were strictly caste-based. But at a later stage, we see the tactical involvement of national leaders and subsequent attempts to incorporate them within the history of the freedom struggle.

[3] In 1888, Sree Narayana Guru challenged the caste hierarchy by installing a stone and consecrating it as a Shiva idol at Aruvippuram, near Thiruvananthapuaram, Kerala. The Ezhavas and other lower castes were not allowed inside Hindu temples then. By consecrating the Shiva idol, Narayana Guru challenged the Brahmin prerogative of consecrating a temple. When Brahmin priests questioned this violation, Narayana Guru sarcastically replied that he had installed the Ezhava Shiva.

Ayyankali became a member of the assembly of Travancore, known as the Sree Moolam Popular Assembly (SMPA) or Praja Sabha, in 1911, representing the backward Pulaya community.

history of Muslims in India has been burdened by the conquests and encounters in India's historical and cultural past, echoes of which mark Muslim identity in India even now. Moreover, prejudices based on the modernist contention of Islamic societies as anti-modern/anti-progressive/anti-women, in contrast to liberal/progressive/feminist societies, provided ample justifications for this omission. This explains the contradictory references to the Mappila Rebellion, Khilafath Movement, and other instances of Muslim participation in the nationalist movement by national and colonial historians.[4] Thus, reformist discourses highlight the Ezhava movements or the movement within the Nambutiri community as indications of Kerala's passage into a liberal and progressive cultural space, whereas the Muslim community's attempts to embrace the modernising ideals of education, democratic rights, women's emancipation, etc., were strictly viewed as a movement within the confines of religion. The rites of passage involved in the transformation of religious reform movements into a cultural renaissance that defines Kerala's secular image do not accommodate Muslims or the Muslim reform movements, reflecting conscious omissions and careful distortions, and leading to the evolution of the Muslim 'other' in the reform discourses, as expressed in V. T. Bhattathirippad's narrative of Aidon. The uncivilised, uneducated Muslim becomes the iconic marker of backwardness in modern cultural expressions in Kerala. In mainstream literature and films, this remained an uncontested reality for a long time. This caricature of the uneducated Muslim and cartoons of political leaders from the community remain a recurrent theme in Kerala's cultural landscape.

Viewing Muslim reform movements in the context of the reform movements in Kerala is problematic. First, there is an already existing category of Muslim reform movements as an offshoot of the wider context of cultural renaissance, within which the reform movements have been incorporated. Another

---

[4] M. T. Ansari (2005a, 36–77) points out how the history of the Mappila Rebellion was reduced to a footnote in the national struggle for independence.

difficulty is viewing the Muslim reform movements as a response to Muslim reform activities and a national political consciousness. Although reform within the Muslim community was influenced by both phenomena, the response of Muslim reform leaders in Kerala to the call of modernity was entirely unique. While it had pan-Islamic tendencies and nationalist inclinations, in the true spirit of reform, the community engaged in a creative cultural and political upheaval. Moreover, the categorical representation of reform movements in the early twentieth century also clashes with Muslim reform activities, which had been transformed into more clearly articulated movements by the 1950s. Another problem with representing Muslim reform movements is that the reform movements in many other communities located the essence of their identity within the Hindu fold. All reform leaders, including Sree Narayana Guru and Ayyankali, rejected conversion as a solution to caste oppression, and this later facilitated entry into the Hindu fold. The historical Temple Entry Proclamation was equally an effort to resist mass conversions (Gopakumar 2008, 76).

The reformer, who is left out in this attempt to negotiate with the Hindu identity, thus carries out the historian's job of documenting the history and reinventing the identity of the Muslim community. How successful were Muslim reformers in general and Muslim women in particular in this effort? That is a relevant question that needs to be engaged with, and yet is disposed of as a resolved category in the 'secular' public sphere of Kerala.

The Bhakti movement of the fifteenth and sixteenth centuries, which continued well into the seventeenth century, was a result of both colonial and native forces that suppressed the free expression of human will, and had a definite impact on the cultural and social lives of Kerala's people. The reform movements of the late nineteenth and early twentieth centuries kept alive its spirit and resistance to forces of subordination.[5] Sreedhara Menon views the cultural context of the Bhakti movement thus:

---

[5] E. M. Sankaran Nambudiripad reads the Bhakti movement as the stimulus behind later reform movements.

The violence that had become a common phenomenon in the political life of Kerala, the social restrictions imposed upon the lower castes, the moral degradation resulting from Devadasi system, the depreciation in the spice market, the recession resulting from the monopolisation of foreign trade by the colonisers and the falling living standards of many, including the farmers, resulted in a melancholic atmosphere.

It is under these circumstances that people turn to piety for solace. Into this scenario, Ezhuthachan made his entry intending a revival of piety movements. (2008, 186)

Menon further describes Thunchath Ezhuthachan's contribution to Malayalam literature and language:

In the 16th and 17th centuries Thunchath Ezhuthachan set a major revolution in the area of learning. The Brahmin monopolisation of Sankrit and the learning of Vedas and Upanishads, upholding 'Sudhrakshara samyuktham durathaha parivarjjayeth',[6] was revolutionised by the literary achievements of Ezhuthachan. The Ezhuthupally system initiated by Ezhuthachan to educate laymen spread all over Kerala. (ibid., 189)

Following this, the trajectory of the reform movements can be mapped in continuation with the efforts of Ezhuthachan and others to disengage education from Brahmins and their monopoly over Sanskrit (Sreedhara Menon, quoted in Nair 2008, 189). At the same time, historical specificities, such as heightened nationalist sentiments and the emerging reform activities all over India would also have contributed to it. However, rather than reading these reform movements as offshoots of those taking place in north India, we need a historical understanding of the resistance they offered to forces of oppression, and see the drive for ethnic, religious, and cultural assertion as reflecting their essence. Parallel to the Bhakthi movement ran a drive for literacy that popularised the Arabic Malayalam script, along with an increased interest in cultural production in the Muslim community. In *Mahathaya Mappila Sahithya Parambaryam* (*The Great Tradition of Mappila*

---

[6] 'The Sudras are denied the privilege of learning the Vedas.

Literature), C. N. Ahammed Moulavi and K. K. Muhammed Abdulkareem documented the early efforts towards a literary and cultural upheaval amongst the Muslims of Kerala: 'Ever since Islam spread in Kerala numerous scholars and writers have lived here. Ibn Bathutha, the 14th century traveller describes his meeting some Muslim scholars and leaders in his travelogue ...' (1978: 129).

As per the *Mahathaya Mappila Sahithya Parambaryam*, the earliest available work in Arabic Malayalam script, *The Mohiyidheen Mala*, was written five years before Ezhuthachan wrote his *Adhyathma Ramayanam.*[7] The structure of narrative poetry, written along the lines of hagiography, was an attempt to historicise the Muslim existence as well as revitalise the community in light of the Portuguese threat. Another important work is *Tuhfat al-Mujahidin,* written in the sixteenth century. The book, which can be considered the first anti-colonial document in history, highlights Portuguese cruelties against the Muslims and talks about the necessity of religious and spiritual awakening amongst Muslims. Thus, the Bhakti movement was not confined to Hindu revival, but had an impact on the Muslim community as well. The reform activities of the late nineteenth and early twentieth centuries extend from this tradition. But instead of concerns with caste oppression as in Hindu reform, Muslims took up questions of education, a return to the scriptures, and colonial resistance. The struggle to resist the Portuguese was a major concern, as the coloniser's presence threatened the social security of Muslims the most. In his Introduction to *Makthi Thangalude Sampoorna Krithikal* (*The Complete Works of Makhthi Thangal,* 2006), M. Gangadharan writes about Veliyamcode Ummar Khazi, who campaigned for the Tax Defiance Movement against the British in Malabar in the early nineteenth century. Gangadharan points out that Ummar Khazi was perhaps the first to start a resistance

---

[7] Roland E. Miller, in *The Mappilas of Malabar* (1976), records the year of writing as 1607. The work itself talks of its construction in Kolla Varsham 782, which supports Miller's contention.

against British tax policies in India (ibid.: 12). Syed Sanah Ullah Makhthi Thangal was the son of one of Ummar Khazi's disciples, and a pioneer of reform movements in the Muslim community. Thangal's anti-colonial resistance sparked a community's aspiration to engage with modernity, redefining the modern in terms of resistance to European culture and revising the category of the native. *Kadora Kudaram* (*The Lethal Weapon*), Thangal's first work, resisted the distortion of both Islam and Hinduism by Christian missionaries.

Partha Chatterjee argued that the reform movements were attempts to equip the native language and society for modern culture, without succumbing to European conventions (2008a: 7). Viewing the Muslim reform movements from this perspective, we find the reformers endeavouring to revise the language, provide universal education, and resist the impact of colonisation. Given the gradual transformation of society from comfortable and familiar homeland to a difficult and contested space where Islam, as a religion rooted outside India, had to struggle for its identity and existence, the reformer's task was two-fold: *first*, assert one's claim to native identity, and *second*, equip the community to join the modern nation. Such an effort was evident from the days of *Tuhfat al-Mujahidin*. As an historian in changing times, the author of *Tuhfat al-Mujahidin* considered it important to document the opulent lives of Muslims before the advent of the Portuguese in Malabar. The dialogues between Sanah Ullah Makhthi Thangal and contemporary society were clearly anti-Western in essence and culture, which countered the orientalist assumptions of Christian missionaries, assumptions that had the coloniser's unflinching support. Significant among his counter-attacks on Christianity was the one on the holy trinity, the backbone of Christian theology (Makhthi Thangal 2006: 29–100). Not only did he challenge the basis of Christian belief, but he also found parallels between Christian and Hindu theology, connecting the holy trinity of Father, Son, and the Holy Ghost and the Hindu concept of the *Tri Murthi* of Brahma, Vishnu, and Shiva. His unique approach to religion, making it available to scientific analysis, heralded the dawn of modernity, along with efforts to reform it from within. A table provided at the end of *Kadora Kudaram* comparing Hinduism and Christianity is an intelligent attempt to mark the religion's transition from a premodern realm to a modern space (ibid.: 97–100).

Makhthi Thangal dealt with the dominance of Islamic civilisation and culture in a markedly anti-orientalist vein in his writings. His arguments were widely supported by quotes from historians and scholars, many of whom were Europeans. As a historian of Islam, Makhthi Thangal claimed that European civilisation was indebted to Islamic culture. He refers to *Darvi*, a book which, according to him, had been written by a French minister, to state that:

> Europe was once totally immersed in darkness. Knowledge of philosophy, science, mathematics, rhetoric, sculpture etc. was extended to them by the Islamic world. In Baghdad, Samarqand, Damascus, Kabaruvan, Egypt, Persia and Cordova there were plenty of institutions of scholarship where knowledge was imparted impartially. The knowledge dissemination during this period was mainly from these areas, and this is precisely where Europeans got the information on various sciences from. (Abdulkareem 2006, 436)

As a true reformer concerned with his community's entry into modernity, Makhthi Thangal discusses education, women's status, and the history of the Muslim community. He emphasised the importance of education and learning of Malayalam and English, and also undertook the translation of the Quran and other religious works in Arabic, as well as the reform of the Arabic Malayalam script. The short work *Ta'leemul Iqwan* on the reformed Arabic Malayalam script was published in Hijra 1310 (AD 1892), and later, in a newspaper, *Tufat al Akbaar*, in the new script in Hijra 1312 (AD 1894) (Ahammed Moulavi and Abdulkareem 1978: 127).

NATIONALISM AND ISLAM IN KERALA

The imagined nation is a problematic space for the Muslim intellectual. The 'spiritual domain' (Chatterjee 2009) of the nation was already an enigma for them, as the space was defined strictly along Hindu traditions. The inside/outside or *ghar/bahar* division may not be a viable construction through which to think of Muslim reform activities, because the nationalist conceptualisation did not take into account identities that fell outside the familiar frame of Hindu practices. Under these circumstances, most historians overlook Muslim reform movements in their urgency to delineate and analyse nationalist and reformist histories along Hindu archives. The nation has always been a confused terrain for the Muslim. While on the one hand a sense of belongingness needs to be asserted, on the other, a premodern religion, from a pan-Islamic perspective, has also to be defended, asserted, and modernised. In the Indian context, the reformers' task has been made tougher because of the syncretic bonds that Islam has forged with Hinduism. Through a Hindu identity that is unequivocally Indian, Hindu reformers laid claim to the spiritual core of the nation (which differs from the Western notion of nation), while at the same time alienating Muslims from this space.[8] The complexity involved in the Muslim engagement with modernity was felt in Kerala as well. Here, it was more troublesome as Islam in Kerala has an entirely different relationship with the state's history, which, being free of the baggage of invasions and attacks, is different from that of the rest of India.[9] In terms of finding a balance between modernity and tradition while reviving language, Muslims could not fit into the models available in other communities. An easier alternative is ignoring Muslim reform attempts, categorising them as strictly religious movements.

Another surprising tactic in mainstream historiography has been to ignore Muslim participation in the history of the

---

[8] Nationalist Hindu attempts to modernise India have been the topic of discussion in many texts. These efforts also positioned Muslims as the antithetical Other (see Gupta 2008).

[9] Perhaps noting this difference, colonial historians have occasionally created tropes; for instance, casting Tipu Sultan in the role of invader and fanatic, and constructing a long history of Tipu's atrocities in northern Kerala. This image was taken up by later mainstream historians.

nationalist movement.[10] The Malabar Rebellion features on the margins of India's struggle for independence and is often treated as a peasants' uprising against feudalism, or even as a display of Muslim fanaticism against Hindus. By the early nineteenth century, the status of Muslims had changed considerably in the political context.

A close analysis of Muslim reform movements in Kerala shows that rather than claiming the nation, their attempts were to modernise the community. In all the discourses on modernity, the ethnographic origins of the community could be traced to the historical roots of Kerala. However, even while focusing on an Islamic past that endorses a strict reading of the Quran and the *Hadith*s, efforts have been made to detach the community from superstitious practices.

Print journalism was one mechanism that Muslim reformers resorted to in order to reach out to the community. More than any other community, print culture played a major role in the reform strategies of Muslims in Kerala. From the 1900s, there circulated hundreds of regional newspapers and magazines, all with the intention to popularise education, highlight the status of women, and discuss the Islamic way of life. The relationship between the State and Muslim reform leaders was interesting, especially when compared to the loyalty exhibited by leaders like Syed Ahmed Khan. Vakkom Maulavi was the patron of Swadeshabhimani Ramakrishna Pillai, who was exiled on charges of treason by the colonial regime. Muslims formed some major organisations during this period: the first was Muhammadeeya Sabha, formed by Makhthi Thangal in northern Kerala. Sheikh Hamadani Thangal formed the Muslim Nishpaksha Sabha, which intended to unite the Muslim brethren. Vakkom Maulavi was initially a part of this movement. In 1905, he started the *Swadeshabhimani* newspaper with Ramakrishna Pillai as his chief editor. *Swadeshabhimani* attacked the rule of the king and his corrupt ways. In 1910, state

---

[10] The songs called *maalas* record the participation of Muslims in the anti-colonial struggle.

intervention led to the press being shut down and the daily was banned. Like most reform leaders, Vakkom Maulavi focused on the political, social, and economic aspects of the community's development, and identified a lack of education as the cause of the community's backwardness. In the article 'The Need of Muhammadeeya Sabha', published in his daily, *Muslim,* he wrote about the necessity for education:

> [T]he Muslims of Kerala are in a pathetic situation. They have not only ignored this reality, being hesitant to take the initiative, but have also been indifferent to the reminders from other communities through newspapers and other sources. Muslims of Kerala have been identified as the ignorant ….
>
> The necessity of a Muslim organisation has reached its heights. If Muslims of Malabar, Kochi and Travancore unite to form an organisation the backwardness of the community can be slowly rectified. Histories have taught us that all communities have risen to development solely through these kinds of organisations and meetings …. (Govindapilla 2009, 51)

While discussing the community's backwardness, reform leaders also pointed to a better future, through education and active involvement with culture in the form of printing and publishing. It is interesting to note that many of them owned their own printing presses,[11] and published widely on the role of Islam in the modern world as well as ways to lead the Muslim

[11] Referring to the contribution of the print media and literature in Bengal, Partha Chatterjee writes that the crucial moment in the development of the modern Bengali language was when the bilingual elite made it a cultural project to provide his mother tongue with the necessary linguistic equipment to enable it to become adequate for 'modern' culture. An entire institutional network of printing presses, publishing houses, newspapers, magazines, and literary societies was created around this time, *outside* the purview of the State and the European missionaries. The language therefore became a zone over which the nation had to declare its sovereignty, and then transform it in order to equip it for the modern world (Chatterjee 2008a, 7). This was problematic for the Muslim in Kerala as Arabic Malayalam was also a major medium of Muslim creativity.

forward as befitted citizens of an emerging nation. Unfortunately, later historians only focused on this backwardness, leaving out Muslim negotiations with modernity. From 1910, the community witnessed a dynamic period of mobilisation through education, writing and publishing, political and social work, and so on, a period that never appears in the mainstream narratives on reform movements. The community, along with its women, engaged in a complex negotiation with religion and modernity in order to relocate itself in the emerging political sphere.

WOMEN IN THE REFORM CONTEXT

The representation of women in the nationalist histories of South Asia has been problematic, and the added identity of Muslim complicates it even further. While revisiting nineteenth-century colonial documents on India, many historians, especially feminist historians, have identified conscious strategies of documenting Indian customs and practices as inferior and thus needing to be rectified.[12] The status of women was a favourite point of entry (Bullock 2002; Metcalf 2006). The native reformer, taking his cues from the colonial master, followed the project of civilising, or perhaps uplifting the status of, their women. In Kerala, this worked in a slightly different manner. Since the Muslim population of this densely populated state is considerable, the reformers had to focus on the plight of the Muslim community. While Muslim reformers took up the issues of education and social awareness, later historians followed the preconceived notions on Islam, depicting the community as backward and their women as suppressed by the customs of this 'primitive religion'. Thus, Muslim women, whose destinies were in the hands of their male masters, remained in the murky world of ignorance and illiteracy, contributing nothing to the cultural renaissance in the documented history of the reform movements. In the nationalist models of reform,

---

[12] Lata Mani's (2009) reading of colonial documents on Sati serves as an example.

the emerging identity of the Hindu woman was both that of a preserver of ancient Hindu values and a symbol of the evolving nation's heritage. Metcalf identifies this phenomenon:

> The social reformers ultimately identified the middleclass, educated housewife with nothing less than the preservation of 'Hindu' religion and culture, and even with India itself as Bharat Mata. The 'New Hindu woman' was at once different from the unreformed, poor, and uneducated women; from English women, who were both a model and a threat; and from non-Hindu, above all Muslim women. To the extent that such an image was at the heart of Hindu cultural nationalism, it helps explain the failure of political nationalism to engage imagination and commitment of large segments of population. (2006, 100)

The identification of the Bengali *bhadralok* female as the new image of the Indian woman, challenging the profile of the 'ideal Victorian woman', distanced other women from the cultural space of the nation. This phenomenon has functioned in all cultural productions and political designs ever since.[13] This formula operated slightly differently in Kerala, owing to the different context in which nationalism had evolved there. One difference lay in who constituted the genteel class in Kerala, corresponding to the Bengali *bhadralok*. The impact of communist movements with their promise of an egalitarian social structure led to the creation of a distinct model for Kerala. The fact that reform movements in Kerala were not strictly upper-class or Hindu-oriented, as they were in Bengal, added to the difference. Although there had been a lot of discussions on women during the reform era, the question that needs further examination is: Was there an apparent model for the 'woman' in this context? Even though the conflation of the Hindu woman with the image of Bharat Mata was assimilated into the cultural space of Kerala in independent India, this was not the case in the reform context. Was there an ideal woman who could uphold tradition in the context of the reform movements

---

[13] Popular movies have cast women's images in this context. The portrayal of Muslim women in mainstream movies and literature has been pathetic.

in Kerala? There were diverse models available, but this diversity was camouflaged by later historians of the reform movements. J. Devika's reading of Malayali[14] modernity views the reform movements as a context that produced gendered individuals:

> Early-twentieth-century reformisms in Malayalee society … put forth an 'order of gender' as the ideal alternative to the existent oppressive order *janmabhedam*, difference-by-birth, *jati*. The individualism they espoused entailed a vision of gender difference, which was immediately organised in terms of a complementary sexual exchange. Ideally, men were to remain within the public domain, and women within the domestic, exercising different sorts of authority and power …. These domains were … determined by the sexual endowments of the body. Women … ought to exercise supervisory authority within the home, … so that the unique and positive dispositions, capacities, inclinations etc. of those within the domestic domain may be well-developed. (2007, 243)

Devika goes on to say that in women's writing of the reform period, especially those of Lalithambika Antarjanam, complementary sexual exchange seemed to have been indefinitely postponed. In her reading, Antharjanam rejects instrumental exchange as the basic nature of the relation between the sexes, and challenges the male project of re-forming women. Devika's critique of the reform project as male attempts to control and redefine female bodies has been echoed by feminists in connection to other reform projects (Gupta 2008; Sangari and Vaid 2009), especially in Bengal. While I agree with Devika's reading of Antharjanam's writings as an oppositional reworking of sexual complementarities (2007, 248), I also realise the impossibility of turning this observation into a general theory of women's participation in the reform context. Modernity was defined differently by different communities. The strained relationship with religion and tradition was common to all reformers, but the negotiations that each community

---

[14] Malayali is one who belongs to Kerala. Devika uses this vernacular term as she insists upon using Keralam instead of Kerala.

adopted to accommodate religion within modernity cannot be generalised. Where women were concerned, these negotiations had wider implications.

I would like to elaborate on this through different readings of the Channaar Rebellion. The Channaar Rebellion of the mid-nineteenth century was spurred by the determination of Channaar women to cover their breasts, in an open refutation of upper-caste strictures that denied women of the lower castes the right to cover their upper bodies. The act of wearing blouses (see, for instance, Devika 2007, 269–73) cannot be read as violence inflicted upon the natives by colonial morality, or as the reformer's attempt to follow colonial standards of morality:

> In turn, the community reformisms gave the idea deeper reach through a variety of means. From the accounts of reformist activities, it seems that often these means involved outright intimidation; even coercion .... The use of violence to clothe women who refused to cover themselves is sometimes mentioned in histories of reform and reformers. (ibid., 273)

What is ignored here is the role of caste in determining a particular dress code for a community. Perhaps the notion of sexuality associated with bare breasts was a colonial import, but denying a particular community access to clothes in light of a revised morality has wider implications. Modernity is context-specific, and each community's negotiations with modernity and the ideals of enlightenment were different. It is in this context that I would like to read the agency of Muslim women in reform movements, and their negotiations with religion and modernity to situate Muslim women in the new world. These mediations mostly functioned independently of male discourses, although there were points of intersection. The language of the new woman was thus a complex domain of multiple interests and loyalties, at times apparently contradictory in terms of its approach to the binary of tradition and modernity.

Within the patriarchal structures that formulate discourses on modernity, women had been portrayed as mere tools in the process of modernising. But in any nation's progress towards modernity, we see a tight link between reformism and feminism. The history of non-European nationalist movements bears testimony to the entry of women in mainstream politics and their active participation in political struggles.[15] However, in documented histories, women become the symbol of community backwardness, as well as markers of its virtue and heritage. This dual role conveniently countered the European critique of oriental women (see Bullock 2002), while at the same time confining them within the same framework of patriarchy that shapes indigenous systems.

The history of the nationalist movement in India is replete with gaps and silences in its documentation of women's participation. Historians attempting to write the history of the reform movements in Kerala have followed the same pattern. It is ironic that most revolutionary acts involved important decisions concerning the plight of women. Clichés abound: the shift of Nambutiri women from the kitchen to the public domain; widow remarriages in the Nambutiri community; the Channaar Rebellion; Pulaya women's refusal to wear stones (variously reported as *Kallayum Maalayum, Kallumaala*, etc.);[16] or even the discussions on women's education. It is indeed notable how discourses on women informed the ideals of reformation. At the same time, historical narratives on the reform movements are crucially silent about female participation in these revolutionary events. Even the records of the Channaar Rebellion of the mid-nineteenth century, a highly woman-centric movement, is unusually silent about its female participants. Look at how the *Kallumaala* rebellion has been narrated by P. Sivadasan in *Kerala Charithram Sambhavangaliloode* (*History of Kerala through Events*):

---

[15] Kumari Jayawardena, in *Feminism and Nationalism in the Third World* (1986), discusses the development of feminism in the historical context of the Third World.

[16] Lower-caste women were forced to wear heavy stones and glass pieces around their necks, marking their backwardness.

Women from the Pulaya community defying the norms of the upper-caste and the police restrictions discarded the stones on their neck in public, under the leadership of Ayyankali and progressive leaders like Changanassery Parameswaran Pillai at the Railway station ground, Kollam. It has been reported that the stones, discarded by them, formed a heap of about four to five feet and remained in the ground for a long time. (2007, 86)

Apart from a few women who belonged to the Hindu upper caste or socially forward segments, such as Arya Pallam, Lalithambika Antharjanam, Devaki Narikkattiri, Ambadi Ikkavamma, A. V. Kuttimalu Amma, and Akkama Cherian, history does not acknowledge the participation of any other women in these movements. In M. N. Vijayan's *Nammude Sahithyam Nammude Samooham* (*Our Literature, Our Society*, 2000), we come across a passing reference to Arya Pallam and the play *Thozhil Kendhrathilekku* (*To the Workplace*).[17] K. N. Ganesh also refers to Tharavathu Ammalu Amma, Ambadi Ikkavamma, T. K. Kalyani Amma, Lalithambika Antharjanam, and K. Saraswathi Amma while discussing the rise in women's movements (Ganesh 2002, 136). Apart from these few instances, women have been excluded from recorded history. Thus, the Channaar Rebellion, the 'Kallayum Maalayum Bahishkaranam' of Pulaya women, and even the widow remarriages that took place in the Nambutiri

---

[17] *Thozhil Kendrathilekku* (1948) is the historic play written and performed by a group of Nambutiri women over half-a-century ago as part of the struggle for their emancipation. The play narrates the life story of Devaki, who left her marital home for 'Thozhil Kendram' (the workplace), which was a free commune of women seeking to make a living for themselves. Many plays written by men on the theme of women's emancipation in the Nambutiri community are celebrated and discussed. But *Thozhil Kendrathilekku* never received attention in the public domain in Kerala until recently, when feminist historians highlighted its historical importance. For the women who wrote and staged the play, it was not merely theatre, but a part of their personal struggles. The first available published copy of the play was printed at Yogakshemom Press, Thrissivaperur, in 1948, although the play is said to have been performed since 1945.

community came to be known after the male reform leaders like Ayyankali or V. T. Bhattathirippad. Of course, they had a major role to play, but discrediting the role of women in these movements while highlighting the male patrons displays the fissures in historiography.

It is important to note that while the reform movements in other communities were marked by revolutionary acts, Muslim reform centred around public talks, gatherings, and most importantly, discussions in journals and periodicals. Hundreds of periodicals associated with the reform leaders were published during this period, but most of these were seen as religious literature. Miller refers to them in *The Mappila Muslims of Kerala*: 'Mappila periodicals tended to be associated with narrow objectives and did not fall into the category of general literature ...' (1976, 290). Haleema Beevi's response to an interview question on the materials published in her weekly, *Bharatha Chandrika*, reveals an altogether different reality:

> The weekly was named *Bharatha Chandrika*. Literature was given priority with the poems of Changampuzha Krishna Pillai, the stories of Vaikom Muhammad Basheer, and so on. Thus *Bharatha Chandrika* was also the learning school for budding writers .... O N V Kurup, Gupthan Nair, Balamani Amma, Kamukara Purushothaman and many important writers of the time used to publish in this. (Beevi 1995, 6)

Reading this testimony against Miller's observation reveals the prejudices of historians, which led them to exclude Muslim periodicals from the discourses on reform movements. Miller's reading was also informed by the preconceived notion of Islam as primitive and anti-modern. Interestingly, reform movements had flourished in the Muslim community, expressed mostly through print and publishing. Many Muslim reformists like Vakkom Maulavi and Haleema Beevi had their own publishing facilities. These periodicals were used widely to mobilise the public.

Image 2.1: Haleema Beevi

Source: File photo, *Prabodhanam Weekly*.

MUSLIM WOMEN AND REFORM MOVEMENTS

The writings of Muslim women during this period, while informed by the wider movements to improve the status of women in society, were situated within the norms of the religion. They were widely circulated between 1920 and 1970 and this makes it difficult to place them in the framework of nationalist discourses against imperialism.[18] Hence, these periodicals cannot be written off as religious literature. In recent times, feminists have revised their views on the position of women in Islam.[19] Even though Muslim reform discourses were situated in the colonial context, they were not strictly nationalist, and reflected a larger humanist perspective

[18] It is to be noted that reform movements amongst the Muslims of Kerala extended beyond the colonial period to the 1970s and 1980s. The contemporary manifestations of political Islam in Kerala may be traced back to Muslim reform movements.

[19] Here, I refer to the challenges that Islam poses to normative conceptions of feminist agency, as discussed in Saba Mahmood (2005).

beyond the frame of the nation. Challenges to imperialism were also mounted beyond the borders of the nation. By the 1940s, the impact of political decisions taken by the Congress and Muslim national leaders alike had turned 'nation' into a fraught concept for Muslims.

K. M. Seethi provided a brief history of periodical literature in the Muslim community of Kerala in the first issue of *Chandrika Weekly*, published on 15 July 1950. He listed a number of publications circulated widely among the Muslims, and referred to Moosakutty Sahib's *Muslim Mahila*, and Haleema Beevi's *Muslim Vanitha* and *Bharatha Chandhrika*, which were entirely dedicated to women. He also referred to a wide readership of Muslim women, which worked as a motivating force for all these journals (Seethi 1950, 4).

Muslim women wrote widely in these periodicals—for example, in *Ansari, Al Islam, Mappila Review*, etc.—and certain special issues were meant for women alone. Haleema Beevi entered the terrain of journalism in 1938 with *Muslim Vanitha,* which was later modified as *Adhunika Vanitha*. Although it discussed issues such as women's education and the need to reform religion and eradicate superstition, it fought hard to survive and finally had to stop publishing. *Bharatha Chandrika* made its entry in 1946, with Vakkom Abdul Khader and Vaikom Muhammed Basheer as co-editors.

Bharatha Chandrika emerged as a daily after a year, and it is surprising to note that the defiance in Haleema Beevi's writings against the oppressive reign of Sir C. P. Rama Swami, the dictatorial Diwan of Travancore, went unnoticed. While acknowledging the recent efforts to reclaim her space in the history of the women's movement in Kerala, it is disturbing to note her absence in discourses on early women's movements. A staunch feminist and reformist, she was also an ardent member of the Indian National Congress. In 1949, the magazine *Azad* was published, with Haleema Beevi as the chief editor. In subsequent years, she took a break from active journalism to emerge as an activist. In 1960, she organised a Muslim women's conference at Perumbavoor, near

Kochi, and in 1970, she started a new magazine titled *Adhunika Vanitha*, with women in all the major posts. In an article published in *Aaraamam* immediately after her death in March 2000, Sasikumar Chelannur wrote:

> Haleema Beevi entered the world of print media when the world of letters was alien to women, especially Muslim women. This Muslim woman journalist is still an amazing presence in the history of print journalism in Kerala as she entered the public arena when women were hesitant to occupy political and public roles. This great woman who fought against the dictatorial rule of Sir C. P. is no longer with us. Her exciting life lies before researchers to be explored. (2000, 11)

What is interesting in this reading is the constant reminder that Haleema Beevi's work did not receive the public attention it deserved, and the iteration of her unusually strange presence in the public sphere. But why did she not get the importance she deserved in recorded history?

Image 2.2: Haleema Beevi with her Husband

Source: File photo, *Prabodhanam Weekly*.

None of the hundreds of journals and tracts in circulation among the Muslims from the 1920s to the 1970s was acknowledged in mainstream documentation. The evolving public sphere in Kerala, despite its secular, modern outlook, failed to accommodate the cultural and political writings of this community.

Apart from Haleema Beevi, who asserted the claims of Muslim women to the political sphere, other women from the community also wrote on the plight of women. For instance, P. Beefathima wrote in the *Mappila Review* of August 1945: 'Men of Kerala do not treat women as per the instructions of religion. If women are ill treated in personal life, it is of course because of the ignorance of the community on the laws of the religion' (p. 40). A quick glance at these journals reveals a number of such reformist ideas, written by women from within the space of religion, yet concentrating on women's agency.

The world over, Muslim women who engaged in discourses of modernity often had a strained relationship with religion. The dialogues of the Muslim women of Kerala with modernity reflect a different trajectory. Without compromising the spiritual realm of the religion, they could debate and discuss modernity, redefining themselves and their community. This redefining never negated tradition, but remained in constant negotiation with it, as reflected in the periodic literature by Muslims on women and by Muslim women writers during the reform era. First, the colonial context in which this literature was published is important. Reformist discourses, especially in the Muslim context, discussed and defended the status of Muslim women and Islam as a response to the Western critique of Islam. The reform attempts of men identified women in general, and Muslim women in particular, in need of reformation. While Muslim women's own ideas of reform were circumscribed by these two aspects, they succeeded in leaving an imprint on the political and cultural domains of the nation. Through their negotiations, even while remaining connected to their social, religious, ethnic, and national communities, they demonstrate a capacity for action in distinct ways.

Responses to colonialism in the reform context emerged in many ways. Unlike the Hindu reformers, Muslim reformers took an anti-European approach, upholding Islam in a wider historical and geographical perspective. In an article titled 'Islam and Women', published in *Al Islam*, Vakkom Maulavi writes:

> It is equally foolish to say that polygamy is established by Islam as a practice, as to say that purdah is a Muslim practice. The so called civilized Greek and Roman men used to keep their women away from other men. Greece which is supposed to be the sacred centre of civilization and the birth place Socrates and Plato used to treat its women like animals. (1918, 32)

The article goes on to defend purdah and the virtues of the Islamic way of life. It claims that all communities practised gender segregation, and that the present critique of purdah stems from the influence of an American culture that allows unrestricted male-female contact, which had previously been allowed only in the nomadic past. The article follows the *Encyclopaedia Britannica* to define purdah as the system that separates men and women, stating that its usage in all oriental communities shows that the practice pre-dated Islam. The article both defends Islam and counters the colonial projection of the religion as the barbaric 'other'.

Many articles in various little magazines attempted to define the Muslim woman as fundamentally different from, and yet privileged over, her European and Hindu counterparts during this time. The reformist attempt was mainly to confront the colonial critique of Islam's treatment of its women, which was later echoed in Hindu nationalist discourses as well. This theme was iterated in several articles published between 1915 and 1960.[20] Read, for instance, the editorial response published in the magazine *Isha'ath* in October 1934 on the widow remarriages in the Nambutiri community, titled 'Rasika Sadanathile Vidhava Vivaham' ('The Widow Remarriage at Rasika Sadanam', 1934):

> The lives of widows in Hindu community have been miserable. In the past they were burnt alive in the funeral pyres of their husbands as per

---

[20] Marakkar (1952, 31–34); and Maulavi (1920) provide strong defences of the Islamic treatment of its women.

Vedic instructions …. Yet Hindus have never extended the widows equal rights with other women or allowed them to remarry. The grievances of widows … has never been attended to by Hindus, the strict followers of the Vedas.

But Islam has answered the plea of widows …. Not only that they were given equal status with other women in the society, their insecurity had been addressed to by the instruction, 'you should marry the widows in your community.' Since this instruction has been strictly followed, widow grievances are absent in Islam. Now, after years of suffering, Hindus have come forward willingly … in this matter ….

This was definitely an attempt to distinguish the Islamic treatment of women from that of Hindus and Christians. There are also articles that discuss the right to property enjoyed by Muslim women, placing them in a better position over Christian women. Since discussions on the plight of women led to discourses on the backwardness of Islam, the reformer's dialogue was shaped by a defence of Islam's treatment of women. Here, the reformist is carving separate identities, defining what is meant by a Hindu or a Muslim, especially in terms of women. Katherine Bullock points out the hierarchical privileging of Christianity over Islam in terms of the status of women in *Rethinking the Muslim Women and the Veil* (2002), which leads to the construction of Europe as superior to the Orient:

> The point of discourse on women was that a nation could not advance while its women were backward. Women as mothers were seen to play a crucial role in educating their children, and thus perpetuating the civilization. Christian mothers (the European mothers) exerted a healthy civilizing influence on their children. Muslim mothers did not. So colonialists, missionaries, and feminists, as well as native elites trying to 'modernize' their countries, all hoped to have access to the Muslim woman in order to influence her, so that the nation might progress. (ibid., 18)

Muhammad Kutty Arimbra, in his article 'Sthree: Padaviyum, Pravarthana Rangavum' ('Woman: Status and Career', 1959), compares women's status in Semitic religions and Islam. He studies various cultures and claims that all civilisations have had their superstitions and rigid restrictions, and that barbarism was the common feature of all ancient tribes. He points to the inferior treatment of women by Jews and Christians, who viewed the woman as the temptress and as the epitome of sin. Critiquing Europe's treatment of its women and defending the status of women in Islam, he states:

> Yet, when did Europe that takes pride in itself as a progressive civilization, an ideal model for all, legally approve of women's rights? Only in the recent past. This is not a reading of the feminist revolution from male perspective, but I am forced to write this due to constant demands from empathizing souls. Even now in many European countries, women's rights have not been properly acknowledged and most of their claims have not been legally accepted (ibid.).

Thus, the aim was to both counter the European critique of women's status in Islam and establish a distinct individuality for the Muslim woman in contrast to the Hindu woman. Hindu reformist efforts to depict the Hindu woman as the symbol of virtue and tradition had to be addressed in the same context. However, this was not as evident in Kerala as it was in Bengal, perhaps because powerful reform movements from the lower castes in the Hindu community had marked Kerala's entry into modernity. Nevertheless, these discourses continued to portray Muslim women as relatively better-off than their Hindu counterparts.

The colonial invaders had constructed a hierarchical ordering of civilisations based on the status of women in the respective societies. Native reformers addressed the same issue; as mentioned earlier, in the Muslim community, women became the central subject of the male reformer's project. In order to be better wives and mothers, as well as the preservers of tradition, women needed to be educated, and their social worlds extended outside their homes. But along with broadening women's social horizons, the domestic world itself was re-formed, and opened to the workings of the modern State. It was the male reformer, though, who determined the style and pattern of female re-forming. Among Muslims in Kerala, this pattern functioned in a slightly different manner. During that period, unlike in northern India, there was no strict observance of purdah among the Muslim women in Kerala. Therefore, the male reformer's role was limited, as compared to the Nambutiri or Hindu upper castes. Unlike the Nambutiri community, what we witness in the Muslim community is not a complete refutation of tradition; on the contrary, we see a reverence for and celebration of tradition here. The reformism in the Muslim community thus discusses how best to follow the religious virtues. While adopting organisational forms and printing technology from modernity, Muslim reformers were careful to not imitate the West, and delineate a way of living distinct from Western society. There is also a careful distancing from Hindu reformist spirituality, which locates the nation and its heritage in its women. While articulating the destiny of Indian Muslims in changing times and acknowledging the need to educate women and extend their domain from the private to the public sphere, they did not pin their cultural hopes only on their women. Gail Minault, in *Secluded Scholars* (1999), identifies such a phenomenon in north India among both Muslims and Hindus. She states that in male reform programmes, women were identified as potential students, as readers of enlightening literature, as subscribers to magazines designed to disseminate new knowledge, and as beneficiaries of the activities of men (ibid., 9).

This was true of Muslim reform movements in Kerala as well. But the distinction between secular and religious positions can be gauged from the difference between male and female discourses on Muslim reform. While male reformists drew on the Islamic intellectual tradition to support reform programmes for women, women's discourses focused on more mundane arenas, articulating issues ignored by men. Their views at times substantiate and at times challenge the male perspectives. The reform programme for women, as charted out by male reformers, mainly centred on women's education, and sometimes on modern welfare mechanisms like health, hygiene, etc., where women were supposed to play a role in safeguarding the family. An article on the importance of breast milk, 'Mulappalinte Kootuthal Pradhanatha' ('The Greater Importance of Breast Milk'), published in *Mappila Review* in 1945, carried a translated excerpt from an article by American scientist and thinker, Alexis Carl. In its conclusion, it observed:

> Modern women are not informed on motherhood and its responsibilities. Some mothers prioritize many other things over child care. They neglect their primary duty. Girls do not get any information or specific training to cope with the responsibilities of life through education. Likewise they do not get privileged status in the community also. (ibid., 15)

Such secular discussions often informed reform concerns about women. Although purdah was a major concern for outsiders wishing to define the community, it was referred to only in terms of defending Islamic law. In this context, let us also discuss a story titled 'Sevika' (the woman in social service), published in *Mappila Review* of 1945. The short story, written by P. A. Muhammad Koya, centres around a girl named Nafeesa, who had a great passion for studying, despite the resistance of the majority in her community. She persevered, ignoring all obstacles. Her notion of education was in accordance with the modern enlightenment view. For instance, when Nafeesa's father bowed to community pressure and asked her to discontinue her studies, she responds, as befitting a modern individual:

> 'You mean I should discontinue studies? I cannot agree to that. Why should the community bother about my studies? Only educated men and women can lead the society and the community to progress. Can we dance according to their tunes? Let them blabber whatever they want.' (ibid., 5)

This spirit of modernity, reflecting the individual's right to choose their priorities, can be seen in much of the literature published in these periodicals. Later in the story, Nafeesa actively participates in disaster management during an outbreak of cholera in the locality. She organises a cholera eradication cell with the aid of neighbourhood women, provides solace to many grieving families, and soon becomes a favourite in her community. Although the story ends with her death from cholera, the message is clear: education is to be given priority over all else. Another aspect is the individualism exhibited by Nafeesa while making her choices. Beyond all this is the message that an educated girl can benefit the community. The shaping of a modern woman who will be productive for both the society and the family forms the core of this story. In those days, the preference of men was for an 'ideal' woman, who could meet the demands of the modern family and society at large. These periodicals have a wide range of entries intended to familiarise women with new methods of childcare and household management. Women were also requested to contribute writings, and the editorials addressed a female readership as well. These discussions and debates took place in the larger context of efforts to open schools and institutions that could impart a secular education to women. The editorial in the *Mappila Review* of October 1945 reported:

> The decision of the Govt. to promote Hobart High School in Madras to a Muslim Women's College is a matter to rejoice for all Muslims .... The Govt. has agreed that from the secondary class onwards women need separate schools. For Muslim women this is a necessity as coeducation is not conducive to Muslim culture and tradition. This has blocked the entry of Muslim women into higher education. There have been grievances regarding separate facilities and reservations for Muslim women's Higher education .... We are happy to know that the Secretary of Tirur Muslim Girls High School, Janab Koyappathodi Ahammed Kutty Saheb has submitted a request to the educational advisor to Madras Govt., Sir Thomas Austin seeking free education in this college and free boarding in the associated hostel for Mappila girls ....
>
> With the establishment of Tirur Muslim Girls High school, Mappila women have developed a greater affinity to higher education. A majority of Mappila women who complete high School may consider higher educational possibilities. Their low financial status

may prevent them from such aspirations. It is the responsibility of the Govt. to encourage such resourceful students. If their economic status alone blocks their aspirations it is a crime on the part of the state not to attend to it. We sincerely hope that Sir Austin succumbs to this demand of Mappila women. (ibid., 29–30)

What we see here is not merely a community's aspiration to higher education, but also a realisation on the part of the modern citizen that the State has a duty to provide welfare services. While tradition and culture are not being relinquished, there is a growing awareness of the State as the institution primarily responsible for its subjects. This transition of power and authority from priests and community elders to the State becomes slowly evident in the reform discourses. At the same time, the Muslim subject retrieves tradition, as is insisted upon by the Quran. A shift from the *hadiths* and other interpretations to the Quran was the trend of the time, as reform leaders initiated projects to translate the Quran to Malayalam. Education, health, hygiene, and various other tools of modernity were often resorted to, not as an embracing of the West, but usually through negotiations.

During the 1940s and 1950s, Muslim women's education was the major fulcrum on which the community's reform attempts were centred. The Muslim Boys English High School was opened in Tirur in 1936, and in 1940, the Muslim Girls High School was started. After a year, boarding facilities were also extended to students. Most Muslim journals published during this period urged the public to send their children to schools. In discussions, modern education was presented as an enlightening tool, required for the individual in her/his journey towards emancipation. Clichéd descriptions of ignorance and backwardness were the key features: 'Does the community hope to progress after pinning down their women to smoke filled kitchens?' queried an Editorial in *Mappila Review* (1945, 49). In 'Sthree Vidhyabhyasam' ('Women's Education'), M. Sheykh Muhammad Maulavi, the principal of Arabic College, Areekkod, exhorted in *Al Manar* (1959, 124): 'The Muslim's Women's Organisation should be able to throw out the demon of ignorance among its women and should improve their cultural and educational standards.' A. K. Abu wrote an article in *Al Manar,* 'Muslim Sthreekalum Vidhyabhyasavum' ('Muslim Women and Education'), which looked to the *hadith*s to approve women's education and harshly rebuked the critics of women's education for being fraudulent manipulators (1960, 260).

The confusion on this issue was also evident amongst scholars. They all agreed to adopt education without compromising their obligations to religious traditions. While analysing these dynamic dialogues, the most striking aspect appears to be their unanimity in terms of their purpose of educating women. K. M. Maulavi, in 'Sthree Vidhyabhyasam', shared his views on women's education:

> It is surprising to see difference of opinion regarding women's education among the followers of a religion that has evidently presented the rights and responsibilities of women and insisted on education for all. Let me draw your attention to certain important aspects of this matter. Muslim women need separate educational institutions. Girls nearing puberty should be educated in these exclusive schools. If possible women teachers need to teach in these institutions. The most important quality of a woman is the purity of her soul and body. She should follow her obligations to her husband. (1953, 12–13)

He discussed the design of a curriculum for girls, intended 'to enlighten her soul, refine her character and make her adept in controlling the family and nurturing good habits in children aiming at preserving the family property and prosperity' (ibid.). Further, such an education would enable the economic and political endeavours of the community. Islamic principles could lead to wisdom and enlightenment. Here, interestingly, he urged Muslim women to get a multilingual education, anchored in Arabic, Arabic Malayalam, and pure Malayalam. Education had to begin with a good understanding of the Quran, leading to learning, '*aqeed, aqlaq, ibadath, haraam* and *halaal*'.[21] Homemaking and childcare

---

[21] What is right and wrong, acceptable and unacceptable, as per the fundamental principles of Islam.

were not exempted—courses on weaving, tailoring, and cooking were included, and were meant to make women resourceful (ibid.). This attempt to reform women in order to modernise homes and train them as community ideals was unique to Indian modernity. Religion plays a central role here, and the male reformer's job was to dictate norms for women's empowerment. Many have observed that the central focus of female empowerment was to relocate caste in modern homes under the guise of reforming women. The general tone of this narrative was emblematic of the anxiety accompanying the central role of women as the carriers of 'tradition' in modern families, rampant in the literature on Hindu reformism:

> Apart from this if they also learn Mathematics, Geography, Sociology that discusses the fall and rise of various communities in human history, National history, and Economics that deals with the prospect of maintaining wealth, they can contribute to the progress of the community as they had contributed in the beginning years of Islam to promote the religion. If a man marries a woman adept in all these areas of knowledge, and hands over the control of the home to her, she will definitely handle all her responsibilities. Moreover, that home evolves as the best school for our children. (ibid.)

This is precisely how modernity assigned roles to women. At the same time, the vital element of preserving tradition becomes a crucial factor here. The woman is thus supposed to adapt to a changing modern world, while at the same time preserving traditions. The image of the ideal woman became something of an obsession within reformist discourses. The need for balance placed an added responsibility on the woman, as this brought the ideologies of tradition and modernity into conflict. Discussions in the larger society on the reform of women's status made this even more problematic: the woman was now responsible for the modern home and the old tradition, leading to increased negotiations with modernity and tradition. In the writings by women during this reform period (1900–70), these negotiations became a dominant theme.

I will now analyse the third aspect of Muslim reform movements in connection with its women: how women included themselves in the reform context and revamped their ways and thoughts as modern individuals without compromising religion or community. I consider the entries of Muslim women in periodicals that represented Muslim engagement with modernity, covering fifty years from 1920 to 1970. The period 1950–70 was crucial for the Muslim community as it witnessed dynamic, critical discourses on religion, with reform dialogues taking place within the well-developed groups of the Nad'wath-ul-Mujahiddin and Jama'ath-e-Islami. Besides these two groups, the traditional *Sunni* Muslims, who usually stick to customs and rituals, also addressed the reform concerns through the formation of the Samastha Kerala Jamiat-ul-Ulema, countering the pan-Islamic *Salafi* influence and focusing on the community's progress. The Nad'wath-ul-Mujahiddin is strongly influenced by the Wahaabi tradition of Saudi Arabia, whereas Jama'ath-e-Islami claims to be the face of political Islam. Many Muslim women, including Haleema Beevi, associated with Nad'wath-ul-Mujahiddin, as it was more open to organising a women's movement. Later, Jama'ath-e-Islami also developed a strong women's wing, as did the Sunnis. During the 1950s and 1960s, most of the women engaged in the reform movement were a part of the women's wing of Nad'wath-ul-Mujahiddin. Many leading Muslim periodicals represented its ethos, and in the beginning, the intent was to confront conservatism in the community and open it up to new avenues of learning without compromising the religious doctrines. *Al Manar*, *Al Farooq*, and *Ansari* were some of the periodicals that reflected a focused dialogue with the conservatives in the community at the beginning of reform, and continued to support this school in the post-independent phase as well. However, the reform wave among Muslim women had started earlier; *Muslim Vanitha*, the first Malayalam magazine meant exclusively for Muslim women, was published in 1938 with a 17-year-old Haleema Beevi as its chief editor. Haleema Beevi spoke about starting the magazine in an interview:

My husband was the inspiration. He was a disciple of Vakkom Maulavi. He was also an Islamic scholar and Arabic teacher. He was running a magazine called *Ansari* then. He was also the editor of this magazine. Constantly referring to the backwardness of Muslim women and the possibility of a women's periodical to inform both the community and its women he instilled interest in me. Women's journals were very few in number then. That is how we started the magazine *Muslim Vanitha*. I was the Managing Editor. Later the name was changed to *Adhunika Vanitha*. It was more than fifty years back .... (Haleema Beevi 1995, 2)

Speaking about its rationale, she said:

Like the name signifies it stressed Muslim women's issues: the importance of their social and educational progress. We tried to free Islam of superstitions and ignorance and to expose the real countenance of religion. The magazine presented a perspective of women's progress and their status in Islam free of any distortions. Besides this, there used to be women's conferences conducted by the magazine every month. We used to have talks on women's issues .... I can recollect a huge meeting in Perumbavoor around that time. Nafeesath Beevi presided over the meeting. (ibid.)

An interesting feature of women's participation in the Muslim reform movement is the presence of political activists. Rather than literature, it was conferences and meetings that were treated as important media. Another important aspect was bringing women together and enlightening them about the necessity of education. Most of the dominant figures placed themselves in the arena of political activism. By the 1950s, the political climate of Kerala had also begun to polarise between the allies of the National Congress and the Left Democratic Front. Nafeesath Beevi was the first Muslim woman to become a lawyer, while Haleema Beevi was a municipal councillor and an ardent participant in the movement against the communist ministry organised by the Indian National Congress in Kerala, the *Vimochana Samaram*. Earlier, Begum T. C. Kunjachumma was elected to the women's committee of the All India Muslim League's 1938 Patna conference as a representative from Malabar. Kunjachumma was a Muslim woman who placed herself within the frame of religion and served as a mediator between the community and the world outside. She used the medium of *Kessu Paattu* (narrative songs) to situate Islam in the context of the nationalist movement. It is stated that through her songs, Kunjachumma marked Kerala's presence in the 1857 independence struggle. A relative of Kottayam Thangal had apparently shouted slogans against the British in public in Thalassery in September 1857, demanding that the British leave India immediately. This warrior was Mayan, who was imprisoned and later executed in jail by the British.[22] Kunjachumma familiarised the local public with many such great figures who are important in the history of Kerala, yet are never represented in mainstream history.

Haleema Beevi's speech at the inauguration of the Muslim women's conference in 1938 referred to the sisterhood within the Muslim community, and the beauty and strength of women's organising power. Speaking of the necessity of women's education, she urged educated women to join the labour force in government institutions in an attempt to foster self-respect. While claiming a part of the modern State, she never compromised on religion; all her arguments favouring education were placed within the context of Quranic verses that present knowledge and learning as imperatives (Devika 2005, 168–73).

Among the early publications of Muslim women is a translation of the Urdu story *Sultana's Dream* by Rokeya Sakhawat Hussain, in *Muslim Mithram* (1927). The well-known feminist utopia reverses Muslim gender roles, placing men in purdah and turning the *zenana* (the part of the house meant for the seclusion of women) into a *mardaana*.[23] This was quite a revolutionary act for the early twentieth century, and the Malayalam translation

---

[22] Kunjachumma's history was narrated in the fifty-eighth part of a serialised newspaper article in *Chandrika Daily* of 14 May 1970 (p. 18), titled 'Charithrathinte Thanka Thalukal', authored by 'K. P.' I located this in the personal collection of a veteran journalist in Calicut, K. P. Kunhi Moosa.

[23] *Mard* means man in Urdu and the term is coined to suggest the seclusion of men in a feminist utopia.

evoked controversy. It is to be noted that the renowned Western feminist utopia, *Herland* by Perkins, was written in 1915, but had to wait till the 1970s to be rediscovered during the feminist revival. The spirit of modernisation is reflected in the publication of this story.[24] The same issue of *Muslim Mithram* also carried an article on 'Muslim Women and Education'. The title page of the journal had an epigraph from A. Sainaba Beevi, Headmistress, that reads: 'To disseminate knowledge to the Muslim / *Muslim Mithram* has born! / Let it live in eternal glory / with the divine blessings of Almighty'. The reformist thought was thus welcoming of secular education, promoted the free movement of women, and tried to equip women to meet the challenges of the modern home. There was also resistance to patriarchal oppression as a spirit of feminism evolved from the reformist ideas. From this context, the community proceeded further to religion and piety. This turn was characteristic of the Muslim reform movement, and the salient feature of Muslim women's engagement with modernity. One reason could be the constant reference to an improper understanding of Islamic principles as the cause of the community's backwardness and its treatment of women. Thus, the secular context of modernisation leads to a better reading of the religion, as religious education, along with secular education, becomes a determining factor. Another reason could be the growing insecurity about the Muslim community's position as a religious minority in the political space of the nation after Partition in 1947. These shifts in the trajectory and motives of the reform ideals are obvious in discussions in the periodicals. After Independence, the community revised its position on women's education, which was made clear in the new perspectives cited by renowned figures like Haleema Beevi.

The decades following the 1930s saw a steady development towards a spiritual understanding of religion on the part of Muslim

---

[24] *Sultana's Dream* cannot be read as a critique of purdah, as Rokeya Sakhawat Hussain's opinion on purdah is quite divided. A complex relationship with modernity is evident in many Muslim women's writings of the time.

women, even in the changing political context. The October 1945 issue of *Mappila Review* carried an article by P. Beefathima, titled 'Muslim Sthreeyude Parathanthratha' ('Muslim Women's Slavery'). The author points to the necessity for a better understanding of the religion, as Islam and its women are often misrepresented and misinterpreted by people from other communities. She explains how Islamic rules have been wrongly followed in Kerala, because of which dowry and other oppressive practices have flourished, and highlights the real Islamic practice of *mahr* that enables women to collect an amount of money from her husband at the time of marriage (Beefathima 1945, 43–45).

In the special issue of *Al Manar* in September 1959, Haleema Beevi responded to the journal's revival in the context of the *Vimochana Samaram* in Kerala. Opening her article with an account of the difficulties and the imprisonment she faced while participating in this movement, she recollects the contribution of periodical literature in making her aware of the rights of Muslim women. She discusses a magazine in Malayalam called *Al Murshid*, which she read as a student:

> My association with *Al Murshid* had been vital in my life and career …. Reading *Al Murshid* for about a year made us realize that many of the conventions that we had been following were un-Islamic and meaningless. We could also see that the general misunderstanding in the community about women's education was due to a lack of proper religious education. *Al Murshid* also provided us with confidence … to confront our opponents through a proper grasping of the superior status that Islam extends to women and the right to education it offers illuminated by the Quran, the *hadiths* and history. (Haleema Beevi 1959a, 87)

She talks about starting *Muslim Vanitha* twenty years earlier, and the revolutionary changes that had occurred in the community since then. Interestingly, she compares Muslim women from different parts of Kerala: the women of Travancore were forward in terms of modern education, yet much inferior to the women of Malabar when it came to knowledge of religion. This propelled her to start *Muslim Vanitha* in Thiruvalla, a part of central Travancore, in order to familiarise them with the religion. There was a notable shift in perspectives on modernity in the later years, when she urged the authorities to seek women's readership for the magazine. The tone of these articles, reflecting a distinct identity of the Muslim woman in changing times, is remarkably different from that of the 'Welcome Speech' at the Muslim Women's Conference, published in *Muslim Vanitha* in 1938 and included in J. Devika's *Herself* (2005, 87-90).

In the November issue of 1959, Haleema Beevi wrote about the Cochin Women's Conference, which had Muslim women delivering religious speeches.[25] Highlighting the importance of Muslim women engaging with matters of faith, she discusses the significance of this conference. While women have made remarkable progress in political, literary, and other social avenues, religious contexts have been the prerogative of men, who often address gatherings comprising both men and women. For Haleema Beevi, the conference heralded the entry of Muslim women in the religious public sphere, who spoke eloquently on the Quran and the hadiths.

> There are plenty of post-graduate and graduate Muslim women in various subjects. But it is in this conference that I witness Muslim women with degrees in Islamic theology … I know many Muslim sisters who can talk in depth for hours on mundane topics and material sciences. Are women not eligible to gain knowledge in religion? Can't they conduct speeches on religion? Won't the history of great women as Islamic scholars repeat? Many others also would have shared thoughts of this kind. I think the Cochin Conference of *Nad'wath-ul-Mujahiddin* replies [to] these questions. (1959b, 197–99)

The shift in focus from secular to religious education is evident

---

[25] Religious speeches meant to bring about greater awareness amongst devotees are a regular feature in the Muslim community. Such a gathering, termed *Matha Prasangam*, is addressed by a renowned scholar and usually conducted by Jamaat committees.

here. The reformer realises the obviously different trajectory that the Muslim woman takes while accommodating modernity. Modernisation thus becomes a project within the religion, as much as it extends the community to the secular world outside. I collected about twenty articles by Muslim women on the spiritual aspects of education, where the demand was to understand religion, in magazines like *Ansari*, *Al Manar*, and *Mappila Review* between 1945 and 1965. There were also poems and stories with repeated appeals to understand religion, rather than merely rendering religious verses without understanding them. A poem in *Al Farooq* titled 'Are We Not Lucky', written by the students of Al Madrassathul Islaamiya, Chendamangallur (1952, 30), reflects upon the status of Muslim women. They identify different categories of Muslim women: one group follows the immoral Western civilisation, while another remains confined to murky kitchens, learning to read Arabic and the Quran without following a single line, considering this enough for a true Muslim. The poem concludes:

> Are we not members of the human species?
> Isn't here anyone to listen to our grievances?
> Are we dull wits to remain in ignorance forever?
> Are women machines meant for cooking and delivering babies?
> (1952, 30)

As I have discussed earlier, Islam's precarious position in relation to colonial modernity underlies all mainstream discourses on Islam. Muslim women's identity in the wider public space is marked by prejudiced notions on the veil, Islam's projection as being outside of civilised modernity, and so on. The discourses initiated by these women in the reform context and their conspicuous position as subjects need to be juxtaposed against stereotyped notions of Muslim women as oppressed by their own community. It is not surprising that Muslim reform movements are misinterpreted and misrepresented, given that in the reform movements in Kerala, non-secular dialogues have often been discursively appropriated within the secular framework of nationalism. Moreover, as in the national context, a political vocabulary denoting difference has developed, which marks Muslim women as being outside the project of 'secular modernisation'. The complex negotiations and mediations that Muslim women resort to call for a revision of the notion of feminist agency, and of the role of liberal thoughts and resistance in determining one's feminist inclinations. The reading of women's reform dialogues becomes problematic in the context of the shift from secular to religious; the binaries of tradition/modernity, veiling/unveiling, or religious/secular do not adequately describe the reform project among Muslim women. As Shamsul Alam says, diverting the focus of Muslim women's discourses to a tradition versus modernity binary overlooks the continuity of patriarchal relations within both traditional and modernist discourses (2006, 235–67). In the newly defined modern configurations of power, gender was re-articulated and re-defined along with other variables of caste, class, and religion. In their engagement with modernity, Muslim women attempted to accommodate the newly defined cultural space, re-defining and internalising modernity integrated with the spiritual strength of Islam, which is usually construed as the antithesis of modernity.

Many Muslim women wrote for journals like *Muslim Mithram*, *Muslim Vanitha*, and *Adhunika Vanitha*, which targeted Muslim women as their specific readers. It is interesting to note how Muslim women reinvented their relationship with tradition in the context of the reform movements. Their conscious negotiations with both religion and modernity reflect political agency and investment, which are otherwise omitted in the reform agenda. While none of the periodicals that presented their engagement with modernity were major or established—many of them circulated for only a short span of time—as a group they provided the space for articulating a community's aspirations, ideas of freedom, and concerns about the limits and boundaries of this freedom as part of their effort to fit into the modern nation. While none of the women who wrote in these journals (with the exception of Haleema Beevi or Thankamma Malik)[26] were major writers, as a group they represented the Muslim woman's voice and how she perceived modernity. The fact that they received little attention from mainstream critics or readers and have been forgotten in the literary or cultural history of Kerala, and even in feminist explorations, testify to the different trajectory taken by our notions of women's freedom, agency, and subjectivity.

At the moment of Independence, the reform trajectory segued into religion, resulting in pan-Islamic alliances. The failure of the State and secular political spaces to incorporate the moral and ethical reform the community had been propagating, along with the strategies of exclusion meant to create a homogenous nation, consolidated normative assumptions on ethics and politics. From that moment on, the secular intellectual embarked on a struggle with vocabularies and strategies in their dealings with the Muslims in Kerala. Entangled in a range of issues, gender in Islam presents an uncertain and ambiguous position for the State. The State and civil society are uncertain when it comes to Muslims. While parochial feminist assumptions project the Muslim encounter with modernity as strained, their obscure position is extended to the protected and privileged minority rights in the modern nation. The withdrawal of religion to the private domain and the imbalance in its actualisation continue to trouble homogenous models of modernity. For instance, the Shah Bano case and the response of the State to discussions related to Muslim personal law had wide repercussions on the political coalitions in Kerala. Left intellectuals mostly praised the Supreme Court verdict and went along with the demand for a Uniform Civil Code. However, such an approach was in keeping with the anti-Islam sentiments of the Right-wing Hindutva forces, and the victimised Muslim woman and the patriarchal and uncivilised Muslim male have been the

---

[26] I would also like to mention that some contributors to these periodicals were Muslim women who held powerful positions in the social system, as politicians, lecturers, teachers, government employees, and lawyers, although none were full-time writers.

dominant images of Muslims in the public sphere ever since. It would appear as though the political and social undercurrents in society would have nothing to do with Muslims, who are viewed as anachronisms in the midst of an intellectually mobilised population. While Muslim engagements with modernity have been problematically represented in the history of Kerala, the political mapping of Muslim women's participation in the reform movements remains unexplored in feminist histories as well.

3

Contemporary Dialogues on Muslim Women in Kerala

Since colonial times, women have been used to define a community's progressive nature. The Europeans use this argument to depict the West as the centre of enlightenment and human rights. Spivak's popular phrase, 'white men saving brown women from brown men', summarises the civilising mission from a gender perspective. The native male, adapting to colonial modernity, internalised these images and set out to reform their women. In Kerala, similar discussions on women's status began with the reform movements. As described in Chapter 2, the reform movements provided the intellectual context for Kerala's burgeoning cultural and political perspectives, which led towards a secular platform. But women were of little importance outside the early twentieth-century reform movements, due largely to the male reformers' efforts to restructure the domestic worlds of their women rather than allow them access to the public world. In the case of the Muslim community, the reform movement was itself an unfinished project, later separating into multiple reformist groups in the second half of the twentieth century. The women's question was never forgotten, and consequently, Muslim women themselves discussed the possibilities of political agency within these movements.

However, the changing geopolitical situation in the subcontinent led to increasing hostility towards Islam and Muslims, and

Muslim women were soon used to formulate a critique of the community. Politically, these critiques differ drastically, ranging from Right-wing hostility towards Islam and minorities to the modern intellectual's apathy. The Left-wing critique of Muslims highlighting Muslim women's backwardness, in synchrony with the Right-wing prioritisation of Muslim women's oppression within Islam, emerges as an effective tool against the community. Intellectual discourses and cultural productions such as literature and cinema depicted Muslim women as oppressed victims of a premodern community, which played into the larger geopolitical agenda of vilifying Muslim men and the community as a whole. This chapter focuses on the cultural representation of Muslim women in contemporary Kerala, and the political implications of debates that forge messy alliances between Right-wing, Left-wing, and feminist positions in discussions on Islamic patriarchy and Muslim women's oppression.

FEMINISM'S VARIED HISTORY IN KERALA

The history of feminism in Kerala highlights various strands and ideological lineages. The matrilineal traditions and practises of many Kerala communities in premodern times and their implications in the formation of social understandings of gender have been discussed in Chapter 1. However, while matriliny and its varied strands provided a strong, women-oriented inheritance, they could not break free of the pernicious influence of caste and class predominant in the precolonial social system. Colonial interventions in social practices and institutions such as marriage were aimed at creating colonial subjects in line with Victorian moral values. The impact of modern education on the deprived classes and their reorientation towards modernity have been studied from various angles. While examining feminist traditions in Kerala, therefore, one needs to address the role of women in anti-caste movements, and a productive feminist discourse ought to encompass Dalit, Muslim, Ezhava, and Christian minority women's agency in their respective political environments. In recent years, we have seen the emergence of strong narratives on the history of Nambutiri and Nair women. Feminist Literary History in Kerala has recorded the voices of writers from dominant classes and castes; from Saraswati Amma to Devaki Nilayangodu, the history of early feminism has been explored as part of mainstream feminist projects.

Since the 1990s, the emphasis has been on excavating the untold stories of mainstream feminist history in Kerala. An important work that needs acknowledgement here is Shamshad Hussain's *Nyoona Pakshathinum Lingapadavikkum Idayil* (*Between Gender and Minority*, 2009), which traces the feminist history of Muslim women in Kerala. Similarly, the strong, politically-oriented voices of Dalit and Adivasi women produced a critique of mainstream feminism in Kerala, foregrounding the voices of women who speak differently. They rejected both the upper-caste monopoly on women's voices in Kerala and the patronising from established feminists, whom they branded 'savarna feminists'. C. K. Janu's *Mother Forest* (2004), a poignant autobiographical account of Adivasi claims to forestland, and Nalini Jameela's powerful life narrative, *The Autobiography of a Sex Worker* (2005), churned the Kerala public sphere, revealing as they did traditions and strands of thoughts that were different from the liberal humanist or Left-liberal positions under which feminism had been patronised in Kerala thus far. While addressing the question of gender, these feminist works see community identity as a strong factor in determining one's social status. Rejecting the universalisation of the experiences of *savarna* women in India, their narratives highlight a different understanding of identity, which encompasses the men of their communities as subjects of caste discrimination, social ostracising, and political annihilation as well. However, the dominant Left intellectual history of Kerala has a tense relationship with identity-based assertions, primarily due to the universal enlightenment values the Left subscribes to. Locating the history of Muslim women and feminism within this complex socio-political environment is a daunting yet interesting task for a feminist historian.

THE LEFT POSITION ON MUSLIM WOMEN

Despite Islam being a heterogeneous set of beliefs and practices, discussions on Muslim women in Kerala have always been motivated by the assumptions and prejudices prevalent in Eurocentric liberal humanist discourses. Orientalist images of the Muslim woman as victim, suppressed by the rigid strictures of Islam and Islamic fundamentalism, rule these discussions. The shortcomings of secular-feminist dialogues that treat religion as an oppressive tool have never been dealt with. The secular perspective that envelops academic discussions in Kerala marks the Muslim woman as an anomaly in the nation's progress towards modernity and development. For them, Islam is oppressive, and its women are waiting to be liberated by the secular, modern intellectual/feminist. Religion (Islam) is not a viable tool for feminist agency, but a homogenised anvil of patriarchy. Representations of Muslim women merge with the Islamophobic discourses of neo-imperialism, with Muslim women as passive victims of their religion and culture. While religion is just one of the loci from which Muslim women derive their subjectivity, the universalised image of the oppressed Muslim woman flourishes in contemporary debates on Islam.

The Shah Bano case (1985) was the first instance of feminist intervention in the legal and political history of Muslim women in post-Independence India. *Mohd. Ahmed Khan v. Shah Bano Begum*, commonly referred to as the Shah Bano case, is a controversial maintenance lawsuit, where the Supreme Court of India delivered a verdict in favour of Shah Bano. As per the verdict, the divorced Muslim woman was eligible for a maintenance amount from her husband, as is a non-Muslim woman. However, pressure mounted by Muslim organisations against the verdict resulted in the Parliament, led by the ruling Congress Party, passing the Muslim Women (Protection of Rights on Divorce) Act, 1986, which reinstated the community's stand on alimony. This meant that the divorced woman's maintenance was restricted to a period of *iddah* (ninety days post the divorce). The law also entrusted the woman's care to her relatives and the waqf. In later judgments, including the Daniel Latifi (Shah Bano's lawyer) case, the Supreme Court of India upheld the validity of the Shah Bano case, thereby nullifying the Act.[1]

The Left and many feminist groups interpreted the Parliament's intervention as a failure of the modern legal system and of democratic rights. E. M. S. Namboodirippad, the general secretary of the Communist Party of India (Marxist) (CPI[M]), demanded in a huge rally in Thiruvananthapuram, the capital of Kerala, that the country be given a common civil code, and asked for the removal of the Sharia if it permitted a man to have several wives.[2] Sharia debates and the ensuing controversies created a permanent fissure between the prominent Left political party in Kerala and the Muslim organisations. However, in later years the demand for

---

[1] The Muslim Women (Protection of Rights on Divorce) Act, 1986 (MWPRDA, 1986) overruled the Supreme Court's decision in *Mohd. Ahmed Khan v. Shah Bano Begum*. The Act upheld that a Muslim husband was responsible for maintaining his divorced wife only for the *iddah* period, shifting her care to the waqf and her relatives after that. *Danial Latifi v. Union of India* challenged the constitutional validity of the Act on the grounds that the law was discriminatory and violated the right to equality guaranteed under Article 14 of the Indian Constitution. It stated that Muslim women are deprived of maintenance benefits provided to other women under Section 125 of the Criminal Procedure Code, 1973. It also argued that the law would leave divorced Muslim women destitute and thus violated the right to life guaranteed under Article 21 of the Indian Constitution. The Supreme Court while upholding the constitutionality of the Act, ruled that a Muslim husband is liable to make 'reasonable' and 'fair' provision for the future of his divorced wife, extending beyond the *iddah* period. The Court's interpretation was based on the word 'provision' in the Act of 1986, thus striking a balance between the constitutional validity of the Act and ensuring support for the divorced Muslim woman.

[2] See https://www.pgurus.com/demand-uniform-civil-code-gathering-momentum-thanks-educated-muslim-women/. This rally marked the beginning of debates on the Sharia in Kerala, with the Left taking a non-compromising position on the UCC. In subsequent contestations, the Indian Union Muslim League, an erstwhile CPI(M) ally, merged with its parent organisation, the Muslim League, leaving the Left camp.

a Uniform Civil Code was used by Hindutva groups to alienate the community from the rest of society. In the backdrop of the demolition of the Babri Masjid in Ayodhya, Uttar Pradesh, in December 1992, and the subsequent erosion of the community's political power, the demand for UCC became a political tool against the minority rights assured by the Constitution. This altered the position of many feminists and the CPI(M) regarding UCC: 'An Umbrella Legislation at this stage would therefore amount to building a skyscraper on the meagre plinth of a cottage,' stated Brinda Karat, General Secretary of All India Democratic Women's Association (AIDWA), a corollary of the CPI(M), in a *Frontline* article in 1995. While this discretion was maintained in national debates, the Communist Party and Left intellectuals never took an open position in relation to the Sharia or the UCC in Kerala. Since the Muslim League had always allied with the Congress Party in Kerala after the Shah Bano verdict, the question of minority rights became ambiguous in the public debates of the liberal Left or Left electoral politics. Therefore, the image of Shah Bano as the victim of rigid religious conservatism and Islamic polygamy created an archaic, anti-modern image for Islam in Kerala. Positing oneself as a secular Muslim and critiquing the community became the only possible, and at times easy, political position for a Muslim choosing to associate with the Left intellectual movements.

CRITICAL INSIDER? THE POSSIBILITY OF INTERNAL CRITIQUE

Who can speak for a community? This question has become a predominant concern in identity politics since the Black identity uprisings from the 1980s. Following this line of thought, the Dalit movement in India has also been debating the issue of who can be called an 'insider' for a long time. This question of identity has been addressed by nuanced approaches from various perspectives. Ranging from Spivak's celebrated question, 'Can the Subaltern Speak?', to the more recent theoretical examinations offered by Saba Mahmood (2008b), Talal Asad, et al. (2008), and others, the right to speak from within or against a community is a loaded issue, carrying the weight of both identity and political power. U. R. Ananthamurthy's idea of a critical insider in Hinduism, challenged vigorously by the Hindutva ideology, is one such position. Sharmila Rege (1998) offered the idea of 'standpoint' in the debate on who can speak on behalf of Dalit women. The idea of a critical insider is an intellectual category, with the agency and subjectivity to frame critique. Originating in enlightenment rationality, the idea of secular critique informs our idea of political agency. In this context, the idea of a critical insider provides a rationale for the secular Left to talk about communities and identities. The 'critical insiders'[3] who take up the role of reformers, criticising the community and mending it from the inside, especially in relation to Islam and women, narrow the focus to *purdah* and the associated oppression that differentiates the Muslim woman from her liberated Western counterparts. In demanding that religion fit into the category of a modern liberal entity, these critics of Islam highlight its incompatibility with modern life. However, this excessive focus on the modern is seldom extended to other religious practices in India.

The Project of Liberating Muslim Women in Kerala

Contemporary debates on women and Islam in Kerala have been generally motivated by an essentialist Left approach that treats women as a homogenous category in need of liberating, despite their heterogenous identities. Viewing Islam from the outside, critics in Kerala saw it as a space of conservatism that stands as an antithesis to modernity. The analytical strategy adopted by Hameed Chendamangallur (2002)[4] is a typical instance of such

---

[3] The term is often used in discussions on Islam in Kerala. The historian M. Gangadharan suggested that Islam in Kerala needed 'critical insiders' (2010: 5–9).

[4] Chendamangallur is a pro-Left intellectual in Kerala, quite active in discussions on 'Islam and its vices in destabilising the secular outlook of the state'. The book referred to here has been widely acclaimed by the Marxist historians of Kerala, including M. N. Vijayan, as a critical journey

a misreading. His book presents purdah as a polarisation of symbols, and connects the defeat of reformist values at the hands of religious fundamentalism in Kerala to Islam. Associating Islam with religious fundamentalism, he urges Muslims in India to identify with the rich heritage of this nation, instead of preaching exclusionary politics or separatism. The responsibility of merging with this heritage seems to lie with the Muslims alone. In an almost naive tone, he insists:

> The Christians of India should admit the legacy of non-Christian Indian tradition and heritage as part of the Christian tradition in India. Likewise, the Muslims of India should admit the legacy of non-Islamic Indian tradition and heritage as part of the Indo-Islamic tradition. Only then we may rise to the perspective of integrating the philosophers varying from Brihaspathi and Buddha to Swami Vivekananda and poets from Valmiki and Vyaasa to Tagore as part of the cultural heritage of entire India and its people. (ibid., 14)

He even demands the integration of Sufi mystics and mysticism within the cultural heritage of India. Splitting the Indian heritage into Hindu, Islamic, or Christian is unrealistic; since culture associates itself with geographies rather than religions, the proper way is to view our culture as Indian culture and our cultural heritage as the Indian cultural heritage (Chendamangallur 2002: 14–16). These arguments present Muslims and Christians as responsible for religious separatism. The responsibility of holding the nation and its heritage together is given to the minorities. Beyond this, there is a dangerous homogenisation of identities that he argues for. His argument is informed by the violent erasure of identities that the modern State seeks in order to maintain its 'secular' functions, and this is also the fundamental position taken on the discussion on purdah in his work. Informed by a superior notion of modernity over tradition and religion, these dialogues identify the modern State

______

that will shake the foundations of 'Islamic fundamentalism and religious conservatism'.

as liberating for the individual, as compared to the oppressive measures of religion.

While it is necessary to engage with the concerns raised by these critiques, the disproportionate reception of the critiques by the mainstream and the concerns raised by practising Muslims bring to light an unintended complex political association between Islamophobic neo-imperialists, Right-wing nationalists, and the secular Left. The heterogeneity of Muslim identity, which includes Islam as a political identity and unites practising and non-practising Muslims through the common thread of 'minority otherness', often escapes the attention of both the political Left and feminists. Problematic in these narratives that accept the critiques raised by non-practising/Islam-bashing/liberal Muslim intellectuals, who profess to speak in the voice of the universal human, is a complete erasure of their Muslim identity. This appears to qualify them to enter a world shorn of the identity concerns raised by Muslims in the contemporary world, and demands that they ignore the threats posed to a minority community by majoritarian fundamentalism as the primary concern, and focus on a critique of the religion from within. While the modern notion of individual rights does necessitate a reform of religious values and practices, the intense focus on such critiques leads to their acceptance into the realm of the 'larger' human rights discourse. Unfortunately, the human rights violations that Muslims themselves experience due to their minority identity, ranging from lynchings to alienation from secular platforms, do not receive the same attention as does the gender critique from within the religion. Thus, a non-practising Muslim woman easily gains entry into a debate on religious practices within Islam, and her opinions are accepted in the Left and liberal discourses. The liberal human at the centre of these arguments, whose rights are being debated and demanded, is reduced to a normative, essentialist, and universal identity. The anomaly in such positions becomes visible when practising individuals from within the religion are alienated from these discourses, rendering them partial and one-sided. The reception accorded to, and acceptance of, non-practising Muslim women by the media and academic forums during the Triple Talaq controversy, which sabotaged the discourse and camouflaged the voices of practising Muslim women, is a recent example.

This exceptionalism necessitates unravelling the social, political, and cultural imbalances that determine the politics of critiques. A universal West-centric notion of women's rights permeates the discussion on Muslim women. Arab feminists have pointed out that Islam practises a relational notion of self, a self that connects one with the community, both culturally and institutionally. However, the classical liberal bourgeoise notion of rights privileging certain forms of political thought undermine other perceptions of the self and embodiment. When such a worldview is extended to critique Islam, complex and diverse systems that have evolved over centuries into the current set of beliefs are overlooked for a simplistic understanding of the religion.

FEMINISM AND MUSLIM WOMEN IN KERALA

In a discussion on contemporary debates around women and Islam in Kerala, the public response to a controversy surrounding Rayana Khazi, a young student from Cherkalam in Kasargode, needs to be analysed. In 2010, she spoke to the media about threatening letters and phone calls that she had received, forcing her to adopt the practice of *purdah*. After Rayana's revelation, the media, and human rights and feminist activists rushed to her aid.[5] In the already volatile public sphere of Kerala, which was grappling with the attack on T. J. Joseph,[6] a college teacher, this

[5] NDTV reported the event; see Youtube under the title, 'She needs better protection from Kerala's Taliban'. See https://www.youtube.com/watch?v=dBWZJADZFpI.

[6] T. J. Joseph, a Malayalam lecturer in a college managed by the Roman Catholic community in Kerala, created a controversy through a mid-term question paper, which allegedly carried an explicit defamation of the Prophet. He was later attacked by a group of young men, who claimed to represent the Popular Front, a Muslim political organisation that is often termed as

was immediately attributed to Islamic fundamentalism. Rayana's issue provided an opportunity to discuss the 'Muslim woman' in public. She became the subject of debates and continued to claim her position within the religion, even though she refused to wear a veil. The discussions finally led to a demand for 'internal public spheres' within the religion to discuss and debate gender. Devika (2010) viewed the issue as an opportunity to counter internal patriarchies in the religion:

> In this particular juncture of the history of our society in which a large number of young Muslim women are gaining education, why is there so much fear, such reticence, about them entering the internal public sphere as full members of the community? I do feel that if these women do manage to break through the barriers—set up variously by Reformer-Men (the older ones, from Rayana's case, seem to deploy either veiled coercion, or resort to cajoling, and the younger men, to just the latter!)—it is they who will strengthen the community beyond all expectations.

This was Devika's response to Jenny Rowena and K. Ashraf's article, 'Rayana R. Khazi and the Spectre of Religious Fundamentalism in the Kerala Public Sphere', in *Kafila.org*. There was a call for an internal public sphere within the community to discuss the possibility of freedom within the religion. But what Devika suggests here is a rather simplified way of viewing the complex layers of a Muslim woman's political identity. Devika's response fails to connect the ethical life of a Muslim and the politics of a minority identity, as well as the tangential structures of power connecting the two. Also, while writing about Rayana, one cannot overlook the politics of Muslim representation in mainstream discourses in an attempt to underline the liberatory potential of feminism. What Devika suggests here—the possibility of the educated Muslim woman taking up the responsibility of speaking

---

extremist. This developed into active debates in the Malayali public sphere on Islamic fundamentalism, leading to all Muslim activists being branded as fundamentalists.

for the community—is not viable in Rayana's case. While Rayana was born a Muslim, the community's response to her faith and identity was not considered while entrusting her with the duty of reforming the community. Such 'feminist' interventions often widen the gap between Muslim everyday lives and 'progressive' narratives. Despite her claims to be a Muslim, community rhetoric stated that Rayana not be accepted as an 'insider' located in Islam without addressing the question of her faith as a Muslim subject, given that Islamic theology stresses Islam as a community belief rather than a personal one. The strong strand of individualism presented in Devika's reading does not take into account the severe impact Rayana's critique had on the vision of Islam as an oppressive domain. Neither does it address the complex Islamophobia underlying public discussions on this issue. On the other hand, the vibrant debates within the community initiated by practising Muslim women never receive such public attention.

The 'internal public sphere' that Devika refers to is a space of contested subjectivities, and one has to tread cautiously when politicising it. This sphere also redesigns its priorities vis-à-vis the larger public sphere outside the community, where brotherhood/ sisterhood or community identity and solidarity are constantly invoked to counter the mainstream alienation. The article also overlooks the intense engagement that young Muslim men and women have with their piety and politics, as practising Muslims, yet as subjects with complete agency. In fact, the Muslim community of Kerala is one of the most vibrant public spaces that boasts of an enriching political and academic engagement, especially because of its young members.

Anouar Majid (2006) asserts the impossibility of thinking of feminism in singular terms. He challenges the Western acceptance of the individual as central to all discourses:

> If the crisis of the individual is one of identity, the solution does not lie in accepting a bourgeois definition of the human, but in examining the historical and cultural background of the prevailing

(western) capitalist equation of the individual with an 'autonomous, contract making self', where the 'self' is conceived as property. (ibid., 78)

Even when we do not accept the West and the East as mutually exclusive rigid categories, the difference between notions of the self in these two discourses need to be emphasised. Reading Rayana as the subject of a productive debate within the community thus issues from a homogenised vision of the self and the concept of freedom itself.[7] Thus, discourses around the Rayana Khazi incident categorically seek to carve an identity that the secular, liberal society would want for the Muslim woman. Also, as the object of these discourses, the Muslim woman's political agency has been determined by the liberal platforms of a monolithic feminism.

Over the years, Muslim women have viewed the question of patriarchy within religion in multiple ways. They have developed complex strategies of discussing, debating, and representing their identities. I do not wish to read Rayana's, or any Muslim woman's, fight within the religion as pointless. Rather, I would say that the feminist impatience to intervene and find advocates for women's rights within the religion springs from their convictions, which in turn issues from their privileged location in the mainstream. Any intervention in a community identity based on practices and embodiments of faith requires ethical self-interrogation and a revision of one's own political location and convictions. This excessive stress on the citizenship rights of the universal human, and the centrality of the 'othering' of Muslim men in

---

[7] Devika's reading of the Hadiya case in 2017, and her assessment of Hadiya's conversion and marriage, likewise adhere to a strong strand of individualism. Beyond the questions of choice, love, and marriage, Hadiya's agency, as she clearly expressed it, was determined by her faith; however, this finds no expression in Devika's analysis of the situation. Her article in *The Caravan,* 'The Hadiya Case Represents the Crossroads Between a Sociological Trend of Muslim Alienation and Self-Assertion by Kerala's Youth', touches upon the Islamophobia involved in restricting a young girl from converting to Islam or marrying the person she loved.

Image 3.1: Muslim Women Protest the Violation of Hadiya's Rights

Source: Lukmanul Hakeem.

these narratives as the oppressor draws on a larger Islamophobic discourse upheld by the mainstream. This was the case in the recent Triple Talaq and UCC discourses as well. The same rights discourses, however, fail to evoke a similar public impact in cases of violence against the Muslim community.

FEMINIST THEOLOGY AND ISLAMIC FEMINISM

One school of feminist theologians demanded a revision of the 'patriarchal' framework of Islam. There have been attempts to read the Quran from the woman's perspective (Wadud 1999), as well as to attribute patriarchy in Islam to the *Hadith*s, the interpretations of the Quran (Mernissi 2002). A reading of the theoretical framework of this school of thought helps to delineate the problematic paradigms subscribed to in the reading of Muslim women.

Image 3.2: Muslim Women Speaking for Themselves

Source: Lukmanul Hakeem.

The Muslim woman emerged as a subject of interest in feminist readings only in the late 1990s. Most feminist anthologies presented before that had never had a separate cultural category for Muslim women. Feminists from the Islamic world marked their entry into the academic arena with discussions on identities and anti-imperialist perspectives, resisting the Eurocentric version of academic feminism. As early as the 1970s, Islamic feminists had begun analysing the plight of Muslim women. This school of Muslim feminism, which ranged from Mernissi to Wadud, has studied Islam from a woman's perspective, and has been critiqued widely for attempting to present an ahistorical version of Islam that has remained unchanged from the time of the Prophet. In their reading of the Quran, they invariably frame Islam as the fundamental category for analysing the lives of Muslim women all over the world. The historical and contextual diversities that shape Muslim women's lives find no place in their analyses.[8] In resorting to this method of analysis, these theologians fail to

---

[8] Khadija Mumtas undertakes an ahistorical interrogation of Islam that I intend to highlight in my analysis of *Barsa*.

conceptualise the possible relationships between Muslim women and other factors in society, such as kinship, or political and economic systems.[9] Moreover, they emphasise a reinterpretation of the scriptures so that religious texts can be made conducive to addressing women's rights. Reasserting this tradition through a feminist reading is problematic, however, as they end up validating a fixed religious category.

Image 3.3: Embodied Faith: Resistance and Agency

Source: Lukmanul Hakeem.

[9] Leila Ahmed's reading of Muslim women stands as an exception. Her work reads Muslim women as a lived reality, rather than as a theoretical abstraction (see Ahmed 1992).

Aysha Hidayatullah's book, *Feminist Edges of the Quran* (2014), discusses the diverse and complex possibilities of the Quranic exegesis. Her comprehensive analysis of contemporary feminist Quranic interpretations explores the dynamic challenges they offer to Islamic tradition, and the way they shape contemporary Muslim views of the Quran. While acknowledging that feminist readings of the Quran played a vital part in developing the nascent field of Quranic *tafsir* (exegesis), she argues that feminist exegetical practices make claims that are not fully supported by the text. She acknowledges the feminist appeal to values of justice and equality, but demands a revision of these positions. She also identifies their work in the modernist movement in Quranic exegesis, where modern values of gender equality and justice are read into the Quran without considering how this practice could be anachronistic. She explains that it is not a feminist's responsibility to justify Quranic verses that could be patriarchal or misogynist—as is often the case with other religious texts as well. So the primary point of reference in feminist exegesis—the modern compatibility of the Quran—needs to be reframed carefully.

Fathima Mernissi and Amina Wadud

This section responds to the feminist readings of the Quran and *Hadiths* by two feminist theologians who were key to exposing the patriarchal misreading of Islam.

Mernissi defines her work, *Women and Islam: An Historical and Theological Inquiry* (1993b), thus:

> This book is not a work of history. History is always the group's language; the official narrative that is pressed between covers of gold and trotted out for ritualistic ceremonies of self-praising. This book is intended to be a narrative of recollection, gliding toward the areas where memory breaks down, dates get mixed up, and events softly blur together, as in the dreams from which we draw our strength. (ibid., 10–11)

In subsequent passages, she speaks of her book as a vessel journeying back in time, seeking a fabulous wind that would swell its sails and send it gliding towards the beginning of Hijra, when the Prophet was a leader opposed to all hierarchies, when women had their place as unquestioned partners in a revolution, where the mosque was an open place and the household a temple of debate. She draws a clear distinction between the authoritative, official history and what she intends to do. She reads between the lines and uncovers the areas blurred by a patriarchal narrative, shedding light on a hitherto distorted truth. Through a study of the women of the Prophet's time and their involvement with his life and preaching, Mernissi shows up how men in positions of power have manipulated reality over time. Starting with the Prophet's army chief Umar, this authority extended to all patriarchal souls intolerant of the great reform the Prophet was bringing about in Arabian society in terms of gender equality.

The problem with such a reading lies in the fact that Mernissi was using the Quran and early Islamic history as the analytical base for explaining women's lives throughout the Islamic world. The same position is adopted by strict 'patriarchal fundamentalists', who also look to the Quran and Hadiths to assert a male hierarchy. The crucial variations visible in women's condition within and across Muslim societies are not accounted for in this reading. Although Mernissi focused on case studies from the Moroccan society she was familiar with, her theoretical argument depended on generalisations across different Muslim societies. Belief becomes the factor that connects the Quran to the Muslim social organisation (DeLamotte, et al. 1997, 80). While these feminists suggest a progressive way of reading the Quran and Islamic history to analyse the lives of women across the Muslim world, new ways of conceptualising the relationship between religion and women need to evolve. When, in many Islamic countries, feminist critiques go hand-in-hand with the ongoing process of 'Westernisation' and debates on the marginalisation and oppression of Muslim women, they end up asserting Western notions of progress and the 'uncivilised' nature of non-Western people.

Wadud (1999), in her progressive reading of the Quran from a feminist perspective, also views the lives of Muslim women as dictated by religion alone. Stating that her work is not 'on the general topic of "Islam and Women"', nor a book 'about Muslim women', Wadud says in her Preface to the second edition:

These books abound on the market. These books are also limited to providing information for general readers about the particular case studies on which they are based. Although various cases are drawn: from history, cultures, nation-states, classes, literature, education, politics, and the like, all of them can benefit from the lens given through reading this book. Quran and Woman contributes a gender inclusive reading to one of those most fundamental disciplines in Islamic thought: tafsir, or Quranic exegesis. (ibid., xv)

The extent to which these perspectives counter the Western imperialist attack on Islamic tradition for denying its women agency is debatable. This is made even more problematic by their definition of feminism, which is exclusively along modern, liberal lines. Even as this reading of the Quranic exegesis makes sense, it indicates a paradigm of modernity that controls all discourses on liberation or claims to political agency. Also, here, the question of gender in Islam is limited to a discourse on the Quran; and Wadud makes no claims of including Muslim women in her discourse beyond this.

Although we see a continuum in the discourses on women's rights in Islam and on Muslim women in colonial discourses on oriental societies, the binary of Muslim women versus religion has been put forth as a symbolic marker of emancipation since the Iranian Revolution of 1978–79. I refer to the Iranian Revolution as a historical moment that marked a feminist nationalism, whose triumph and complexities continue to influence discourses on Islamic feminism.

The controversial veil (*chador*), a full-length garment worn by many women in the early demonstrations, did not necessarily mean female submission. Iranian women reported that the veil was worn as a symbol of mourning and of resistance to the Shah. Many women wore veils for the first time during the revolution, vowing not to remove them until the Shah was gone. The veils also come in handy for concealing weapons and leaflets! (Hill 1979)

Women were active participants in this movement to dethrone Shah Reza Pahlavi II, who was considered a representative of US imperialism. Feminists, the Left, and religion came together for the first time to form an unusual confluence in the history of revolutions. In reports, this was recorded as a broad revolutionary coalition of political groups comprising Leftists, nationalists, Islamists, and social forces, including women and men of the middle class, working classes, intellectuals, etc.

Michel Foucault's celebration of the Iranian Revolution is a much debated topic, as the dethroning of the Shah also led to a widespread suppression of women's rights in the later phase (Afary and Anderson 2005). For much of the revolution, French intellectuals had been in solidarity with the Islamic cause. But by March 1979, when a series of rules was created to curtail women's rights in the family as well as in public life, protests against this began to garner public attention. Perhaps it was this moment that led to the diverging of the paths of religion and the discourses on rights.

In India, it was B. R. Ambedkar and Muhammad Ali Jinnah who brought religion into the critical discourses against the embedded upper-caste Hindu religiosity of Gandhian nationalism. In our country, it is impossible to think about the nation outside of religion, and therefore liberatory politics cannot be imagined without including religion either. Gender is not constructed as a secular formation in India, as Muslim, Hindu or Dalit are categories that dictate what it means to be a man or a woman. This is the complex terrain of women's rights in India, and a key point to consider while addressing the question of gender. Theology, modernity, and gender are thus problematically interwoven in the Indian context.

Barsa: A Feminist Reading of Islam, Muslims, and Women in Kerala?

Barsa, a novel published in 2007 by Khadija Mumtas, puts forth 'haunting and agonizing' (see Wikipedia, https://en.wikipedia.org/wiki/Barsa) questions through its protagonist Sabitha, a doctor from Kerala working in Saudi Arabia, who also happens to be a convert to Islam. The novel led to immense fame for its author, as well as a significant position among the Left intellectual groups in the state. Mumtas, a doctor by profession, has other notable works to her credit: *Athmatheerthangalil Munginivarnnu, Doctor Daivamalla, Purushanariyatha Sthreemukhangal, Athuram*, etc. She is presently the Vice-Chairman of the Kerala Sahitya Akademi and an Academic Council member, Thunchathezhuthachan Malayalam University, Tirur. Mumtas began her literary career with *Athmatheerthangalil Munginivarnnu*, which was first serialised in *Chandrika* weekly and later published as a novel by Current Books in 2004. She shot to fame with *Barsa*, which was a great critical and popular success. Critics declared that the book denoted a milestone in Malayalam literature, and claimed that it presented a 'realistic' narrative of the restrictions that bind the lives of Muslim women.

While as a fictional enterprise it cannot claim any substantial aesthetic merit over many other works of Malayalam fiction, the novel received several accolades, including the renowned Sahitya Akademi Award (2010). The title, *Barsa*, a term used by Fatima Mernissi in *Women and Islam* (1993b), refers to a woman who has removed her veil. In my reading of *Barsa*, I intend to present the problematic construction of the Muslim woman as an ahistorical category, a victim of an unchanged, timeless religion. My concern also extends to the construction of Islam as anti-modern in the novel, and I shall disclose how the novel projects the popular stereotypes of Islam usually upheld in Islamophobic imperialist contexts. *Barsa* is mostly written in the form of Sabitha's interior monologues. As the novel progresses, we learn that Sabitha had converted to Islam after her marriage to a Muslim doctor. The chapters focus on Sabitha's contemplations on the rigidity of Islam, as experienced through the trivial, everyday events at her workplace.

The author contextualises *Barsa* right at the beginning through an introduction that links her writing to a long tradition of thought that she terms as belonging to the 'Islamic feminists'.[10] The names she lists include Fatima Mernissi, Asma Barlas, and Asra Nomani. Many later feminist interpreters from the Muslim world have accused Asma Barlas and Fatima Mernissi of having followed a modern methodology to analyse women in Islam.

Through the eyes of her narrator, Sabitha, Mumtas views Islam in a similar manner. Sabitha had been born into a Hindu family and had converted to Islam after her marriage (rather, it was her conversion that made the marriage possible). She travelled to Saudi Arabia with Rashid, her doctor husband. The entire narrative focuses on Sabitha's critique of Islam as witnessed in Saudi Arabia, specifically her responses to her experiences at the hospital. Marriage and conversion have been presented through a romantic visual, reflecting the idealised vision of a society that allows religious syncretism. In the context of allegations that the Muslim community uses marriage as a tool for conversion, the portrayal of marriage and Sabitha's subsequent conversion in this work is a little untoward. However, it also states clearly that it was Sabitha who had to convert; open to the marriage, her family accepted this proposal. Sabitha's childhood associations with the religion made it easy for her to fit into the community. By situating marriage and conversion within contemporary debates, the author appears to undercut the previous romantic notion of conversion.

In fact, in recent times, an accusation labelled 'love-*jihad*',[11]

---

[10] I have reservations about the use of this term to describe Muslim women's political agency, as it carries a referent of an 'always the same Islam' and Muslims.

[11] In September 2009, Justice K. T. Sankaran rejected the anticipatory bail plea of two Muslim men and ordered the Director-General of Police to conduct a probe into 'love-*jihad*'. In the same month, a court in Bangalore ordered a similar probe during the hearing of a *habeas corpus* petition. The woman in question was an adult, but the court ordered her to stay with

which stems from Right-wing ideology, has emerged, which claims that Muslim men use love and marriage as convenient tools to lure Hindu women towards Islam. In this context, Sabitha's conversion cannot be viewed as an innocent act. The romantic representation of Sabitha and Rashid's relationship takes place within a *faux* secular framework that ignores contemporary realities. Instead, this relationship is given an idealised form that harks back to the 'cultural renaissance'. On the other end, this ideal also caters to the Sangh Parivar's allegation of forced conversions to Islam by hinting that Sabitha's conversion was the only possible way to actualise their love.

Universal Feminist Agency in *Barsa*

Sabitha in *Barsa* views herself as a Muslim through the lens of the Quran and Islamic history, with constant parallels drawn between her life and those of women in Islam's history. Sabitha's identity sometimes merges with Hajira Beevi, the mother of Ismail, or Aysha, the Prophet's young wife. There are stream-of-consciousness episodes where the narrator meanders through the minds of women in Islamic history. Parallel incidents are strategically placed to support this juxtaposition of identities. The opening chapter presents the ritual of *Hajj*, the last of the five diktats that a Muslim should observe. Sabitha's participation in the ritual is reflexive; her narrative challenges both its spirituality and essence. Here, she invokes Hajira, whose life had been determined by men, including an extremely masculine 'God'. Her rebellious words seem to give her agency. Hajira says:

---

her parents until it had been made clear that she had indeed married for love. The controversy had a huge impact on the public perception of inter-religious marriages involving young Muslim men in Kerala. There emerged an immediate coalition between the Hindu and Christian upper classes in Kerala against this phenomenon labelled 'love-*jihad*'. The Catholic Church circulated 'guidelines' to its subjects to protect their women from the seduction of Muslim men (*Kerala Kaumudi Daily*, 5–8 October 2009).

> Have you not celebrated *Id'ulAzha*, the great day commemorating the sacrifice of Ibrahim? Have you not also listened to the story of the great father who obliged to God's order to sacrifice his only son? …. the only son whom he had abandoned, and had been brought up by his poor mother contesting the heat and storm of the desert? That is masculinity! The greatness of unflinching piety, stubbornness, that sets out to materialize God's orders even at the expense of blood ties. We, the women are just inferior. The one who searches for water for her son even while encountering death …. (Mumtas 2008, 19)

This rebellious tone continues, reducing the complexities of religious observance to a monolithic reading of the patriarchal values embedded in Islamic practices. The narrator challenges the authors of the Hadiths, arguing that what they attributed to the Prophet were misinterpretations:

> I looked into heaven. It was full of virtuous men. I looked into the hell. It was filled with women. (They disobeyed their men!) You should obey! Cover the beauty of your hair. Stretch your *hijab* to your face and to the breasts too. Never remove the black apparel. At night please your men like prostitutes. Live in harmony with his other wives and slave women …. Then you can enter heaven along with them. No, not with them! They get young and delicate women—as delicate as they have been maintained inside the shell of an egg—as their partners. (ibid.)

At one point, Hajira's concerns are juxtaposed with Sabitha's and her anxieties about gender injustice in Islam. Sabitha seems an inappropriate subject to raise these questions as her subjectivity has in no way been determined by the domineering masculinity of Islam. She might work in Saudi Arabia—as do countless others from Kerala—but Islamic history is not the sole determinant of her destiny as an individual. She had only come to Saudi Arabia in search of material prospects, and then found herself restricted by the norms of a foreign land. It is not clear why Sabitha is presented as the conduit through which to examine the issue of patriarchy in Islam. Essentialising her identity through a universal Islam negates her own historical and socio-political realities. Further, the author fails in building the character of Sabitha as someone invested and educated in the religion, leading the reader to question the premise of Sabitha's concerns. In the discipline of Gender Studies, new avenues are opened up that relate forces of domination to specific cultural contexts and challenge the view of resistance as the only viable form of political agency. However, from this perspective Mumtas' *Barsa* reflects an uninformed and illogical representation of feminist agency. Every feminist story is entangled within multiple aspects of life: while faith plays a role, it is not the only defining factor.

Yet another universalised vision of feminist agency is offered through the description of Sukayna. In a passing reference to the murder of Hassan, the Prophet's grandson, along with his family at Karbala in Iraq, Sabitha refers to Sukayna, the daughter of Hassan. She is the only one left alive in the family. Her multiple marriages are presented as a challenge to male chauvinism; she had demanded monogamy from her partners, who were smitten by her beauty and scholarship. Those violating the contract were even made to face the law. Sukayna is presented as a free spirit who engaged in legal debates, ridiculing the men whom she brought before the court. A favourite among feminist historians, she is compared with Thathrikkutty[12] as an example of rebellion against 'male hypocrisy'. Praises are showered on her for being '*Barza*', the woman who refuses to cover her face. As the one who refuses to accept defeat, the one who surprises and motivates women, the symbol of feminist aspiration, Sukayna is highlighted as a model for Muslim women (Mumtas 2008, 86). This description of Sukayna as the sole agent of Muslim women's feminist aspirations is both ahistorical and highly problematic, as it reads Muslim womanhood as an essentialised identity that remains constant over time and space. Sukayna is, in fact, a recurring image in all feminist narratives on Islam. Mernissi (1993b) devoted three pages to Sukayna's attributes, a description that resonates with *Barsa*:

> ... a barza woman is one who does not hide her face and does not lower her head. And the dictionary adds that a barza woman is one who 'is

---

[12] The rebellious Nambutiri woman in the history of Kerala.

seen by people and who receives visitors at home'—men, obviously. A barza woman is also a woman who has 'sound judgement'. A barza man or woman is someone 'known for their *aql* (reasoning)'. Who are they, these Muslim women who have resisted the *hijab*? The most famous was Sukayna, one of the great-grand daughters of the Prophet through his daughter Fatima, the wife of Ali .... (Mernissi 1993b: 191–92)

Anyone reading this passage cannot but notice the similarities between the two descriptions. There are other instances where *Barsa* appears an almost literal translation of some of these texts. Let us look into the arguments that evolve in this context. First, while Mernissi locates her text within Islamic history and offers a reading of Islam from a woman's point of view, *Barsa* locates itself among the twentieth (or even the twenty-first) century Muslim woman, and seeks to establish that the reality that Sukayna had confronted in the initial years of Islam continues to exist. But neither Sabitha nor any other woman in Islam possesses Sukayna's courage. This vision of the woman as an abstract entity, de-contextualised and representing Muslim women all over the world, proves inadequate under present circumstances. While Mernissi presented Sukayna as a model for the liberated woman first in 1984 at a conference, where she claims to have been vehemently attacked, and then subsequently in *Women and Islam* (1993b, 191–93), it was important for her to counter the Western notion of Muslim women as victims. Mernissi (1993a) has spoken about Muslim women who have defied the odds and risen to political power, thereby showing that the erosion of women's rights enforced by a male-constructed legal framework could not silence or immobilise women entirely (Majid 2006, 67). Even when one objects to the interpretation of rights and staunch individualism in Mernissi's perception of women in Islam, the historical context and her investment in the study of Muslim women's predicament, thereby inaugurating the feminist *tafsir* (a progressive interpretation of Quran), make her an inspiring presence in the field of Islamic feminism.

But *Barsa*, written some twenty years later in the context of a Western feminist discourse that freezes Muslim women in time, space, and history, is an anachronism. While Muslim feminists like Nawal El Saadawi and Fatima Mernissi had challenged the grand narratives of Islamic patriarchy, the contrapuntal critique had been necessary to mark their entry into new avenues of feminism. However, in a context where women from marginalised worlds revise their strategies to counter the essential notions of freedom, liberty, and equality that Western feminism upholds and asserts, entering the feminist public sphere not in terms of negations within structures of domination but through constant negotiations, *Barsa*'s representation of the Muslim woman as a category affected only by gender hierarchy is flawed and prejudiced.

ISLAMOPHOBIA: IS *BARSA* A PREJUDICED FEMINIST READING AGAINST ISLAM?

It would not be incorrect to state that *Barsa* reinforces contemporary prejudices against Islam. The campaign against Islamic nations in the West is always steered by discussions on Muslim women as victims of their community. By portraying the Muslim woman as a subject of the religion, suppressed by its male-oriented norms, Western feminists assert a cultural supremacy over other women.

The category of 'Third World' in Western feminist discourses can become problematic, as we can see in the 'save Afghan women' campaign. 'East' and 'West', or 'First World' and 'Third World' are not rigid, mutually exclusive categories. The interconnected networks of power that run through these categories do not go unnoticed. At one point, the reader might even be confused as to who the 'Muslim woman' represented in *Barsa* really is. If Sabitha is the symbol of the Muslim woman, this construction is anomalous, as she does not fit into the context of her narration. She is a convert who is not native to Saudi Arabia, and her identity is not reflected in any of the historical female figures discussed. The Muslim woman who is denied control over her own life is at the centre of Sabitha's discourse. While she reflects sympathetically on the plight of victim women, the reality of the narrative undercuts her own argument.

Many of the Muslim women presented in the novel are in control of their own lives, making choices and proving that the veil need not be an obstruction to their aspirations. Doctor Shamsad, a native of Saudi Arabia, who chooses her sexuality, relationships, and life, is one such woman. However, Sabitha does not approve of her, describing her as a wanton woman, forever engaged in banter with other doctors and seeking men across nationalities. Adopting a condescending, moral tone, Sabitha says that Shamsad had not ensnared any men yet, and speculates that the men were perhaps put off by the legal formalities attendant upon marrying a Saudi Arabian woman, the possible friction between cultures, or the pride that is so much a part of Saudi women. Saudi Arabian natives receive four times the salary that foreign employees get, so a relationship with Shamsad carries the temptation of immense wealth. Although not an exceptional beauty, Shamsad is pleasant (Mumtas 2008, 118).

This description reflects the narrator's 'high moral bearing'. Sabitha is torn between two contradictory beliefs: her prejudiced view of women in Islam and the real women she encounters in the hospital. These women do not conform to her image of Muslim women as victims, and her disappointment is reflected in her moral judgements. It is noteworthy that it is Sabitha, the supposedly liberated woman who claims a secular lineage and professes emancipation, who labels Shamsad as a woman of wanton desires. She is the one who sits in moral judgement over men and women in the novel. She is shocked to learn that Shamsad watches Hindi movies, and by the fact that she leaves her face uncovered. While the novel's dominant narrative discusses and celebrates Sabitha as *barza*, the woman whose mind and face are open, the author's prejudices and moral apprehensions form a sub-text that proves that Sabitha is neither *barza* nor approves of it.

Sabitha's vulnerability, the high moral ground she appropriates for herself, and her inability to be accommodating and open are evident in the way she judges many of the characters. She is bothered by the extra attention paid to her by Iqbal, the senior doctor, and prays to God to get him married at the earliest. Her own conscience finds herself guilty. In one instance after another, it is made clear that Sabitha, the woman chosen to reflect the free spirit of Muslim women, is the one most controlled by moral inhibitions. Her critique of Islam emerges from her own frustrations.

Subscribing to popular misconceptions about Muslim men, Sabitha refers often to the Muslim male's sexual virility. Further, some of the interpretations suggest an inadequate historical understanding of the Islamic past, which is clear from the representation of the Prophet's multiple marriages. His wives, mostly beautiful and wise, are thus viewed as mere objects, ruled by jealousy and insecurity whenever a new wife enters the family. Finally, the novelist even suggests that the restrictions on Muslim women might have evolved from the insecure psyche of the 'ageing Prophet' (Mumtas 2008, 118), who worried about his beautiful wives. Aysha's disappearance for a few hours with a young soldier when returning from the war had triggered rumours. These allegations are repeated in a conscious effort to distort the story. When the reference, 'Muhammad is old. Consider his nine beautiful wives! How young Aysha is! How can he satisfy them any way' (ibid., 114), is placed in the midst of a discourse on Islam and gender, religion is twisted to suit a problematic gender discourse. Following this, the narrator directly relates the assumed flaws in the Prophet and his wives to gender in Islam, which is structured by an ageing Prophet, disturbed by the challenges to his masculinity:

One day at the peak of the Prophet's silence and uneasiness[13] Allah began to speak through the Prophet's tongue on the admonition for defaming the Prophet's wives, with a warning not to look at them as sexual objects. He granted them permission to leave the marriage if at all they had wanted and cautioned on the impossibility of

---

[13] As a result of the rumours against his wives and the sexual insecurity accompanying his ageing.

relationships with men even after his death if they decided to remain as his wives. (ibid.)

Sabitha's reduction of Islamic principles to personal issues between the Prophet and his wives trivialises the spiritual context of Islam, and marks the political space of the narrative as disruptive and vicious. My interest lies not in a theological defence of the narrator's arguments, but rather, in highlighting the disruptive strategy undertaken in *Barsa*, which resonates with contemporary dialogues against Islam.

Double standards in sexual freedom are what intrigues Sabitha the most. She is disturbed by the controls placed on female sexuality while men are allowed multiple sexual partners. Sabitha's life is in no way affected by polygamy, which is extremely rare among the middle-class, educated Muslims of Kerala. Given this, her intense response to polygamy and much of her concerns are at a distance from her lived reality. Therefore, such references appear to arise solely from a necessity to adhere to the popular imagination of Islam.

Muslim men are portrayed as lustful, with an uncontrolled sexual appetite. There is an incident of female circumcision in *Barsa*, which Islam is blamed for. A Sudanese doctor requests his friend to circumcise his wife, whose 'civilised parents' had saved their daughter from this 'primitive' custom during her childhood. The narrator underlines the incident through a reductionist statement on the plight of women, whose bodies serve as mere tools for men. Female circumcision is attributed to the sexual drive of the Muslim man and his warped belief that female genital mutilation leads to greater sexual pleasure for him. Even educated Sudanese men succumb to this belief.[14] Sabitha's omniscient eye approximates a panopticon, scrutinising the 'other'. At the end of every observation she adds her 'evaluation', which is invariably prejudiced against Arab culture. At times, the reader cannot but

---

[14] Many decolonial feminists have labelled efforts to use female circumcision to tarnish Muslims and the Third World as unfair. In reality, this custom is often a region/clan-specific practice (Mohanty 2006).

see that her knowledge seems to precede her experience, and she searches for instances to justify her prejudices. As an outsider in Saudi Arabia in search of better prospects and wealth, Sabitha should be a powerless and passive expatriate bound by the legal and political authority of a foreign country. But she escapes this passivity by unleashing a critique of the religion that shapes the legal and political basis of State operations, including the health system into which Sabitha enters. Therefore, as a narrator Sabitha is definitely unreliable: her narrative is in constant danger of effacement, in line with the precarious subjectivity of the Muslim woman.

India vs. Saudi Arabia: *Barsa's* Internalised Hierarchies and Uneven Comparisons

Multiple instances highlighting her apprehensions, jealousy, and insecurity are placed as contrapuntal to Sabitha's status as the powerful subject providing a 'sensible critique'. Inevitable comparisons between women in Saudi Arabia and in India creep into the narrative. Sabitha's comparison of the maternity rooms in Kozhikode Medical College (Kerala), where she completed her medical degree, with the hospital in Saudi Arabia is interesting; Sabitha speaks of the severe scrutiny that doctors and employees in the hospital come under from patients' relatives, who report any perceived misbehaviour to the *Mudir* (Director). In her hometown, a maternity ward in Kozhikode Medical College is often marked by two or more helpless, screaming women in the same bed, spattered by a concoction of amniotic fluid and faeces, with their wet clothes dishevelled. She compares this situation with the proud and confident women in Saudi Arabia, wrapped in tidy white clothes, loudly demanding a solution to their intense pain, ordering, '*Th'aaliyadhakthura, th'aali sister, shoofiana*' ('Doctor, come here, Sister, you too examine me'). She further states that Saudi Arabian and Mazarin women are the loudest; Indian, Pakistani, Bangladeshi, and Burmese women do not fuss, perhaps due to their genes, or the consciousness of their inferior status as wives of low-paid employees (Mumtas 2008, 102).

Here, the narrator appears disappointed to find that women in Saudi Arabia are conscious of their rights in hospitals, in contrast to her hometown, run by a secular State. While as a nation Saudi Arabia follows Islamic law, it also maintains the welfare machineries of a modern State. Health is one system that brings the power of the State home to its subjects. The terrible description of patients in her hometown ironically shows how women, as subjects, have been repressed by the mechanisms of the modern State. Sabitha's critique therefore develops from an inferior position, and from her disappointed realisation of how different women in a Muslim country were from the prejudiced view held of them. Other instances reveal Sabitha as a jealous and prejudiced narrator: she is awestruck upon hearing a Saudi Arabian woman asking about the length of the cervical dilation while considering if she had the time to go home and return for the delivery. She exclaims to Waheeda, her colleague, 'How informed these Arab women are on medical issues! Is there a possibility of our women asking their doctor about the status of their cervical dilation ever?' (Mumtas 2008, 30). Waheeda replies that these women interrogate and understand everything, and also know how to use their knowledge at the right time. No one can defeat them when it comes to rhetoric, an Arab strength since time immemorial; yet at the same time, they are not diffident about their ignorance in scientific matters. In fact, they consider the foreigners '*Ajami*' (dumb) (ibid.).

Sabitha is also acutely aware of the economic disparities between Saudi Arabia and India. Her disappointment takes the form of jibes; she attributes the 'arrogance' of Saudi citizens to the petroleum wealth of their nation, suggesting that had it not been for petroleum, the country would have lagged far behind her 'civilized nation'.

Her criticism of Saudi Arabia often ignores the wide human resources it invites, and the support that it offers to many national economies, including that of Kerala. When she does remark on it, she chooses to portray it only as exploitation. The sexual exploitation of maids is a generalised trope in the novel, referring once again to the extreme sexual appetites of Arab men. The *mahr* system[15] and other Islamic practices that support women have been presented as fraudulent in actual practice. Sabitha's expectations of Muslim women and her actual experience with women in Saudi Arabia are entirely different. The disparity between these two images results in the disruption of Sabitha's entire narrative. We have seen how women in Islamic history were intertwined with the person of Sabitha; similarly, the Islamic State and men are superimposed onto each other in the novel. Thus, the State that casts doubt on Sabitha's fidelity is juxtaposed with Sabitha's husband Rashid, the Muslim male. Such instances abound; even Dr Iqbal, with his two fellowships from London, behaves like a conservative Muslim after his marriage. After his marriage to a traditional Sudanese woman and his promotion, he seemed to transform into a subject of religion and the Islamic State. He cannot but represent the torturer, the imposing Muslim man in Sabitha's narrative.

Sabitha presents the Prophet as an ordinary mortal, described in terms of desires and emotions. It is intriguing to note the complete erasure of the Prophet's spiritual aura in her interpretation of Islamic history. Sabitha is unwilling to accept any contextual explanations of polygamy offered in Islamic history or the Hadiths. According to her, the Prophet was an ageing man, driven by both his sexual aspirations and insecurities. In her retelling of the story of the Khyber War and its aftermath from the perspectives of the Prophet's young wives, Aysha and Ummu Selma, the women are presented as jealous, and worried about the impact that beautiful Jewish women might have on the vulnerable Prophet. Abu Hureira, a male attendant in the harem, brings them news of the war, and his 'exaggerated report' adds fuel to the fire of their envy. The wife of Kinaina, commander of the Ban Nadir army, is presented as dainty. When the army reached the

---

[15] The custom of giving money to the bride at the time of marriage, a reversal of the dowry system.

harem after defeating the fort, everyone was spellbound by her exceptional beauty. Rasool (the Rabbi) wrapped her in the shawl that hung on the gates of the fort. Everyone then realised that Muhammad desired her; after all, such a beautiful and aristocratic woman was quite unapproachable for an ordinary mortal. The anxiety among people was whether she would be taken as a slave woman or a wife (Mumtas 2008, 111).

A conversation between Sabitha and Waheeda about Indonesian maids provides yet another instance of generalisation about Muslim male sexuality:

> Most of them are over thirty five, though they don't look so. Fair and slim as they are, the Arabs are fond of them …. Most of them insert Copper-T or implants before coming here. They are well aware of the dangers involved. Doctor Waheeda chuckled …..'Are you not convinced? The dialectics of master and slave woman is not new in Arabia. Earlier they were possessed as captives of war. Today they are imported from other countries in the arrogance of petro-dollars. Can the Arabs come out of a habit that is embedded in their genes?' (ibid., 31)

The only parallel that strikes Sabitha is that of Soopi Muthalali, the local Muslim landlord, and his rumoured relationship with his maid back in her hometown. Despite the intricate caste system deeply rooted in Kerala and its prolonged history of upper-caste Hindu exploitation, the only example that Sabitha could think of in this context concerned a Muslim. The convert Sabitha's Hindu past, which she never rejects, is kept alive and informs the political context of her comparison. This prejudiced view of Muslim men recurs in her description of Waheeda's husband and family, too. The doctor's children are grown, and study in their hometown. Once a year, her husband and children visit and stay with her for about two months. Yet it is said that her husband's presence is more difficult to tolerate than the loneliness of living alone the rest of the year. Trivialising their sexual relationship, she states that Waheeda gets a urinary infection whenever her husband visits. Family visits are clearly not a happy occasion, and can only be tolerated for short spans of time (Mumtas 2008, 32).

Sabitha's stern morality finds Waheeda's life as a lone female unacceptable. Her own insistence on accepting her visa only if her husband received clearance as well is held up as a symbol of her virtue and devotion, and signals her apprehensions about living 'alone'. Therefore, she feels the need to explain Waheeda's living alone in terms of her 'demanding husband', who gives her nothing but 'urinary infections'. These generalisations and allegations feed into Sabitha's reading of Islam as a material rather than a spiritual religion.

Arab women's indifference to their men's wanton desires is attributed to the provision in Islamic law that permits polygamy. A conversation between Sabitha and Waheeda alludes to how Arab women are silently complicit in the sexual exploitation of their maids:

> Once they reach here, even before they learn the language the Arab owner tells her of his need through gestures. They will be asked not to lock the doors of their rooms. If they do not comply with it, there will be physical harassment. Recently we heard the story of an Indonesian *Khaddama* [Arabic for maid] who jumped down from her window and committed suicide. Arab women do not seem to have any problem with this. Otherwise he may marry again. There would be lots of money involved in the marriage. (Mumtas 2008, 31–32)

Apart from portraying the Arab male as lustful, the narrative hints at a subversion of the fundamental systems of support that Islam offers its women. The *mahr* system is intended to improve the status of women within Islam, and also counter the pre-Islamic tradition of dowry. My intention is not to refer to Islam as a space of female emancipation; I am well aware of the internal patriarchies that women have faced in the theological and historical existence of Islam. But I am concerned about the subject position of Sabitha as a 'critical insider'. Adding to this ambiguity, the author carefully places the narrator at the threshold of the religion as a newly converted Muslim. Her observations can be viewed diplomatically as both within and outside the religion. In the Introduction, the author refers to a remark made by her friend Civic Chandran, 'You are not Taslima Nasreen'; this, she states, gave her confidence. It also hints at her diplomacy and the equivocal position she intends to take vis-à-vis religion. The implied fear underlying the comparison with Taslima Nasreen shows her nervousness at the prospect of being exiled from Islam. She preferred to be simultaneously on the inside and the outside, where she is allowed to critique the religion from within while representing it to the intellectual audience outside, and thereby fill the dire need for 'secular modern Muslim women' in Kerala.

It is difficult to imagine Sabitha as a 'critical insider' not because of her status as a convert, but rather because of the ambiguous position she places herself in with respect to the religion. The term 'critical insider' needs elaboration and further exploration in our political discourse. Identity may not be the only determinant of critique, but the critique does not stand alone as an ahistorical entity. Multiple experiences may constitute the Muslim identity: spiritual, political, constitutional, and so on. But while subscribing to a reform of the religion from within, it is also important to position one's critique at a distance from Islamophobia. Further, religious conversion is a complex phenomenon in a country like India. Since Independence, Hindu majoritarianism has grown increasingly anxious about the question of conversion. I have discussed 'love-jihad' and the Hindu Right's resistance to conversion in the Conclusion. The narrator's status as a convert gives the narrative a precariousness related to this complex history of contemporary conversions.

Sabitha's discussion of Arab men and their sexuality needs to be read against the contemporary realities of the 'modern nation' from which she hails. Surrounded by stories of sexual abuse, scams, and inhuman rapes, women in Kerala do not feel secure in their everyday lives. While Sabitha presents Arab men as symbolising an insatiable sexuality, the reality in her home country tells a different story. The security that the Islamic law of Saudi Arabia provides its women, and the capital punishment extended to rapes and sexual exploitation do not form part of Sabitha's narrative. This conflict between the narrator's prejudices and contemporary reality casts doubts on the author's intentions, thwarting the credibility of her arguments.

Barsa's Critical Acclaim

As a novel, *Barsa* positions itself in relation to contemporary discussions on Islam in Kerala. *Barsa* was an instant success in a market flooded by books on Islam and Muslim women, especially in the post-9/11 context of Islamophobia and discourses on Islamic fundamentalism. In a world polarised into pro-Islamic and anti-Islamic groups, the environment in Kerala, too, was conducive to debates on Islam as a lost project in the history of the renaissance. Literary historiography in Kerala has always excluded Muslim literature, and has adopted a somewhat partisan attitude vis-à-vis Islamic anti-colonial literature or representing the modern literature of Muslim writers. The failure of the renaissance and its ideal project of cultural secularism are reflected in the careful exclusions in literary histories (Tharamel 2007, 23–29). Muslim writers have never been welcomed in mainstream histories; even secular writers like Vaikom Muhammad Basheer have not been completely accepted, and their reputations have fluctuated. In his Introduction to *Barsa*, A. P. Kunjamu mentions the context in which Muslim lives have been placed in many Malayalam novels. Unfortunately, these contexts have been homogenised and made uniform to suit a liberal discourse, or at times ignored and banished to the margins of a dominant Hindu discourse.

Kunjamu considers *Barsa* the sole attempt to describe Muslims lives from the perspective of the marginalised, viewing the novel as the reading of Islam by a Muslim woman (Kunjamu 2008, 14). While there is a conscious and organised effort to marginalise Muslim writers, what adds to *Barsa*'s reputation is its approval of the victim status of Muslim women. The more *Barsa* underlines the backwardness of the Muslim community, the greater its approval and acceptance by the mainstream. The 'confession' in the Preface on the social responsibility of the individual to ask questions makes the book an important document on the resisting Muslim woman: her resistance marks her entry into the modern world. Likewise, there are only two inevitable choices before the Muslim woman: she can either discard the *purdah*, reveal herself, and thus be *barza*, liberated, or she can remain veiled and oppressed. When Kamala Das converted to Islam, discussions in mainstream journals were directed at the possibility of her writing *My Story* (2009) as a Muslim woman. After the poet's death, Thaha Madayi asked a couple of questions:

Why do Muslim women of Kerala always veil their experiences? Even in a time of innumerable autobiographies and biographies why do not Muslim women publish their narratives like the beautiful *Mappila Pattu*?[16] …. If a Muslim woman had written *My Story*[17] what would have happened? Such a thought is relevant now. (Madayi 2009, 46)

Subsequently, he provides the answers:

A community that had ostracised N. P. Muhammad and similar reformers cannot be expected to accept Surayya.[18] Not only that she wouldn't be accepted, she would also be defamed. The sympathy extended to Surayya at her death wouldn't have been extended to Madhavikkutty had she been a Muslim by birth. (ibid.)

Madayi argues that a great work like *My Story* could exist only because Madhavikkutty was not a Muslim. Had she been a Muslim (and here, he draws a parallel between the renowned author and his illiterate grandmother, Asyumma, as Muslims), she would have spent her days in prayer and Quran recital, and would have died without revealing her 'self' to the world, without leaving behind any symbol of her existence. He clarifies that his is not a communal argument and that it is his testimony as a Malayali Muslim, throwing open a challenge to possible opponents to counter his argument through the necessary evidence and provide a transparent narrative of the Muslim woman's self (Madayi 2009, 46).

[16] Traditional Muslim songs.
[17] The controversial autobiography of Madhavikkutty/Kamala Das.
[18] The name taken by Madhavikkutty after her conversion to Islam.

Here, the author again invokes the binaries of revealing and not revealing. Madhavikkutty, who wrote such a revealing autobiography, is a veiled woman in Islam. I would like to extend this argument to ask: Why should 'revealing' become the only viable political agency for a woman? How could the author conclude unilaterally that his grandmother, who had lived the pious life of a Muslim woman, had 'wasted' her life? The *barza*, the unveiled woman, thus becomes a potent symbol in all our discussions of female emancipation. It is also the only viable agency for a woman. The woman who negotiates with her familiar context, the one who fits within the confines of religious compulsion, is not liberated. Madhavikkuty, as a woman revealing her personal space, is in a way the symbol of our liberal aspirations. The controversial autobiography, informed by the longings of Malayali modernity, also represents the free woman in our cultural representations. Madayi's critique also presents the complex position of Muslim women within the genre of autobiography. The Muslim woman, an anomaly in the liberal-secular space, is thus represented in our literary and cultural productions as the eternal outsider. Through her clothing, vocabulary, and also her victim status, she is marked in our movies and literature as alien. Most popular movies represent her as a victim; a backward, suppressed woman in the backyards of our culture.

Madhavikkutty's conversion to Islam thus violates this popular notion of Islam: the free woman turning to Islam and embracing victimhood is confusing, and sabotages the normative idea that all individuals seek liberation from forces of oppression. The dialogues that took place around the conversion highlighted contradictory interpretations amongst critics. The *barza* woman is liberated and the author of *My Story* is *barza*, while the veiled woman is a victim. Thus, *barza* is also our archetype of the free woman; the one who opens her life to interpretation and observation is making a statement about her existence. Self-narration allows for an assertion of one's existence. But the political context of this self-narration turns it into a compulsory disclosure, at least in the case of confessions. The sinner confessing to be the 'disciplined subject' is the other extreme of this self-narration, as in the case of religious confessions. However, in modern contexts, revelations secure one's subjectivity within the progressive domain. Thus, a woman's unwillingness to speak out or open up in public, is viewed as a threat to this progressive project. This obsession with disclosure is a popular trope of modernity. The implications of unveiling in the colonial context is discussed elsewhere in this book.

The woman who discards her veil is acceptable to modernity, to the secular State, and to liberal intellectuals. Thus, Mumtas' *Barsa* secures a stable, prominent position in literary history, where many other Muslim writers have failed. The fissures in the literary and cultural historiography of Kerala are evident in the conspicuous absences of Muslim women writers[19] and reformers in our histories. By conforming to the image of the Muslim woman demanded by the public, *Barsa* and Mumtas succeed where Haleema Beevi or Puthoor Amina had failed. *Barsa* owes its specious appearance to its overlooking of 'location' and 'conversion' as important anthropological aspects, thereby exposing the discursive limitations of modern critique.

Barsa attributes to Islam all the Middle Eastern cultural practices. Arab feminist discourses of the post-orientalist phase critiqued the primacy accorded to universalised Western liberal assumptions on women's rights over culture-specific practices, and successfully delineated a space of articulation for Arab women outside the male-centric Arab nationalism. *Barsa* pays no attention to these developments. Discarding what appears to be a bourgeois definition of human, they define women's subjectivity through practices that may appear as subjugation when studied through Western concepts of individualism. The critique of Islam and the Arab world as anti-modern and misogynist stems from a privileged discourse that needs no legitimation in

---

[19] The genre of *Mappilapattu* (Mappila songs) is not explored in this work. Many women authors and singers have popularised this genre, and there is a strong women's agency in the oral tradition of Mappila creativity.

an Islamophobic context. This critique, raised by Mumtas and various 'secular Muslims', is situated in a hierarchical framework of modern liberal assumptions against Islam, geo-political imbalances that privilege the West, and a majoritarian anti-Muslim populism in India.

Those who applaud *Barsa* consider it a realistic representation of the Muslim woman's aspiration for freedom. On the other hand, criticism of Barsa originates from a defence of Islam's hierarchical ordering of gender. Both readings fail to note the essentialist identity that the work attributes to Muslim women. They hardly speak for women in Islam; women present spiritually and materially within Islam are seen only as vulnerable victims. The narrative point of view conforms to the existing secular critiques of Islam, and offers no new understanding of the complexity of Muslim women's identity. The focus on a universal Muslim woman, not shaped by either historical or social conditions, is perhaps *Barsa's* greatest failure, a failure evident in popular responses to the novel. P. K. Pokker, the prominent Left intellectual, reads *Barsa* thus:

> Writers have realized the factors inherent in the formulation of one's identity along with the ideological premises of representing the self. The philosophical premises and living conditions that reflect the identity crisis exclusively experienced by Muslim women, different from that of men, have been discussed here specifically because Barsa represents the identity of the Muslim woman. The author of this work has been approached as a Muslim woman because the problematic space discussed in the novel can be narrated only by a woman and is inherent only in Muslim lives. (2008, 14).

Pokker identifies the conflicting ideologies and hidden dangers that the work reflects through the rather careless Preface, which seems to contradict the entire narrative. In the Preface, the novelist recollects a debate on the theme of 'Muslim/non-Muslim', where a speaker from the 'Hindu' team allots to the Quran the responsibility of laying the foundation for both the spiritualist and the terrorist. Mumtas' response, that she shared his concern, is rather revealing, given that she is attempting a work on Muslim women; it discloses her insensitivity to the political machinations to homogenise all Muslims as terrorists. Pokker rightly points out that this Preface sabotages the possibility of reading *Barsa* as a progressive document. But he fails to see how the narrative portrays the Muslim woman as a homogenised, ahistorical entity by conflating the plight of Aysha with that of any other Muslim woman, as well as through the trope of merging identities, which the narrator makes use of at times. The question of Aysha's chastity becomes a concern for Sabitha, which is later reflected in her life when her husband and the State, representing male supremacy in the text, place her under scrutiny on charges on infidelity.

Pokker's idealisation of cultural renaissance as the liberating point for Kerala, marking its entry into modernity, leads him to equate this with the great Malayalam poet Kumaranasan's impatience with questions on Sita's fidelity in *Chinthavishtayaya Sita* (*Pensive Sita*). In his reading, Sabitha's resistance to systems of oppression marks her feminist agency. He extends his argument further: 'The female circumcision that takes place in Sudan is not in practice openly in other parts of the world. But it is awful to note the possibility of establishing such grotesque systems to satiate the male desire' (Pokker 2008, 17). Here, the author makes clear his concept of freedom and political agency, while striking a chord with the established critique of Islam as the 'Other' of modernity. In his discourse, the veil becomes a symbol that represents the victim—the Muslim woman. Her ignorance and uncivilised existence are manifest in practices such as female circumcision, taken to represent the community.

Here, one might wonder whether the author's omission of the geographical and cultural location of this practice is deliberate. Such a perspective might dilute the desired effect of placing Islam as the sole perpetrator of heinous practices. In Pokker's reading, the Muslim woman represents one entity, while Islam becomes the only determinant of her status. Thus, women in Saudi Arabia, Sudan, and Kerala are victims of their religion, Islam, which also curtails their political agency. Islam becomes the barbaric Other of the civilised values of the renaissance.

Feminism's Universalism and Counter-Perspectives

Sara Farris' important work, *In the Name of Women's Rights: The Rise of Femonationalism*, examines the demands for women's rights put forth by strange allies: Right-wing nationalist political parties, neoliberals, feminist theorists, and policymakers. Focusing on migrant Muslim women in contemporary France, Italy, and the Netherlands, Farris uses the term 'femonationalism' to explain the co-option of feminist themes by anti-Islamic and xenophobic campaigns. By presenting Muslim men as dangerous oppressors of women, these groups use feminist discourse to justify their racist rhetoric and policies. While adhering to a Right-wing rhetoric of 'saving Muslim women', the Left and feminists in India unknowingly play into the hands of the larger agenda to ostracise the Muslim male. Jasbir Puar's *Terrorist Assemblages: Homonationalism in Queer Times* argues that homonationalism serves to both domesticate and control queer life in the US and further the persecution of others, including Sikh, Muslim, and Arab groups. Liberal discourses on queer politics in the US often fall into the category of a homonormative nationalism, where queerness is equated with white homosexuality, thereby portraying the marginal identities of Muslim, Arab, and South Asian as outcastes and justifying their persecution. Both works highlight the dangers of adhering to linear narratives of liberatory politics without studying the layered complexities of the power politics underlying such formations. In the context of Kerala, the Left and feminist narratives on Muslim women need to be reframed and deliberately delinked from Right-wing agendas and international geopolitical interests. By forming strange alliances with the Right-wing persecutors of Muslim men, the Left and feminist politics in Kerala unintentionally add to narratives on Muslim alienation.

Conclusion

*T*here have been very few engaged studies on women and Islam in Kerala.[1] In the reform movements and later progressive discourses, Muslim women were portrayed as passive victims. Illiterate and destitute—these are the two adjectives often associated with Muslim women in these discourses. I have tried to contest these images through a nuanced reading of the state of women in general, and Muslim women in particular, during the pre-reform period, and through presenting Muslim women as active participants in reform movements. Presenting an alternative history of Muslim women brings out the prejudices inherent in mainstream historiography, and its commitment to liberal modernity. In her engagement with immediate cultural and social contexts, the Muslim woman used different modes of participation, none of which has been explored significantly.

The Arabic-Malayalam script, the special script used by the Muslim community in Kerala, was the medium of communication and education in premodern times. Reformers in the community emphasised the need to learn Malayalam and English, attributing the community's backwardness to the insistence on using this script. But the accessibility of this script to all Muslims, without reservations of class or gender, points

[1] Shamshad Hussain's work, *Nyunapakshathinum Lingapadavikkumidayil* (2009), on the Muslim women of Kerala, needs to be acknowledged here. It is the first of its kind to attempt a serious engagement with women and Islam in Kerala.

to a more egalitarian society that had once thrived amongst the Muslims. It is to be noted that during this time, caste had played a major role in denying Sanskrit education to lower-caste Hindus. When dismissing the entire community of Muslims as illiterate, this medium, with its rich traditions and various genres of literature, was not taken into account. The Madrassa education of the premodern past also included songs and *baiths* (Arabic poetry). The Mappilas had songs on almost every aspect of everyday life, ranging from resistance to colonial rule and hagiographies of saints to celebratory occasions like marriages, ear piercings, ritualistic ablutions after childbirth, etc. Domestic and public spaces are intertwined in these songs, reflecting the socio-cultural engagements of the Mappilas.

Women played a major role in the production and circulation of Mappila literature. Many women were involved in the literary tradition of *paatukettu*, which roughly translates to making songs.[2] Songs written in the Arabic-Malayalam script could be found in many traditional families and women had the sole possession of these songs, which were passed down from generation to generation. These manuscripts were called *sabina edukal* (the sabina folios). Groups of women would sing songs like *Nafeesath Maala* (*Hagiography of Nafeesa*) and *Mohiyudheen Maala* (*Hagiography of Sufi Saint Shaykh Mohiyudheen*) during childbirth, as a means to alleviate labour pains. Given the presence of such a lively tradition, the remnants of which exist even in contemporary society, it is illogical to view Muslim women as helpless, illiterate victims. With the emergence of print, many of these oral engagements died out, and the role of secular modernity in disabling several such premodern practices cannot be overlooked. The definition of cultural engagement as an activity

---

[2] In Malabar, there are women who both write and sing such songs during celebrations. This tradition of songs was also used in more powerful representations of the struggles of the Mappilas against the Portuguese and the British. There are plenty of songs valourising the warriors of the 1921 Mappila rebellion.

outside the domestic arena, and the determination of the female domestic space through a gendered structuring of the public domain, both of which took place during the reform period, aided the extinction of these practices. However, there was still a strong female presence in the twentieth-century Mappila literary tradition, in the form of P. K. Haleema and Puthoor Amina. A magazine called *Niza-ul-Islam*, meant for Muslim women, was published in the 1920s in the Arabic-Malayalam script.[3]

The scope of this book does not allow a detailed reading of women's authorial presence, both oral and written, in the Mappila literary tradition. But I do point towards the possibility of and necessity for further research into Mappila literature, viewing it as a feminist cultural endeavour. Rather than considering Mappila literature as sites of exotic ethnographic possibilities, the theoretical propositions emerging from them need to be engaged with. There has been almost no effort on the part of literary critics or cultural theorists to study Mappila literature as a political medium, or to delineate the political dialogue that this literary tradition carries on with the public sphere. My focus on premodern Muslim women in Chapter 1 centred on the role of women as interlocutors in a dynamic society at the cusp of transition. I attempted a nuanced reading of the social milieu of premodern times to show women as mediating between religions and rituals. The active agency of women as promoters of Islam was later transferred to more spiritual platforms, where subaltern communities challenged the universalised version of an 'aristocratic' Islam.

The political positions proposed by Muslims in India in connection to women in the reform context are analysed in the following chapter. Chapter 2 focused on reform movements in Kerala and the strong presence of Muslim women therein. Through the many 'little magazines' in circulation at the time, Muslim women pondered over the possibilities of negotiating between religion and modernity. The exclusion of Muslim reform

---

[3] Shamshad Hussain provides an image of the front cover of a 1929 issue in *Nyoonapakshathinum Lingapadavikkumidayil* (2009, 48).

movements and Muslim women's agency from mainstream histories of the reform movements in Kerala reveals the flaws in mainstream historiography.

While dealing with the question of historiography, I attempted to engage critically with the idea of secular history in order to unsettle the normative political positions within feminist and liberal scholarships. Saba Mahmood (2004) points out that critique is a 'situated' practice that abides by the protocols of what is considered normative within a particular historical moment. She presents the impossibility of a teleological understanding of history and the need to explore the possibility of a remaking of the self through an engagement with 'another' perspective. This approach to history challenges the certainty of one's own political commitments, but also makes it important to re-think them from within the context of 'subjectivation'. Regarding this openness to a 'radical Other', Mahmood elaborates:

> This does not mean that one has to adopt the lifestyles of medieval women, or that one stops fighting against the oppressive and unjust practices imminent to one's own life. To do so would be only to mimic the same teleological certainty that we have been criticizing under the register of secular history in the first place. It does mean, however, to keep open the possibility that one can come to question the contingent importance of emancipation and freedom … in a manner that one did not think was possible when one embarked upon an inquiry in the first place. (ibid., 579)

So feminist historiography, as has been attempted here, definitely highlights the need to revise our notions of history as an essentially secular category. Secular rationality has revised our notions of law, knowledge, and forms of modern governmentality; at the same time, it has also revised institutions of religious life.[4] These reflections make academic debates on the religious and the secular more nuanced; however, the excessive emphasis on the modern

---

[4] For more on this, see Asad (2003); Chandlier and Davidson (2009); Mahmood (2009).

as a binary vis-à-vis religion tends to interpret everyday lives in relation to faith as 'religious extremism'.[5] A similar discussion evolved out of feminist interventions in the Rayana controversy, mentioned in Chapter 3. The chapter also reads the popularity of the novel *Barsa* among secular-liberals as a reflection of their sympathy with the critique of Islam that the novel highlights. Locating the novel in contemporary Kerala, where the Muslim community and Muslim women are transposed onto the polarised realms of fundamentalism and victimhood, respectively, the chapter also studies some of the prevalent discourses on Muslim women. My reading of *Barsa* and the arguments that follow proffers the idea that the secular-liberal principles of freedom and emancipation associated with feminism and other Left-liberal imaginaries cannot be considered universal.

By universalising a particular vision of freedom and emancipation located in the Western imagination, possible 'other modes of articulation' and ways of conceptualising political agency have been compromised. The policies of the secular State also blatantly ignore the inherent contradictions within its own conception, a contradiction that became all too apparent in the issue of Rayana Khazi. As a citizen of the secular liberal-democratic State, she has the right to her choice of clothing. But the same State also claims to offer a freedom of religion that allows religious structures to uphold their beliefs and codes of moral behaviour.[6]

[5] My own article in the leading Malayalam weekly, *Mathrubhumi*, titled 'Islamile Sthree' ('Women in Islam', 2010), has been interpreted in terms of religious extremism. Maina Umaiban, a budding Malayalam writer who claims a secular Muslim identity, criticised the argument, which had challenged the generalisation of liberal aspirations, calling it fundamentalist. Hameed Chendamangallur (2010) pointed out that many Muslim intellectuals, especially women, are committed to an 'intellectual *jihad*'.

[6] The tension prevailing in Kerala at the time of this writing, concerning the conversion and subsequent marriage of Hadiya, is an example of this complexity. The secular State and the court, by seeking an NIA report on Hadiya's conversion to Islam and her marriage to a Muslim, seem to believe that under normal circumstances, no woman would choose to convert to Islam. Thus, the secular agencies of the State, the judiciary and the

While conceptualising the Muslim woman's existence, it is also important to take into account the minority status of Muslims in India. The normative disposition of the legal system and the mechanisms of the State, skewed as they are towards the majority culture and religion, often clash with the claims of equality, freedom, and secularism. The intervention of the court in the context of 'love-jihad' in Kerala or the judgments pronounced in legal cases related to the Babri Masjid demolition and various communal conflagrations challenge the notion of an impartial execution of law. Justice Sankaran's controversial 2009 order to the Government of Kerala to probe into allegations regarding the coerced conversions of Hindu and Christian girls to Islam revealed the prejudices that underlie the legal mechanism in the country.[7] The secular-liberal principles of freedom of speech and religion are thus not neutral mechanisms for the negotiaton of religious differences, but prove partial to certain normative conceptions of religion, subject, language, and injury (Mahmood 2009, 861). Given this indifferent legal framework, the suggestions for a Uniform Civil Code accentuate the problematic realm of jurisprudence in the country. The Shah Bano case and the discourses it evoked centred on a critique of the Sharia and its gender imbalances. However, beyond the law and its liberal manifestations, there needs to be a greater understanding across religious differences and a vision of the ethical traditions and intersubjective norms that provide the basis of legal arguments. There is a need to address the complexity involved in translating ethical and religious norms across cultures while discussing the Muslim woman.

Muslim women scholar-activists who critically study the foundational texts of Islam have challenged these canonical texts and conventional histories. The danger underlying such thinking has been discussed in the earlier chapters. The formation of the All India Muslim Women's Personal Law Board (AIMWPLB)

---

executive, act in accordance with the Islamophobic prejudices prevalent in contemporary society.

[7] See note 11, Chapter 3, this volume.

and many Muslim women's NGOs are attempts on the part of Muslim women in India to develop a dialogue amongst themselves, with the religion, with the community, and at a wider level, with the society on issues related to women. While locating themselves within the community, these organisations address issues pertaining to child custody, guardianship and adoption, women's rights in the marital home, marriage and divorce, *mahr* (dower), etc. The Muslim Women's Rights Network, whose all-India meeting was held in 2005 in Lucknow, discussed the role of the State in protecting women's rights, the impact of communal violence on Muslim women, and the challenges that lie ahead for Muslim women's activism (Vatuk 2008, 500–01). These initiatives undoubtedly reflect the community's attempt to develop a politically vibrant dialogue with contemporary realities. At the same time, when women become prominent participants within the Muslim public sphere, they do not contest their identity as Muslims. However, it may be misleading to view these organisations as platforms to address the politics of gender alone, since they also engage with the pressing realities of living in India as members of a minority community and address the internal discrepancies within the apparently secular framework of the nation. Sylvia Vatuk differentiates between Islamic feminist activists and Islamist women (ibid.). Studying the discourse on women in contemporary Islamic reform movements, she finds that they all share a preoccupation with the need for women to conform to 'Islamically prescribed norms' of modest behaviour and appearance. She charts out the different trajectories of Islamist women and Islamic feminists:

> 'Islamist' women, 'less concerned with the advancement of women's rights than with the advancement of Islamization' seem to have little in common with the Islamic feminist activists .... the Muslim women's rights 'movement', ... is not concerned with identifying or enforcing particular standards of dress or deportment, teaching women, how to become better Muslims or encouraging them to pray more regularly. Its leaders are indeed outspokenly critical of ... reformer's attempts to control women's behaviour .... their attitudes

seem to reflect a conception of religion that is very far from that of the Islamists, one that sees religious faith and modes of observance as private matters, to be negotiated by each individual between herself and God. (ibid., 517–18)

It is precisely this conception of political agency that I have been attempting to contest through this book. Certain liberal assumptions frame Vatuk's discourse: by defining the rigid categories of Islamists and Islamic feminists, she attempts to prioritise the individual over religion. In my engagement with active Muslim women's organisations such as the Girls' Islamic Organisation (GIO), I came across very firm, pious, practising Muslim women actively engaged in debates related to gender equality. What is different in their position is their awareness of the haunted Muslim identity in India. Their responses are balanced; they do not make use of a sophisticated gender discourse to alienate Muslim men or the community, as is often done by the 'liberated' Muslim feminists Vatuk speaks of. Aware of the current political status of Muslims in India, they attempt a more inclusive feminism. She pits her ideal Islamic feminist against its antithetical other, the Islamist, to posit an essential identity of the progressive individual. By presenting religion as a private matter to be resolved between the individual and God, Vatuk abides by the normative prescription of the modern secular State that demands a retreat of religion to the private sphere.

It is this complexity in the term 'Islamic feminism' that has led me to carefully exclude it from my discourse. My own feminist convictions lead me to view feminism as a movement that can provide the theoretical grounding for all kinds of identity struggles, rather than as an emancipatory movement of one particular kind. Such a feminist sensitivity accommodates women in *purdah* within its fold without raising questions about choice in matters of clothing. This feminism does not emphasise individualism or the liberal assumptions of a European modernity, but develops as a tradition that conceptualises different histories and modes of thought. It is precisely this different trajectory of feminism that books like *Women Writing in India* (Tharu and Lalitha 2006) have presented before us.

In their conceptualisation of the Muslim woman, feminist discourses have framed her along two binaries—progressive and anti-religion, or religious and therefore oppressed. Between these two binaries are plenty of other positions that feminism needs to explore. Charles Hirschkind and Saba Mahmood (2002) discuss the portrayal of the Muslim woman as a victim of Islamic fundamentalism, pointing out how young women's decision to veil, an act of modesty as per Islamic norms, is interpreted as opposing the notion of freedom as defined by social conventions:

> This points out the degree to which the normative subject of feminism remains a liberatory one: one who contests social norms ... but not one who finds purpose, value, and pride in the struggle to live in accord with certain tradition sanctioned virtues. Women's voluntary adoption of what are considered ... patriarchal practices are often explained by feminists in terms of false consciousness, or an internalization of patriarchal social values .... A Muslim woman can only be one of two things, either uncovered, and therefore liberated, or veiled, and thus still to some degree, subordinate .... Can our daily activities and life decisions really be captured and understood within this logic of freedom or captivity? (ibid., 352–53)

This is an important proposition in terms of the agency of Muslim women. We need to conceptualise women in Islam outside the logic of this binary opposition. Those values and practices that liberal-progressive individuals espouse may not always form an ideal human existence. Our imaginative possibilities for the Muslim woman centre around misogyny and patriarchal violence. Our ability to conceive of Muslim women beyond these set patterns determines the credibility of our discourses on these women. While viewing the veil as an oppressive measure, the reality of the veil and the harem as modes of sociality that connect the Muslim woman to her immediate public sphere is often ignored.

Besides the problematic position of the Muslim woman in terms of her existence outside the realm of a particularly defined emancipatory politics, in India, the fact of being a part of a religious minority complicates matters further. There is an inherent hostility in the depiction of Muslims that one needs to counter while working towards an impartial history. My engagement with women and Islam in Kerala is an attempt to present Muslim women as subjects of a differently conceived notion of religion, shaped by different variables of time, region, class, ethnicity, etc. In my endeavour to locate the Muslim woman of Kerala at specific moments in Kerala's history, I have presented her as a heterogeneous subject whose agency is not determined by a singular political formation. In her negotiations with religion and the larger society, she expresses her political concerns in ways that might be termed religious conformism by liberal secularism. As much as I explore the possibility of feminism within the category of Muslim, I also reconnoitre the obvious omissions and distortions in conventional historiography in order to project a particular vision of the nation. In doing so, I am well aware of the possible dangers involved, as there is every chance of these analytical reflections being read against the dichotomous characterisation of 'religious extremism' and 'secular necessity'. By challenging the normative claims of secular reasoning, one indeed faces the charges of supporting religious fundamentalism. While I am conscious of my location in academia within a secular epistemic framework, I am attempting here to think of other epistemic possibilities, and thereby not restricting my understanding to one particular structure. Being critical of secularism and its definition of religion does not translate to supporting religious fundamentalism. A complex understanding of the limitations of the categories we subscribe to while framing feminist positions and definitive norms of modernity is the least one can ask for in contemporary India.

Bibliography

Abdulkareem, K. K. Muhamed (compiled). 2006. *Makthi Thangalude SampoornaKrithikal* (*The Complete Works of Makthi Thangal*). Kozhikode: Vachanam.

Abdulkareem, K. K. Muhamed, and K. Aboobacker. 2005. *Mahakavi Moyinkutty Vaidyarute Sampoorna Krithikal* (*The Complete Works of Mahakavi Moyinkutty Vaidyar*), 2 vols. Kondotty: Mahakavi Moyinkutty Vaidyar Smaraka Committee.

Abdu Raheem, C. T. 2008. *Oru Malayali Musliminte Veritta Chinthakal* (*Unique Thoughts of a Malayali Muslim*). Kozhikode: Olive.

Abu, A. K. 1960. 'Muslim Sthreekalum Vidhyabhyasavum' ('Muslim Women and Education'). *Al Manar* 5 November, 260.

Abu-Lughod, Lila. 2002. 'Do Muslim Women Really Need Saving? Anthropological Reflections on Cultural Relativism and its Others'. *American Anthropologist* 104 (3), 783–90.

————. 2008. *Local Contexts of Islamism in Popular Media*. Amsterdam: Amsterdam University Press.

Abu, O. 1970. *Arabi Malayala Sahitya Charithram* (*History of Arabic Malayalam Literature*). Kottayam: SPCS.

————. 1991. 'Mappila Sahithyam' ('Mappila Literature'), Kerala State Mappila Song Lovers Association, Fifteenth Annual Souvenir, November, 33–38.

Afary, Janet, and Kevin B. Anderson. 2005. *Foucault and the Iranian Revolution: Gender and the Seductions of Islamism*. Chicago: University of Chicago Press.

Agamben, Giorgio. 2005. *State of Exception*, Kevin Attell (trans.). Chicago: University of Chicago Press.

Ahamed, B. Muhammed. 2006. *Mappila Folklore*. Kozhikode: Samayam.

Ahammed Moulavi, C. N., and K. K. Muhammed Abdulkareem. 1978. *Mahathaya Mappila Sahithya Parampariam* (*The Great Tradition of Mappila Literature*). Kozhikode: Azad.

Ahmad, Aijaz. 2004. *On Communalism and Globalisation: Offensives of the Far Right*. New Delhi: Three Essays Collective, 2e.

Ahmad, Imtiaz, and Helmut Reifeld (eds). 2004. *Lived Islam in South Asia: Adaptation, Accommodation and Conflict*. New Delhi: Social Science.

Ahmed, K. M. (ed.). 2006. *Mahakavi Moyinkutty Vaidyar Padanangal* (*Studies on Mahakavi Moyinkutty Vaidyar*). Kondotty: Mahakavi Moyinkutty Vaidyar Smaraka Committee.

Ahmed, Leila. 1992. *Women and Gender: Historical Roots of a Modern Debate*. New Haven: Yale University Press.

Ahmed, Rafiuddin. 2007. 'The Bengal Muslims, 1876–1901: A Quest for Identity'. In Rafiuddin Ahmed, Mushirul Hasan, and Barbara Daly Metcalf (eds), *India's Muslims: An Omnibus*. New Delhi: Oxford University Press.

Ahammed Musliar, K. P. 1996. *Beema Palli Charithram* (*History of Beema Palli*). Thiruvananthapuram: Beemapalli.

Ahmed, Nazir. 1903 [1869]. *Mirat ul-Arus: The Bride's Mirror—A Tale of Domestic Life in Delhi Forty Years Ago*, G. E. Ward (trans.). London: Henry Frowde.

Ajithkumar, N. 2004. *Kerala Samskaram* (*Kerala Culture*). Thiruvananthapuram: Cultural Publications Department.

A. K. A. 1932. 'Ajnathayo Asooyayo?' ('Ignorance or Jealousy?'). *Isha-Ath* March, 329–30.

Akbar, M. J. 2005. *India: The Siege Within. Challenges to a Nation's Unity*. New Delhi: Roli.

Akhtar, Shaheen, and Moushumi Bhowmik (eds). 2008. *Women in Concert: An Anthology of Bengali Muslim Women's Writings (1904–1938)*. Kolkata: Stree.

Al Madrassathul Islaamiya, Chendamangallur. 1952. 'Njangalkku Bhaagyamille?' ('Are we not Lucky?'). *Al Farooq* March, 30.

Alam, Muzaffar. 2008. *The Languages of Political Islam in India: C. 1200–1800*. Ranikhet: Permanent Black.

Alam, S. M. Shamsul. 2006. In Therese Saliba, Carolyn Allen, and Judith A. Howard (eds), *Gender, Politics and Islam*, 235–67. Hyderabad: Orient Longman.

Algar, Hamid. 1988. *The Roots of the Islamic Revolution*. Malappuram: Islamic Foundation.

Amin, Shahid. 2005. 'Representing the Musalman: Then and Now, Now and Then'. In Shail Mayaram, M. S. S. Pandian, and Ajay Skaria (eds), *Subaltern Studies XII: Muslims, Dalits, and the Fabrications of History*, 1–35. New Delhi: Permanent Black.

———. 2006. 'On Retelling the Muslim Conquest of North India'. In Partha Chatterjee and Anjan Ghosh (eds), *History and the Present*, 24–43. New Delhi: Permanent Black.

Anderson, Benedict. 1991. *Imagined Communities: Reflections on the Origin and Spread of Nationalism*. London: Verso.

Ansari, M. T. 2002. 'In the Interstices of India: Islam and the Processes of Nation-Formation'. Ph.D. thesis, CIEFL, Hyderabad.

———. 2005a. 'Refiguring the Fanatic: Malabar 1836–1922'. In Shail Mayaram, M. S. S. Pandian, and Ajay Skaria (eds), *Subaltern Studies XII: Muslims, Dalits, and the Fabrications of History*, 36–77. New Delhi: Permanent Black.

———. 2005b. 'Self/Other Problematic and the Question of Islam'. *Journal of Contemporary Thought* 21, 83–95.

Aquil, Raziuddin, and Partha Chatterjee (eds). 2008. *History in the Vernacular*. Ranikhet: Permanent Black.

Arimbra, Muhammad Kutty. 1959. 'Sthree: Padaviyum, Pravarthana Rangavum' ('Woman: Status and Realm of Action'). *Al Manar* 5 October.

Arunima, G. 1995. 'Matriliny and its Discontents'. *India International Centre Quarterly* 22 (2–3), 157–67.

———. 2003. *There Comes Papa: Colonialism and the Transformation of Matriliny in Kerala, Malabar: C. 1850–1940*. Hyderabad: Orient Longman.

Asad, Talal. 1993. *Genealogies of Religion: Discipline and Reasons of Power in Christianity and Islam*. Baltimore: Johns Hopkins University Press.

———. 2003. *Formations of the Secular: Christianity, Islam, Modernity*. Stanford: Stanford University Press.

Asad, Talal, Wendy Brown, et al. 2008. *Is Critique Secular? Blasphemy, Injury, and Free Speech*. Berkley: The Townsend Center for the Humanities, University of California.

Ayoub, Mahmoud M. 2006. *Islam: Faith and History*. Oxford: Oneworld.

Bahauddin, K. M. 1992. *Kerala Muslims: The Long Struggle*. Trivandrum: Modern.

———. 2004. *Kerala Muslimkal: Cheruthunilpinte Charithram* (*Muslims of Kerala: History of Resistance*). Kozhikode: Islamic, 2e, rev.

Balakrishnan, P. K. 1987. *Jathivyavasthithiyum Keralacharithravum* (*The Caste System and Kerala Society*). Kottayam: SPCS.

Balakrishnan, P. V. 1981. *Matrilineal System in Malabar*. Calicut: Mathrubhoomi.

Bandyopadhyay, Sekhar (ed.). 2010. *Nationalist Movement in India: A Reader*. New Delhi: Oxford University Press.

Basu, Amrita. 1999. 'Resisting the Sacred and the Secular'. In Patricia Jeffery and Amrita Basu (eds), *Resisting the Sacred and the Secular: Women's Activism and Politicized Religion in South Asia*, 3–14. New Delhi: Kali for Women.

Batool, Essar, Ifrah Butt, Munaza Rashid, Natasha Rather, and Samreena Mushtaq. 2016. *Do You Remember Kunan Poshpora?* New Delhi: Zubaan.

Beckerlegge, Gwilym (ed.). 2008. *Colonialism, Modernity, and Religious Identities: Religious Reform Movements in South Asia*. New Delhi: Oxford University Press.

Beefathima, P. 1945. 'Muslim Sthreeyude Parathanthratha' ('Muslim Women's Slavery'). *Mappila Review* August, 40–45.

Bendrey, V. S. A. 1944. *Study of Muslim Inscriptions: With Special Reference to the Inscriptions Published in the 'Epigraphia Indo-Moslemica' 1907–1938*. Bombay: Karnatak.

Benhabib, Seyla, et al. 1995. *Feminist Contentions: A Philosophical Exchange*. New York: Routledge.

Benjamin, Walter. 1977. *Illuminations*, Hannah Arendt (ed.), Harry Zohn (trans.). London: Fontana.

Bhadra, Gautam, Gyan Prakash, and Susie Tharu (eds). 2005. *Subaltern Studies X: Writings on South Asian History and Society*. New Delhi: Oxford University Press.

Bhagavan, Manu, and Anne Feldhaus (eds). 2009a. *Claiming Power from Below: Dalits and the Subaltern Question in India*. New Delhi: Oxford University Press.

———. 2009b. *'Speaking Truth to Power': Religion, Caste, and the Subaltern Question in India*. New Delhi: Oxford University Press.

Bhasin, Kamala, and Nighat Said Khan. 2005. *Feminism and its Relevance in South Asia*. New Delhi: Women Unlimited.

Bhaskaran. 2004. *Mother Forest: The Unfinished Story of C. K. Janu*. Translated from the Malayalam by N. Ravi Shanker. New Delhi: Women Unlimited.

Bhaskaranunny, P. 2000. *Pathonpatham Noottandile Keralam (Kerala in the Nineteenth Century)*. Thrissur: Kerala Sahitya Akademi.

———. 2005. *Keralam Irupatham Noottandinte Arambhathil (Kerala at the Beginning of the Twentieth Century)*. Thrissur: Kerala Sahitya Akademi.

Bhattacharya, Neeladri. 2008. 'Predicaments of Secular Histories'. *Public Culture* 20 (1), 57–73.

Bhattathiripad, V. T. 2005. 'Uma's Story', V. C. Harris (trans.). *Haritham* 17, 56–65.

Bhavnani, Kum-Kum, John Foran, and Priya A. Kurian (eds). 2003. *Feminist Futures: Re-imagining Women, Culture and Development*. New Delhi: Zubaan.

Bose, Sugatha. 1997. 'Nation as Mother: Representations and Contestations of India in Bengali Literature and Culture'. In Sugatha Bose and Ayesha Jalal (eds), *Nationalism, Democracy and Development: State and Politics in India*, 50–75. New Delhi: Oxford University Press.

Brass, Paul R. 2003. *The Production of Hindu-Muslim Violence in Contemporary India*. New Delhi: Oxford University Press.

Buchanan, Francis. 1988. *A Journey from Madras through the Countries of Mysore, Canara, and Malabar, for the Express Purpose of Investigating the State of Agriculture, Arts and Commerce; The Religion, Manners, and Customs; The History Natural and Civil and Antiquities*, Vol. 2. New Delhi: Asian Educational Services.

Bullock, Katherine. 2002. *Rethinking Muslim Women and the Veil: Challenging Historical and Modern Stereotypes*. London: International Institute of Islamic Thought.

Burns, Robert M. (ed.). 2006a. *Historiography: Critical Concepts in Historical Studies*, Vol. 1, *Foundations*. London: Routledge.

———— (ed.). 2006b. *Historiography: Critical Concepts in Historical Studies*, Vol. 2, *Society*. London: Routledge.

————. (ed.). 2006c. *Historiography: Critical Concepts in Historical Studies*, Vol. 4, *Culture*. London: Routledge.

Butler, Judith. 1997. *The Psychic Life of Power: Theories in Subjection*. Stanford: Stanford University Press.

————. 1999. *Subjects of Desire: Hegelian Reflections in Twentieth Century France*. New York: Columbia University Press.

————. 2000. *Antigone's Claim: Kinship between Life and Death*. New York: Columbia University Press.

————. 2006. *Precarious Life: The Powers of Mourning and Violence*. London: Verso.

————. 2007. *Gender Trouble: Feminism and the Subversion of Identity*. New York: Routledge.

Butler, Judith, Ernesto Lacalu, and Slavoj Zizek. 2000. *Contingency, Hegemony, Universality: Contemporary Dialogues on the Left*. London: Verso.

Butler, Judith, and Gayatri Chakravorty Spivak. 2007. *Who Sings the Nation State? Language, Politics, Belonging*. Kolkata: Seagull.

Centre for Women's Development Studies (ed.). 2003. *Shifting Sands: Women's Lives and Globalization*. Kolkata: Stree.

Chaitanya, Krishna. 1971. *A History of Malayalam Literature*. Hyderabad: Orient Longman.

Chakravarti, Uma. 2009. 'Whatever Happened to the Vedic *Dasi*? Orientalism, Nationalism and a Script of the Past'. In Kumkum Sangari, and Sudesh Vaid (eds), *Recasting Women: Essays in Colonial History*, 27–87. New Delhi: Zubaan.

Chakravarti, Uma. 2009. *Gendering Caste Through a Feminist Lens*. James Chandlier and Arnold I. Davidson (eds), *The Fate of Disciplines*. Chicago: University of Chicago Press.

Chandra, Bipin. 2006. *Nationalism and Colonialism in Modern India*. Hyderabad: Orient Longman.

Chatterjee, Partha. 2006a. 'Introduction: History and the Present'. In Partha Chatterjee and Anjan Ghosh (eds), *History and the Present*, 1–23. New Delhi: Permanent Black.

———. 2006b. *The Politics of the Governed: Reflections on Popular Politics in Most of the World*. New Delhi: Permanent Black.

———. 2008a. 'Introduction: History in the Vernacular'. In Raziuddin Aquil and Partha Chatterjee (eds), *History in the Vernacular*, 1–24. Ranikhet: Permanent Black.

———. 2008b. 'The Nation and its Women'. In *The Partha Chatterjee Omnibus: Nationalist Thought and the Colonial World, The Nation and Its Fragments, A Possible India*. New Delhi: Oxford University Press.

———. 2008c. *The Partha Chatterjee Omnibus: Nationalist Thought and the Colonial World, The Nation and Its Fragments, A Possible India*. New Delhi: Oxford University Press.

———. 2009. 'The Nationalist Resolution of the Women's Question'. In Kumkum Sangari and Sudesh Vaid (eds), *Recasting Women: Essays in Colonial History*, 233–53. New Delhi: Zubaan.

Chatterjee, Partha, and Pradeep Jeganathan (eds). 2005. *Subaltern Studies XI: Community, Gender and Violence*. New Delhi: Permanent Black.

Chatterjee, Partha, and Anjan Ghosh (eds). 2006. *History and the Present*. New Delhi: Permanent Black.

Chelannur, Sasikumar. 2000. 'Pradhama Muslim Pathradhipa Haleema Beevi' ('Haleema Beevi: The First Muslim Woman Editor'). *Aaraamam* March, 7–11.

Chendamangallur, Hameed. 2002. *Pardayude Manasastram* (*The Psychology of Purdah*). Thiruvananthapuram: Melinda.

———. 2010. 'Pothusammathikalile Chathikkuzhikal' ('Pitfalls in Accepted Norms'). 16 May, 8–19.

Cherif, Mustapha. 2008. *Islam and the West: A Conversation with Jacques Derrida*, Teresa Lavender Fagan (trans.). Chicago: University of Chicago Press.

Cherian, P. J. (ed.). 1999. *Perspectives on Kerala History: The Second Millennium: Kerala State Gazetteer*, Vol. 2, Part 2. Thiruvananthapuram: Kerala Gazetteers.

Chernilo, Daniel. 2007. *A Social Theory of the Nation-State: The Political Forms of Modernity Beyond Methodological Nationalism*. London: Routledge.

Childers, Erskine B. 2002. *The West and Islam: Amnesia and Antagonism*. Kedah Darul Aman: TERAS.

Cooke, Miriam. 2001. *Women Claim Islam: Creating Islamic Feminism through Literature*. New York: Routledge.

Cooper, Elizabeth. 1983. *The Harim and the Purdah: Studies of Oriental Women*. New Delhi: Bimla Publishing House.

Dabashi, Hamid. 2009. *Post-Orientalism: Knowledge and Power in Time of Terror*. New Burnswick: Transaction.

Dale, Stephen Frederic. 1980. *Islamic Society on the South Asian Frontier: The Mappilas of Malabar: 1498–1922*. Oxford: Clarendon.

———. 2007. 'Trade, Conversion, and the Growth of the Islamic Community in Kerala'. In Rowena Robinson and Sathianathan Clarke (eds), *Religious Conversion in India: Modes, Motivations and Meanings*. New Delhi: Oxford University Press.

Das, Kamala. 1999. 'I Am Allah's Handmaiden', Interview with Venu Menon. *Outlook*, 27 December.

———. 2009. *My Story*. New Delhi: HarperCollins.

DeLamotte, Eugenia C., Natania Meeker, and Jean F. O'Barr (eds). 1997. *Women Imagine Change: A Global Anthology of Women's Resistance from 600 B. C. E. to Present*. New York: Routledge.

Department of Archaeology, Government of Kerala. n.d. *Arakal Kettu*. Thiruvananthapuram: Department. of Archaeology.

———. n.d. *Arakkal Museum: Kannur*. Thiruvanthapuram: Department of Archaeology.

Derrida, Jacques. 1998. 'Monolingualism of the Other; or, The Prosthesis of Origin'. In *Cultural Memory in the Present*, Patrick Mensah (trans.). Stanford: Stanford University Press.

Desai, Neera, and Usha Thakkar. 2007. *Women in Indian Society*. New Delhi: National Book Trust.

de Souza, Eunice (ed.). 2004. *Purdah: An Anthology*. New Delhi: Oxford University Press.

Devasia, Anitha. 1999. 'A Translation of O. Chandumenon's Indulekha (1889) with a Critical Introduction'. Ph.D. thesis, submitted to CIEFL, Hyderabad.

Devika, J. (ed. and trans.). 2005. *Her-Self: Early Writings on Gender by Malayalee Women: 1898–1938*. Kolkata: Stree.

———. 2007. *En-gendering Individuals: The Language of Re-forming in Twentieth Century Keralam*. Hyderabad: Orient Longman.

Devika, J. 2010. Response to Jenny Rowena and K. Ashraf, 'Rayana R. Khazi and The Specter of Religious Fundamentalism in the Kerala Public Sphere'. *Kafila.org*. Available at http://kafila.org/2010/09/22/rayana-r-khazi-and-the-specter-of-religious-fundamentalism-in-the-kerala-public-sphere-jenny-rowena-kashraf/#comment-11236.

———. 2017. 'The Hadiya Case Represents the Crossroads Between a Sociological Trend of Muslim Alienation and Self-Assertion by Kerala's Youth'. *The Caravan*.

Doi, Abdur Rahman I. 2006. *Women in Shariah*. Kuala Lumpur: A. S. Noordeen, 5e.

Dube, Leela. 1994. 'Conflict and Compromise: Devolution and Disposal of Property in a Matrilineal Muslim Society'. *Economic and Political Weekly* 21 May, 1273–84.

———. 1995. 'Matriliny and Islam in Lakshadweep'. *India International Centre Quarterly* 22 (2–3), 169–80.

Dube, Saurabh (ed.). 2007. *Historical Anthropology*. New Delhi: Oxford University Press.

Dutta, Madhusree, Flavia Agnes, and Neera Adarkar (eds). 1996. *The Nation, the State and Indian Identity*. Calcutta: Samya.

Eaton, Richard M. 2002. *The Rise of Islam and the Bengal Frontier, 1204–1760*. New Delhi: Oxford University Press.

Eck, Diana L., and Devaki Jain (eds). 1986. *Speaking of Faith: Cross-Cultural Perspectives on Women, Religion and Social Change*. New Delhi: Kali for Women.

Editorial. *Mappila Review* October 1945, 29–30.

El Saadawi, Nawal. 1986. 'Towards Women's Power, Nationally and Internationally'. In Diana L. Eck and Devaki Jain (eds), *Speaking of Faith: Cross-Cultural Perspectives on Women, Religion and Social Change*, 248–63. New Delhi: Kali for Women.

Esposito, John L. (ed.). 1983. *Voices of Resurgent Islam*. New York: Oxford University Press.

Esposito, John L., and John O. Voll. 2001. *Makers of Contemporary Islam*. Oxford: Oxford University Press.

Esposito, John L., John O. Voll, and Osman Bakar (eds). 2008. *Asian Islam in the 21st Century*. Oxford: Oxford University Press.

Farouqui, Ather (ed.). 2009. *Muslims and Media Images: News versus Views*. New Delhi: Oxford University Press.

Fernea, Elizabeth Warnock. 1998. *In Search of Islamic Feminism: One Woman's Global Journey*. New York: Anchor.

Forbes, Geraldine. 2004. *Women in Modern India. The New Cambridge History of India*, Vol. 4. Cambridge: Cambridge University Press.

———. 2008. *Women in Colonial India: Essays on Politics, Medicine, and Historiography*. New Delhi: Chronicle.

Foucault, Michel. 2003a. *The Birth of the Clinic: An Archaeology of Medical Perception*, A. M. Sheridan (trans.). London: Routledge.

———. 2003b. *The Essential Foucault: Selections from The Essential Works of Foucault 1954–1984*, Paul Rabinow and Nikolas Rose (eds). New York: New.

———. 2005. *The Hermeneutics of the Subject: Lectures at the College de France, 1981–82*, Frederic Gros (ed.), Graham Burchell (trans.). New York: Palgrave Macmillan.

Freedman, Estelle B. (ed.). 2007. *The Essential Feminist Reader*. New York: The Modern Library.

Freeman, Rich. 2004. 'Genre and Society: The Literary Culture of Premodern Kerala'. In Sheldon Pollock (ed.), *Literary Cultures in History: Reconstructions from South Asia*, 437–500. New Delhi: Oxford University Press.

Fruzzetti, Lina, and Sirpa Tenhunen (eds). 2006. *Culture, Power, and Agency: Gender in Indian Ethnography*. Kolkata: Stree.

Galletti, A., A. J. Van Der Burg, and P. Groot (trans.). 1911. *The Dutch in Malabar*. Madras.

Gangadharan, M. 2006. 'Introduction'. In K. K. Muhamed Abdul Kareem (compiled), *Makthi Thangalude Sampoorna Krithikal (The Complete Works of Makthi Thangal)*. Kozhikode: Vachanam.

———. 2007. *Mappila Padanangal*. Kozhikode: Vachanam, 2e.

———. 2008. *The Malabar Rebellion*. Kottayam: DC.

———. 2010. 'Orotta Islam; Vere Vere Muslingal' ('One Islam: Diverse Muslims'). Interview with Thaha Madai. *Mathrubhoomi* 23 May, 5–9.

Ganesh, K. N. 1997. *Keralathinte Innalekal (Yesterdays of Kerala)*. Thiruvananthapuram: Department of Cultural Publications, Government of Kerala, rev. edn.

———. 2002. *Kerala Samooha Padanangal (Studies in Kerala Society)*. Pathanamthitta: Prasakthi.

Ghosh, Anindita (ed.). 2007. *Behind the Veil: Resistance, Women, and Everyday in Colonial South Asia*. Ranikhet: Permanent Black.

Gilman, Charlotte Perkins. 1980. *Herland*. New York: Dover.

Golley, Nawar Al-Hassan (ed.). 2007. *Arab Women's Lives Retold: Exploring Identity through Writing*. New York: Syracuse University Press.

Gopakumar, P. F. 2008. *Keraleeya Navodhanam (Renaissance in Kerala)*. Thiruvananthapuram: Chintha, 2e.

Gopalakrishnan, P. K. 1984. *Keralathinte Samskarika Charithram (Cultural History of Kerala)*. Thiruvananthapuram: Kerala Bhasha Institute, 2e.

Gopalankutty, K. 2007. *Malabar Padanangal*. Thiruvananthapuram: Kerala Bhasha Institute.

Gopal Panikar. 2006. *Malabar and its Folk*. New Delhi: Asian Educational Services 2e, rev.

Gottschalk, Peter. 2001. *Beyond Hindu and Muslim: Multiple Identity in Narratives from Village India*. New Delhi: Oxford University Press.

Gough, E. Kathleen. 1955. 'Female Initiation Rites on the Malabar Coast'. *The Journal of the Royal Anthropological Institute of Great Britain and Ireland* 85 (1–2), 45–80.

Govindapilla, P. 2004. *Kerala Navodhanam: Oru Marxist Veekshanam (Reformation in Kerala: A Marxist Perspective)*. Thiruvananthapuram: Chinta, 2e.

———. 2009. *Kerala Navodhanam*, Vol 2. *Mathacharyar Mathanishedhikal (Kerala Renaissance*, Vol. 2, Religious Preceptors, Religious Rebels). Thiruvananthapuram: Chinta, 2e.

Greene, Gayle, and Coppelia Kahn (eds). 1993. *Changing Subjects: The Making of Feminist Literary Criticism*. London: Routledge.

Grosby, Steven. 2007. *Nationalism: A Very Short Introduction*. New Delhi: Oxford University Press.

Gundert, Hermann. 1992. *Keralolpathiyum Mattum*, Introduction by Scaria Zacharia. Kottayam: DC.

Gupta, Charu. 2008. *Sexuality, Obscenity, Community: Women, Muslims, and the Hindu Public in Colonial India*. New Delhi: Permanent Black.

Habib, Irfan. 2007a. *Essays in Indian History; Towards a Marxist Perception*. New Delhi: Tulika.

——— (ed.). 2007b. *Religion in Indian History*. New Delhi: Tulika.

Haleema Beevi, K. M. 1959a. 'Anubhavangalilekku Orethinottam' ('A Cursory Glance at My Experiences'). *Al Manar Special Issue* 5 September, 87–90.

———. 1959b. 'Kochin Vanitha Sammelanam' ('Cochin Women's Conference'). *Al Manar* November, 197–200.

———. 1960a. 'Sthreeyekkurichulla Chintha' ('Thoughts about Women'). *Al Manar Visheshal Prathi* September, 172–75.

———. 1960b. 'Samudaya Sthapanngaleyum Prasthanangaleyum Varthedukkuvanum Valarthiyedukkuvanum Sthreekalkkulla Kazhivu Vanpichathanu' ('Women Have Great Prowess to Create and Foster Institutions and Movements of the Community'). *Al Manar* 5 November, 343–50.

———. 1978. 'Njangale Avaganikkunnathu Nallathinalla' ('It Won't Be Good to Avoid Us'). *Kripa* July, 30–34.

————. 1995. 'Oru Pathradhipayude Ormakal' ('Memories of an Editor'). Interview with Basheer Randathani. *Chandrika Azhchappathippu* 8 July, 6–9.

Halley, Janet. 2008. *Split Decisions: How and Why to Take a Break from Feminism*. New Jersey: Princeton University Press.

Hasan, Mushirul. 2007a. 'Introduction'. In Mushirul Hasan, Barbara Daly Metcalf, and Rafiuddin Ahmed, *India's Muslims: An Omnibus*, ix–xxiv. New Delhi: Oxford University Press.

————. 2007b. *Legacy of a Divided Nation: India's Muslims since Independence*. In Mushirul Hasan, Barbara Daly Metcalf, and Rafiuddin Ahmed, *India's Muslims: An Omnibus*. New Delhi: Oxford University Press.

————. 2010. 'The Muslim Break Away'. In Sekhar Bandyopadhyay (ed.), *Nationalist Movements in India: A Reader*, 159–72. New Delhi: Oxford University Press.

Hasan, Mushirul, and M. Asaduddin (eds). 2002. *Image and Representation: Stories of Muslim Lives in India*. New Delhi: Oxford University Press.

Hasan, S. Nurul. 2008. *Religion, State, and Society in Medieval India: Collected Works of S. Nurul Hasan*, Satish Chandra (ed.). New Delhi: Oxford University Press.

Hasan, Zoya. 1999. 'Gender Politics, Legal Reform, and the Muslim Community in India'. In Patricia Jeffery, and Amrita Basu (eds), *Resisting the Sacred and the Secular: Women's Activism and Politicized Religion in South Asia*, 71–88. New Delhi: Kali for Women.

Hasan, Zoya, and Ritu Menon. 2005. 'Introduction'. In Zoya Hasan and Ritu Menon (eds), *In a Minority: Essays on Muslim Women in India*, 1–17. New Delhi: Oxford University Press.

————. 2006. *Unequal Citizens: A Study of Muslim Women in India*. New Delhi: Oxford University Press.

———— (eds). 2005. *In a Minority: Essays on Muslim Women in India*. New Delhi: Oxford University Press.

Hashim, Iman. 1999. 'Reconciling Islam and Feminism'. *Gender and Development* 7 (1), 7–14.

Heath, Jennifer (ed.). 2008. *The Veil: Women Writers on its History, Lore, and Politics*. Berkeley: University of California Press.

Heredia, Rudolf C. 2007. *Changing Gods: Rethinking Conversion in India*. New Delhi: Penguin.

Hidayatullah, Aysha A. 2014. *Feminist Edges of the Qur'an*. Oxford: Oxford University Press.

Hill, Monica. 1979. 'The Iranian Revolution and Women's Rights'. Available at https://socialism.com/fs-article/the-iranian-revolution-and-womens-rights/.

Hirschkind, Charles, and Saba Mahmood. 2002. 'Feminism, the Taliban, and Politics of Counter-Insurgency'. *Anthropological Quarterly* 75 (2), 339–54.

Hossain, Rokeya Sakhawat. 1993. *Sultana's Dream and Selections from the Secluded Ones*. New York: Feminist Press.

Hussain, Asaf. 1988. 'Islamic Awakening in the Twentieth Century: An Analysis and Selective Review of the Literature'. *Third World Quarterly* 10 (2), 1005–23.

Hussain, K. T. 2008. *Kerala Muslingal: Adhinivesa Virudha Porattathinte Prathyayasasthram* (*Muslims of Kerala: The Ideology of Anti-Imperialist Struggle*). Kozhikode: Islamic.

Hussain, Moulavi Ashfaq. 1935. *Rakthasrukkal* (*Tears of Blood*), Abdulla Alyamani (trans.). Kochi: Janaki.

Hussain, Shamshad. 2009 *Neunapakshathinum Lingapadavikumidayil: Keralathile Muslim Sthreekalekurichulla Padanam* (*Between Minority and Gender Justice: A Study on the Muslim Women of Kerala*). Thiruvananthapuram: Kerala Bhasha Institute.

Ibrahim Kunju, A. P. 1978. 'Islam in Kerala'. *Journal of Kerala Studies* 8 (1–4), 593–602.

———. 1981. 'Social Change Among the Muslims of Kerala'. *Journal of Kerala Studies* 11 (1–4), 199–204.

———. 1989. *The Mappila Muslims of Kerala: Their History and Culture*. Thiruvnanthapuram: Sandhya.

———. 2007. *Medieval Kerala*. Thiruvananthapuram: International Centre for Kerala Studies, University of Kerala.

Innes, C. A. 1997. *Malabar Gazetteer*, Vols 1 and 2, F. B. Evans (ed.). Thiruvananthapuram: Kerala Gazetteers.

International Solidarity Network. 2003. *Knowing Our Rights: Women, Family, Laws and Customs in the Muslim World*. New Delhi: Zubaan.

Ivekovic, Rada, and Julie Mostov (eds). 2004. *From Gender to Nation*. New Delhi: Zubaan.

Jacob, Alexander. 1992. 'Kannur'. *Maithree Mela*, 26–40.

Jameela, Nalini. 2005. *The Autobiography of a Sex Worker*, J. Devika (trans.). Chennai: Westland Books Pvt. Ltd.

Jayawardena, Kumari. 1986. *Feminism and Nationalism in the Third World*. London: Zed.

Jeffery, Patricia. 1999a. 'Agency, Activism, and Agendas'. In Patricia Jeffery and Amrita Basu (eds), *Resisting the Sacred and the Secular: Women's Activism and Politicized Religion in South Asia*, 107–22. New Delhi: Kali for Women.

Jeffery, Patricia, and Amrita Basu (eds). 1999b. *Resisting the Sacred and the Secular: Women's Activism and Politicized Religion in South Asia*. New Delhi: Kali for Women.

Jeffrey, Robin. 1978. 'Matriliny, Marxism, and the Birth of the Communist Party in Kerala'. *The Journal of Asian Studies* 38 (1), 77–98.

———. 1993. *Politics, Women and Well Being: How Kerala Became 'A Model'*. New Delhi: Oxford University Press.

———. 1994. *The Decline of Nair Dominance: Society and Politics in Travancore: 1847–1908*. New Delhi: Manohar.

———. 2005. 'Legacies of Matriliny: The Place of Women and the "Kerala Model"'. *Pacific Affairs* 77 (4), 647–64.

John, Mary. 2009. 'Reframing Globalisation: Perspectives from the Women's Movement'. *Economic and Political Weekly* 44 (10), 46–49.

Kabeer, Humayun. 1995. *Muslim Rashtreeyam 1906–1947* (*Muslim Politics, 1906–1947*), P. P. Umer Farooq (trans.). Kozhikode: Aksharam.

Kadakkal, Ashraf A. (ed.). 2007. *Sacharinte Keralaparisaram* (*Kerala in the Context of the Sachar Report*). Kozhikode: Other.

Kandiyoti, Deniz. 1991. 'Women, Islam and the State'. *Middle East Report* November–December, 9–14.

Kannabiran, Kalpana. 2014. 'Annihilation by Caste: Lessons from Budaun and Beyond'. *Economic and Political Weekly* 49 (26–27), 14.

Kannabiran, Kalpana, and Vasant Kannabiran, 1991. 'Caste and Gender: Understanding Dynamics of Power and Violence'. *Economic and Political Weekly* 14 September.

Karam, Azza M. 1998. *Women, Islamisms and the State: Contemporary Feminisms in Egypt*. London: Palgrave.

Karat, Brinda. 1995. 'Uniformity vs. Equality: The Concept of Uniform Civil Code'. *Frontline* November, 82–84.

Kareem, C. K. 1976. *Kerala Charithra Vicharam* (*Musings on Kerala History*). Thiruvananthapuram: Charithram.

———. 1983. *Muslim Samudayavum Samskaravum* (*Islamic Society and Culture*). Thiruvananthapuram: Charithram.

———. 1997. *Keralathinteyum Kerala Muslingaludeyum Charithram* (*History of Kerala and Muslims*). Edapally: Charithram.

Kathirikoya, N. (ed.). 2009. *Mappila Kaladarsanam* (*The Philosophy of Mappila Art*). Thrissur: Kerala Sahitya Akademi.

Katrak, Ketu R. 1992. 'Indian Nationalism, Gandhian "Satyagraha", and Representations of Female Sexuality'. In Andrew Parker, et al. (eds), *Nationalisms and Sexualities*, 395–406. New York: Routledge.

Kazim, Lubna (ed.). 2005. *A Woman of Substance: The Memoirs of Begum Khurshid Mizra (1918–1989)*. New Delhi: Zubaan.

Khadeejakunji, E. 1932. 'Abalakalude Rakshithavu' ('Guardian of the Helpless'). *Isha-Ath* 3 (1–2), 1–5.

Khadiri, Shamsulla. 1954. *Pracheena Malabar* (*Ancient Malabar*), V. Abdul Khayoom (trans.). Kozhikode: Bushra.

Khaldun, Ibn. 2008. *Muquaddima*, Muttanisseril M. Koyakutty (trans.). Kottayam: DC.

Khan, Nyla Ali. 2009. *Islam, Women and Violence in Kashmir: Between India and Pakistan*. New Delhi: Tulika.

Khan, Qadir Husain. 1910. *South Indian Musalmans: A Dissertation*. Madras: Brahmavadin.

Korieh, Chima J., and Philomina Okeke-Ihejirika (eds). 2009. *Gendering Global Transformations: Gender, Culture, Race, and Identity*. New York: Routledge.

Kosambi, Meera (ed. and trans.). 2008. *Feminist Vision or 'Treason Against Men'? Kashibai Kanitkar and the Engendering of Marathi Literature*. Ranikhet: Permanent Black.

Koya, S. M. Mohamed. 1983. *Mappilas of Malabar: Studies in Social and Cultural History*. Thiruvananthapuram: Sandhya.

K. P. 1970. 'Kunjachumma'. *Chandrika* 14 May, 18.

Kumar, Sukrita, Paul, and Malashri Lal (eds). 2009. *Speaking for Myself: An Anthology of Asian Women's Writing*. New Delhi: Penguin.

Kumar, Udaya. 2008. 'Autobiography as a Way of Writing History: Personal Narratives from Kerala and the Inhabitation of Modernity'. In Raziuddin Aquil and Partha Chatterjee (eds), *History in the Vernacular*, 418–48. Ranikhet: Permanent Black.

Kunjan Pilla, Ilamkulam. 1971. *Kerala Charithrathile Iruladanja Edukal* (*The Dark Folios of Kerala History*). Kottayam: SPCS.

Kunjamu, A. P. 2008. 'Muslim Woman Reads Islam and Life'. In Khadeeja Mumtas, *Barsa*. Kerala: DC Books.

Kunjahammed, K. E. N. 2000. 'Varenya Navodhaanathinte Athirukal: Varenya Samudaayangalile Navodhaanavum Malayala Sahithyavum' ('The Boundaries of the Elite Renaissance: The Renaissance in Elite Communities and Malayalam Literature'). In M. N. Vijayan (ed.), *Nammude Sahithyam Namuude Samooham, 1901–2000*, Vol. 2, 41–117. Thrissur: Sahitya Akademi.

Kunjimuhammed, P. 1957. 'Abalayude Vilapam' ('The Wail of the Helpless'). *Al Manar* 5 February, 262.

Kunjiraman Nambiar, T. H. (comp.). 2007. *Mappilaramayanavum Nadanpattukalum*. Kottayam: DC.

Kunjumuhammed, P. T. 2006. 'Malayali Muslim Innum Innaleyum' ('Malayali Muslim: Today and Yesterday'). Interview with Rafeeq Ahmed. *Mathrubhoomi Weekly* 19 November, 73–77.

Kurup, K. K. N. n. d. *Dutchukarum Adirajavum Kannur Saint Angelo Kottayum* (*The Dutch, Adirajah and the St. Angelo Fort in Kannur*) Kozhikode: Malabar Institute for Research and Development.

———. 1995. *Adhunika Keralam: Charitra Gaveshana Prabandhangal* (*Modern Kerala: Research Papers in History*). Thiruvananthapuram: Kerala Bhasha Institute.

———. 1998 *Nationalism and Social Change: The Role of Malayalam Literature*. Thrissur: Kerala Sahitya Akademi.

———. 2002. *The Ali Rajas of Cannanore*. Calicut: Publication Division, University of Calicut.

———. 2006. *The Legacy of Islam (Kerala)*. Kannur: Samayam.

———. 2009. *Thalasseriyile Keyimar* (*Keyis of Thalassery*). Thiruvananthapuram: Kerala Bhasha Institute.

Kusuman, K. K. (ed.). 2003. *Issues in Kerala Historiography*. Thiruvananthapuram: International Centre for Kerala Studies, University of Kerala.

Kutty, V. M. 2007. *Mappilapattu: Charithravum Varthamanavum* (*Mappilappattu: Past and Present*). Thiruvananthapuram: Kerala Bhasha Institute.

Kutty, V. M. M. n. d. *Munambam Muthu: Albhuthakaramathil Alpam* (*The Pearl of Munambam: A Little from its Miracles*).

K. V. M. 1967. *Keralam Videseeyarude Drishtiyil* (*Foreign Perspectives on Kerala*). Calicut: P. K. Brothers, 2e.

Lateef, Shahida. 1990. *Muslim Women in India: Political and Private Realities: 1890s–1980s*. New Delhi: Kali for Women.

Latheef, N. K. A. 1994. *Mappila Saili* (*Mappila Style*). Kochi: Namaskara.

Layoun, Mary. 1992. 'Telling Spaces: Palestinian Women and the Engendering of National Narratives'. In Andrew Parker, et al. (eds), *Nationalisms and Sexualities*, 407–23. New York: Routledge.

Lichter, Ida. 2009. *Muslim Women Reformers: Inspiring Voices against Oppression*. New York: Prometheus.

Lloyd, Moya. 2005. *Beyond Identity Politics: Feminism, Power and Politics*. London: Sage.

Logan, William. 2004. *Malabar Manual*, 2 vols. New Delhi: Asian Educational Services.

Ludden, David (ed.). 2005. *Reading Subaltern Studies: Critical History, Contested Meaning, and the Globalisation of South Asia*. New Delhi: Permanent Black.

Madan, T. N. (ed.). 2008. *Religion in India*. New Delhi: Oxford University Press.

Madhavan Nair, K. 2007. *Malabar Kalapam* (*Malabar Rebellion*). Kozhikode: Mathrubhoomi, 4e.

Madayi, Thaha. 2009. 'Matham Mariya Kutty' ('The Converted Kid'). *Pachakuthira* October, 44–48.

Mahmood, Saba. 2001. 'Feminist Theory, Embodiment and the Docile Agent: Some Reflections of the Egyptian Islamic Revival'. *Cultural Anthropology* 16 (2), 202–36.

———. 2004. 'Women's Agency within Feminist Historiography'. *The Journal of Religion* 84 (4), October, 573–79.

———. 2005. *Politics of Piety: The Islamic Revival and the Feminist Subject.* Princeton: Princeton University Press.

———. 2006. 'Secularism, Hermeneutics and Empire: The Politics of Islamic Reformation'. *Public Culture* 18 (2), 323–47.

———. 2008a. 'Interview'. In Nermeen Sheikh (ed.), *The Present as History: Critical Perspectives on Global Power*, 148–71. New Delhi: Stanza.

———. 2008b. 'Is Critique Secular?' *Public Culture* 20 (3), 447–52.

———. 2008c. 'Secular Imperatives'. *Public Culture* 20 (3), 461–65.

———. 2009. 'Religious Reason and Secular Affect: An Incommensurable Divide?' *Critical Inquiry* 35 (4), 836–62.

Mai, Mukhtar. 2007. *In the Name of Honour: A Memoir*, Linda Coverdale (trans.). London: Virago.

Majid, Anouar. 2006. 'The Politics of Feminism in Islam'. In Therese Saliba, Carolyn Allen, and Judith A. Howard (eds), *Gender, Politics and Islam*, 53–94. Hyderabad: Orient Longman.

Malieckal, Bindu. 2005. 'Muslims, Matriliny, and *A Midsummer Night's Dream*: European Encounters with the Mappilas of Malabar, India'. *Muslim World* 95 (2), 297–316.

Mamdani, Mahmood. 2006. *Good Muslim, Bad Muslim: Islam, the USA, and the Global War Against Terror.* New Delhi: Permanent Black.

Mandalamkunnu, Sainudheen. 2007. *Kerala Muslim Navodhanam: Charithram, Varthamanam, Vimarshanam (Muslim Renaissance in Kerala: History, Present, Critique).* Thrissur: Kaizen.

Mani, Lata. 2009. 'Contentious Traditions: The Debate on *Sati* in Colonial India'. In Kumkum Sangari, and Sudesh Vaid (eds), *Recasting Women: Essays in Colonial History*, 88–126. New Delhi: Zubaan.

Marakkar, A. M. 1952. 'Islamil Sthreekalkkulla Sthanam' ('Status of Women in Islam'). *Al Farooq* March, 31–34.

Mathew, George. 1989. *Communal Road to a Secular Kerala.* New Delhi: Concept.

Maulavi, K. M. 1953. 'Sthree Vidhyabhyasam'. ('Women's Education). *Ansari, Nabidina Visheshaal Prathi* 15 November, 10–12.

Maulavi, Vakkom. 1918. 'Nammude Sthreekal' ('Our Women'). *Al Islam* April, 27–30.

———. 1920. 'Aamukham: Sthree Purusha Bandham' ('Introduction: Man-Woman Relationship'). In Shaykh Mushir Hosain Khidwai, *Sthreekal Islam Mathathil* (*Women Under Islam*), K. Peer Muhammed and M. Ahmedkannu (trans.), 1–9. Kozhikode: Islamic Grandhaavali.

Mayaram, Shail. 2006. *Against History, Against State: Counter-Perspectives from the Margins*. New Delhi: Permanent Black.

Mayaram, Shail, M. S. S. Pandian, and Ajay Skaria (eds). 2005. *Subaltern Studies XII: Muslims, Dalits, and the Fabrications of History*. New Delhi: Permanent Black.

Menon, I. K. K. 1998. *Kunhali Marakkar*. Calicut: Mythri.

Menon, M. P. S. 2005. *Malabar Samaram: M. P. Narayana Menonum Sahapravarthkarum* (*Malabar Rebellion: M. P. Narayana Menon and his Colleagues*) Kozhikode: Islamic Grandhaavali, 2e.

Menon, Nivedita. 2004. *Recovering Subversion: Feminist Politics Beyond the Law*. New Delhi: Permanent Black.

——— (ed.). 2001. *Gender and Politics in India*. New Delhi: Oxford University Press.

Mernissi, Fatima. 1993a. *The Forgotten Queens of Islam*. Minnesota: University of Minnesota Press.

———. 1993b. *Women and Islam: An Historical and Theological Enquiry*, Mary Jo Lakeland (trans.). New Delhi: Kali for Women.

———. 2002. *Islam and Democracy: Fear of the Modern World*, Mary Jo Lakeland (trans.). New York: Basic, 2e.

Metcalf, Barbara D. 2006. *Islamic Contestations: Essays on Muslims in India and Pakistan*. New Delhi: Oxford University Press.

———. 2007. 'Islamic Revival in British India: Deoband, 1860–1900'. In Mushirul Hasan, Barbara Daly Metcalf, and Rafiuddin Ahmed (eds), *India's Muslims: An Omnibus*. New Delhi: Oxford University Press.

Miller, Roland E. 1976. *Mappila Muslims of Kerala: A Study in Islamic Trends*. Bombay: Orient Longman.

Minault, Gail. 1999. *Secluded Scholars: Women's Education and Muslim Social Reform in Colonial India*. New Delhi: Oxford University Press.

——— (trans.). 1986. *Voices of Silence: English Translation of Khwaja Altaf Hussain Hali's Majalis-un-Nissa and Chup ki Dad*. Delhi: Chanakya.

Moghadam, Valentine M. 1992. 'Revolution, Islam and Women: Sexual Politics in Iran and Afghanistan'. In Andrew Parker, et al. (eds), *Nationalisms and Sexualities*, 424–46. New York: Routledge.

———. 2003. *Modernizing Women: Gender and Social Change in the Middle East*. London: Lynne Rienner, 2e.

———. 2006. 'Islamic Feminism and its Discontents: Towards a Resolution of the Debate'. In Therese Saliba, Carolyn Allen, and Judith A. Howard (eds), *Gender, Politics and Islam*, 15–52. Hyderabad: Orient Longman.

Moghissi, Haideh. 2002. *Feminism and Islamic Fundamentalism: The Limits of Postmodern Analysis*. London: Zed.

Mohamad, J. Raja. 2004. *Maritime History of the Coromandel Muslims: A Socio-Historical Study on the Tamil Muslims 1750–1900*. Chennai: Director of Museums, Govt. Museum.

Mohamed, K. M. 1981. 'Influence of Hinduism on the Muslims of Kerala'. *Journal of Kerala Studies* 2 (1–4), 111–18.

Mohammed Ali, V. 2003. *Arabisahithyam* (*Arabic Literature*). Thiruvananthapuram: Kerala Bhasha Institute, 3e.

Mohammed, Sayed P. A. 1962. *Kerala Muslim Charithram* (*History of Kerala Muslims*). Kozhikode: Sandhya.

Mohammed, U. 2007. *Educational Empowerment of Kerala Muslims: A Socio-Historical Perspective*. Calicut: Other.

Mohan, Sanal. 2008. '"Searching for Old Histories": Social Movements and the Project of Writing History in Twentieth-Century Kerala'. In Raziuddin Aquil and Partha Chatterjee (eds), *History in the Vernacular*, 357–90. Ranikhet: Permanent Black.

Mohanty, Chandra Talpade. 2006. *Feminism Without Borders: Decolonizing Theory, Practising Solidarity*. New Delhi: Zubaan.

Moomin, A. H. n. d. *Towards Islam*. Colombo: Diamond.

More, J. B. P. 2004. *Muslim Identity, Print Culture and the Dravidian Factor in Tamil Nadu*. Hyderabad, Orient Longman.

Moulavi, Vakkom. 1918. 'Nammude Sthreekal' ('Our Women'). *Al Islam* April, 27–30.

———. 1992. *Vakkom Moulaviyude Deepika Otta Valiathil* (*Vakkom Moulavi's Deepika in One Volume*). Thiruvananthapuram: Vakkom Moulavi Foundation.

Moya, Paula M. L., and Michael R. Hames-Garcia (eds) 2003. *Reclaiming Identity: Realist Theory and the Predicament of Postmodernism*. Hyderabad: Orient Longman.

Muhammadukannu, K. 1927. 'Muslim Sthreekalum Vidhyabhyasavum' ('Muslim Women and Education'). *Muslim Mithram* 1 (7), 208–13.

Muhammadali, V. P. 2007. *Mappilappattukal Noottandukaliloode*. Kottayam: Current.

Muhammad Koya, P. A. 1945. 'Sevika' ('The Woman in Social Service'). *Mappila Review* August, 4–6.

Muhammad Maulavi, M. Sheykh. 1959. 'Shree Vidhyabhyaasam'. *Al Manar* 5 October, 124.

Muhammed Kunji, P. K. 2008. *Muslimingalum Kerala Samskaravum* (*Muslims and Kerala Culture*). Thrissur: Kerala Sahitya Akademi, 3e.

Muhammed Kutty, K. M. 1959. 'Sthree: Padaviyum Pravarthna Rangavum' ('Woman; Status and Career'). *Al Manar* 5 December, 209–12.

Muhammed, Shibu. 2007. *Charithrathinte Mudranangal: Malayala Pathrapravarthanathinte Vikasavum Parinamavum* (*The Imprints of History: The Growth and Evolution of Journalism in Malayalam*). Thiruvananthapuram: Kerala Bhasha Institute.

Mukhopadhyay, Maitrayee, and Shamin Meer. 2004. *Creating Voice and Carving Space: Redefining Governance from a Gender Perspective.* Amsterdam, KIT.

Mukhopadhyay, Swapna (ed.). 2007. *The Enigma of the Kerala Woman: A Failed Promise of Literacy.* New Delhi: Social Science Press.

'Mulappalinte Kootuthal Pradhanatha' ('The Greater Importance of Breast Feeding'). *Mappila Review* October 1945, 12–15.

Mumtas, Khadija. 2008. *Barsa.* Kottayam: DC.

————. 2011. 'Ummayude Neettiyezhuthanu Njan' ('I Am an Extension of My Mother'). Interview with Maina Umaiban. *Mathrubhoomi Weekly* 18 January, 22–28.

Nair, Lalitha. 1981. 'Abolition of Devadasi System in Kerala'. *Journal of Kerala Studies* 7 (1–4), 61–76.

Namboothiri, N. M. (ed.). 1998. *Vellayute Charithram* (*Vella's History*). Sukapuram: Vallathol Vidyapeedom.

Namboothiri, N. M., and P. K. Sivadas (eds). 2009. *Keralacharithrathinte Nattuvazhikal.* Kottayam: DC.

Nanda, Meera. 2005. *The Wrongs of the Religious Right: Reflections on Science, Secularism and Hindutva.* Gurgaon: Three Essays.

Narayanan, M. G. S. 1973. *Aspects of Aryanisation in Kerala.* Trivandrum: Kerala Historical Society.

Needham, Anuradha Dingwaney, and Rajeswari Sunderrajan (eds). 2007. *The Crisis of Secularism in India.* Ranikhet: Permanent Black.

Nicholson, Linda (ed.). 1997. *The Second Wave: A Reader in Feminist Theory.* New York: Routledge.

Nomani, Asra Q. 2007. *Standing Alone in Mecca: A Pilgrimage into the Heart of Islam.* New Delhi: HarperCollins.

Nora, Pierre. 2006. 'Between Memory and History: *Les Lieux de Memoire*'. In Robert M. Burns (ed.), *Historiography: Critical Concepts in Historical Studies*, Vol. 4, *Culture*, 284–302. London: Routledge.

Padmanabha Menon, K. P. 2001. *History of Kerala: Written in the Form of Notes on Visscher's Letters from Malabar*, T. K. Krishna Menon (ed.), 4 vols. New Delhi: Asian Educational Services.

Pampirikkunnu, Pradeepan. 2011. 'Nationalism, Modernity, Keralaness: A Subaltern Critique'. In K. Satyanarayna and Susie Tharu (eds), *No Alphabet in Sight*, 556–69. New Delhi: Penguin.

Pandey, Gyanendra. 2006. *The Construction of Communalism in Colonial North India*. New Delhi: Oxford University Press, 2e.

Pandey, Gyanendra, and Yunas Samad. 2007. *Fault Lines of Nationhood*. New Delhi: Roli.

Panikkar, K. N. 1992. *Against Lord and State: Religion and Peasant Uprisings in Malabar, 1836–1921*. Delhi: Oxford University Press.

Panikkassery, Velayudhan. 2007. *Kerala Charithra Padanangal (Treatises on Kerala History)*. Kottayam: Current, 2e.

———. 2008. *Keralolpathi*. Kottayam: Current.

Pannoor, Pakkar (ed.). 1998. *Mappila Kaladarpanam (The Mirror of Mappila Art)*. Kottayam: SPCS.

Parameshwaran, P. 2001. 'Pativrata Puraskaram Vasavadattakko?' ('Chastity Award to Vasavadatta?'). *Janmabhoomi*, 7 November.

Parasher-Sen, Aloka. 2007. *Subordinate and Marginal Groups in Early India*. New Delhi: Oxford University Press, 2e.

Parker, Andrew, et al. (eds). 1992. *Nationalisms and Sexualities*. New York: Routledge.

Perks, Robert, and Alistair Thomson (eds). 1998. *The Oral History Reader*. London: Routledge.

Pilla, K. K. 1994. 'Nayanmar, Ezhavarum Thiyyarum, Muslimgal' ('Nairs, Ezhavas and Thiyyas, Muslims'). *Vannerinadu* March, 108–10.

Pokker, P. K. 2008. 'Sthree Mukhavaranam Neekkumbol' ('When the Woman Unveils'). *Desabhimani* 14 September, 12–17.

Pollock, Sheldon (ed.). 2004. *Literary Cultures in History: Reconstructions from South Asia*. New Delhi: Oxford University Press.

Raghavan, Puthuppally. 2001. *Kerala Pathra Pravarthana Charithram (History of Newspapers in Kerala)*. Kottayam: DC.

Ramachandran Nair, Adoor K. K. 1969. *Kerala Charithasakalangal (Fragments of Kerala History)*, 2 vols. Kottayam: National.

Ramachandran Nair, Panmana. 2008. *Sampoorna Malayala Sahitya Charithram (A Comprehensive History of Malayalam Literature)*. Kottayam: Current.

Ramanunni, K. P. 2010. 'Ivarekkondu Enthanu Cheyyuka?' ('What Could be Done with These?'). *Pachakkuthira* February 32–38.

Randathani, Hussain. 2007. *Mappila Mulims: A Study on Society and Anti-Colonial Struggles*. Calicut: Other.

Rao, Anupama (ed.). 2005. *Gender and Caste: Issues in Contemporary Feminism*. London: Zed Books.

'Rasikasadanathile Vidhava Vivaham' ('Widow Remarriage at Rasikasadanam'). Editorial, *Isha-Ath* October 1934, 175–76.

Raveendran, T. K. 1975. 'Umayamma Rani (1677–1684 AD): The First Woman Ruler of Venad (Travencore)'. *Journal of Kerala Studies* 2, 17–23.

Ravi Varma, K. T. 2004. *Marumakkathayam: Gothra Marumakkathayavum Vadakkan Sampradayangalum* (*Matriliny: Tribal Matriliny and Northern Systems*). Thiruvananthapuram: Kerala Bhasha Institute.

Ray, Sangeeta. 2000. *En-Gendering India: Women and Nation in Colonial and Postcolonial Narratives*. London: Duke University Press.

Rege, Sharmila. 1998. 'Dalit Women Talk Differently: A Critique of "Difference" and Towards a Dalit Feminist Standpoint Position'. *Economic and Political Weekly* 33 (44), WS39–WS46

———. 2006. *Writing Caste, Writing Gender: Narrating Dalit Women's Testimonios*. New Delhi: Zubaan.

———. 2013. *Against the Madness of Manu: B. R. Ambedkar's Writings on Brahmanical Patriarchy*. New Delhi: Navayana.

Rizvi, S. Ameenul Hasan. 1983. *Muslim Personal Law and the Modern Bait-ul-Hikmat*. New Delhi: Crescent.

Robinson, Francis. 2008. *Islam, South Asia, and the West*. New Delhi: Oxford University Press.

Robinson, Rowena, and Sathianathan Clarke (eds). 2007. *Religious Conversion in India: Modes, Motivations, and Meanings*. New Delhi: Oxford University Press.

Roy, Anupama. 2005. *Gendered Citizenship: Historical and Conceptual Explorations*. Hyderabad: Orient Longman.

Roy, Arundhati. 2012. 'Interview with Channel 4', 22 December. Available on https://www.youtube.com/watch?v=tjzl4xAhrao.

Ruthven, Malise. 2006a. *Islam in the World*. Oxford: Oxford University Press, 3e.

———. 2006b. *Islam: A Very Short Introduction*. New Delhi: Oxford University Press.

Safi, Omid (ed.). 2006. *Progressive Muslims: On Justice, Gender and Pluralism*. Oxford: Oneworld.

Saidabeevi, B. S. 1954. 'Islamile Rashtra Samvidhanam' ('The Political System in Islam'). *Ansari* 5 November, 100–04.

Said, Edward W. 1994. *Culture and Imperialism*. London: Vintage.

———. 1995. *Orientalism: Western Conceptions of the Orient*. London: Penguin.

———. 1997. *Covering Islam: How the Media and the Experts Determine How to See the Rest of the World*. New York: Vintage, rev. edn.

Said Mohammed, P. A. 1996. *Kerala Muslim Charithram* (*History of Kerala Muslims*). Kozhikode: Al Huda, 5e.

Sainababeevi, A. 1927. 'Mangalam'. *Muslim Mithram* 1 (7).

Saliba, Therese. 2006. 'Introduction: Gender, Politics and Islam'. In Therese Saliba, Carolyn Allen, and Judith A. Howard (eds), *Gender, Politics and Islam*, 1–14. Hyderabad: Orient Longman.

Saliba, Therese, Carolyn Allen, and Judith A. Howard (eds). 2006. *Gender, Politics and Islam*. Hyderabad: Orient Longman.

Sangari, Kumkum. 1999. *Politics of the Possible: Essays on Gender, History, Narrative, Colonial English*. New Delhi: Tulika.

Sangari, Kumkum, and Uma Chakravarti (eds). 2001. *From Myths to Markets: Essays on Gender*. Shimla: Indian Institute of Advanced Studies.

Sangari, Kumkum, and Sudesh Vaid. 2009. 'Recasting Women: An Introduction'. In Kumkum Sangari and Sudesh Vaid (eds), *Recasting Women: Essays in Colonial History*, 1–26. New Delhi: Zubaan.

———— (eds). 2009. *Recasting Women: Essays in Colonial History*. New Delhi: Zubaan.

Sangster, Joan. 1998. 'Telling our Stories: Feminist Debates and the use of Oral History'. In Robert Perks and Alistair Thomsun (eds), *The Oral History Reader*, 87–100. New York: Routledge.

Sarkar, Mahua. 2008. *Visible Histories, Disappearing Women: Producing Muslim Womanhood in Late Colonial Bengal*. New Delhi: Zubaan.

Sarkar, Sumit. 2007. *Beyond Nationalist Frames: Relocating Postmodernism, Hindutva, History*. New Delhi: Permanent Black.

Sarkar, Sumit, and Tanika Sarkar (eds). 2007. *Women and Social Reform in Modern India: A Reader*, 2 vols. Ranikhet: Permanent Black.

Sarkar, Tanika. 1987. 'Nationalist Iconography: Image of Women in 19th Century Bengali Literature'. *Economic and Political Weekly* 21 November, 2011–15.

————. 1999a. 'Woman, Community, and Nation: A Historical Trajectory for Hindu Identity Politics'. In Patricia Jeffery and Amrita Basu (eds), *Resisting the Sacred and the Secular: Women's Activism and Politicized Religion in South Asia*, 89–106. New Delhi: Kali for Women.

————. 1999b. *Words to Win: The Making of Amar Jiban: A Modern Autobiography*. New Delhi: Kali for Women.

————. 2003. *Hindu Wife, Hindu Nation: Community, Religion and Cultural Nationalism*. New Delhi: Permanent Black.

Sarkar, Tanika, and Urvashi Butalia (eds). 1996. *Women and the Hindu Right: A Collection of Essays*. New Delhi: Kali for Women.

Seethi, K. M. 1950. 'Keralathile Muslim Pathra Pravarthanam' ('Muslim Journalism in Kerala'). *Chandrika Weekly* 15 July, 4.

Sen, Amiya P. 1993. *Hindu Revivalism in Bengal 1872–1905: Some Essays in Interpretation*. Delhi: Oxford University Press.

Sen, Indrani. 2008. *Woman and Empire: Representations in the Writings of British India (1858–1900)*. Hyderabad: Orient Longman.

———— (ed.). 2008. *Memsahibs' Writings: Colonial Narratives on Indian Women*. Hyderabad: Orient Longman.

Shaikh, Nermeen. 2008a. *The Present as History: Critical Perspectives on Contemporary Global Power*. New Delhi: Stanza.

————. 2008b. 'Interview with Saba Mahmood'. In *The Present as History: Critical Perspectives on Contemporary Global Power*, 148–71. New Delhi: Stanza.

————. 2008c. 'Interview with Talal Asad'. In *The Present as History: Critical Perspectives on Contemporary Global Power*, 205–24. New Delhi: Stanza.

————. 2008d. 'Interview with Abu-Lughod, Lila'. In *The Present as History: Critical Perspectives on Contemporary Global Power*, 143–47. New Delhi: Stanza.

Shariati, Ali. 1987. *Marxism and Other Western Fallacies: An Islamic Critique*, R. Campbell (trans.). Malappuram: Islamic Foundation.

————. n. d. *Religion versus Religion*, Laleh Bakhtiar (trans.). Kozhikode: Other.

Sherin B. S. 2010. 'Islamile Sthree' ('Women in Islam'). *Mathrubhumi* 29 August, 52–59.

————. 2018. 'Intersections of Justice: Gender, Law Reform and the Muslim Question in India'. *Women's Link* 22 (2).

Siddique, S. 2008. 'Beemapalli Uroos: Vivaranam, Visakalanam' ('Beemapalli Uroos: Description, Analysis'). M. Phil Dissertation, Sree Sankaracharya University of Sanskrit, Kalady.

Siddiqui, Kalim. 1988a. *Beyond the Muslim Nation-States*. Malappuram: Islamic Foundation.

————. 1988b. *The Islamic Movement: A Systems Approach*. Malappuram: Islamic Foundation.

————, et al. 1988. *The Islamic Revolution: Achievements, Obstacles and Goals*. Malappuram: Islamic Foundation.

Sivadasan, P. 2007. *Keralacharithram Sambhavangaliloode* (*History of Kerala Through Events*). Thiruvananthapuram: Chintha.

Sivasankaran Nair, K. (trans.). 1996. *Nieuhof Kanda Keralam* (*The Kerala that Nieuhof Saw*). Thiruvananthapuram: Kerala Gazateers Department.

Smith, Robertson. 1907. *Kinship and Marriage in Early Arabia*, Stanley A. Cook (ed.). London: Adam and Charles Black.

Spivak, Gayatri Chakravorty. 1988. *In Other Worlds: Essays in Cultural Politics*. New York: Routledge.

Sreedhara Menon, A. 1987. *Kerala Samskaram (Kerala Culture)*. Kottayam: SPCS.

———. 1988. *Kerala Charithra Silppikal (The Makers of Kerala History)*. Kottayam: SPCS.

———. 2007. *A Survey of Kerala History*. Kotayam: DC.

———. 2008. 'Samskarika Pashchathalam' ('The Cultural Background'. In Panmana Ramachandhran Nair (ed.), *Sampoorna Malayala Sahitya Charithram (A Comprehensive History of Malayalam Literature)*, 181–95. Kottayam: Current.

Sreekumar, Sharmila. 2009. *Scripting Lives: Narratives of 'Dominant Women' in Kerala*. Hyderabad: Orient BlackSwan.

Strasser, Ulrike. 2004. 'Early Modern Nuns and the Feminist Politics of Religion'. *The Journal of Religion* 84 (4), 529–54.

Sunder Rajan, Rajeswari. 2003. *The Scandal of the State: Women, Law, and Citizenship in Postcolonial India*. New Delhi: Permanent Black.

Tagore, Soumyendranath. 1982. *Peasant Revolt in Malabar, 1921*, K. K. N. Kurup (trans.). Calicut: Sandhya.

Tejani, Shabnum. 2007. *Indian Secularism: A Social and Intellectual History: 1890–1950*. Ranikhet: Permanent Black.

Thaha, Muthana (comp.). 2007. *Vakkom Abdul Khadarinu G-yude Kathukal (G's Letters to Vakkom Abdul Khadar)*. Thiruvananthapuram: Kerala Bhasha Institute.

Thankamma Malik, M. 1958. 'Prathikaram' (*Vengeance*). *Ansari* September, 14–17.

Tharamel, Umar. 2006. *Isalukalude Udyanam: Mappilapattukal (The Garden of Rhythms: Mappila Songs)*. Chengannur: Rainbow.

———. 2007. 'Pinjippoya Edukal: Thula Veena Navodhaana Vyavahaarangal' ('Tattered Folios: Flawed Discourses on Renaissance'). *Mathrubhoomi Weekly* September, 23–29.

Tharu, Susie. 1996. 'The Impossible Subject: Caste and the Gendered Body'. *Economic and Political Weekly* 1 June, 1311–15.

———. 2009. 'Tracing Savitri's Pedigree: Victorian Racism and Image of Women in Indo-Anglian Literature'. In Kumkum Sangari and Sudesh Vaid (eds), *Recasting Women: Essays in Colonial History*, 254–68. New Delhi: Zubaan.

Tharu, Susie, and K. Lalitha (eds). 2006. *Women Writing in India*, 2 vols. New Delhi: Oxford University Press.

Tharu, Susie, and Tejaswini Niranjana. 1996. 'Problems for a Contemporary Theory of Gender'. In Shahid Amin and Dipesh Chakrabarty (eds), *Subaltern Studies IX: Writings on South Asian History and Society*. New Delhi: Oxford University Press.

Trivedi, Harish, et al. (eds). 2007. *The Nation across the World: Postcolonial Literary Representations*. New Delhi: Oxford University Press.

Turabi, Hasan. 1993. *Women in Islam and Muslim Society*. London: Milestones.

Turner, Bryan S. (ed.). 2003a. *Islam: Critical Concepts in Sociology*, Vol. 1, *Islam as Religion and Law*. London: Routledge.

———. 2003b. *Islam: Critical Concepts in Sociology*, Vol. 4, *Islam and Social Movements*. London: Routledge.

Ubaid, T. 1991. 'Mahakavi Moinkutty Vaidyar'. *Kerala State Mappila Song Lovers Association: Fifteenth Annual Souvenir* November, 41–43.

Uberoi, Patricia. 2009. *Freedom and Destiny: Gender, Family, and Popular Culture in India*. New Delhi: Oxford University Press.

Umri, Sayed Jalaluddin. 2000. *The Rights of Muslim Woman: An Appraisal*. New Delhi: Markazi Maktaba Islami.

Utas, Bo (ed.). 1983. *Women in Islamic Societies: Social Attitudes and Historical Perspectives*, Studies on Asian Topics 6. London: Curzon.

Vallikkunnu, Balakrishnan. 2008. *Mappila Sahithyavum Muslim Navodhanavum* (*Mappila Literature and Muslim Renaissance*). Calicut: Yuvatha.

Van Der Veer, Peter. 2006. *Imperial Encounters: Religion and Modernity in India and Britain*. New Delhi: Permanent Black.

'Vanitha Sammelanam' ('Women's Conference'). *Al Manar* 5 April 1961, 351–56.

Vatuk, Sylvia. 2005. 'Muslim Women and Personal Law'. In Zoya Hasan and Ritu Menon (eds), *In a Minority: Essays on Muslim Women in India*, 18–68. New Delhi: Oxford University Press.

———. 2008. 'Islamic Feminism in India: Indian Muslim Women Activists and the Reform of Muslim Personal Law'. *Modern Asian Studies* 42 (2–3), 489–518.

Vijayan, M. N. (ed.). 2000. *Nammude Sahityam Nammude Samooham 1901–2000* (*Our Literature, Our Society 1901–2000*), Vol. 2. Thrissur: Kerala Sahitya Akademi.

Vijayasree, C., et al. (eds). 2007. *Nation in Imagination: Essays on Nationalism, Sub-Nationalisms and Narration*. Hyderabad: Orient Longman.

Viswanathan, Gauri. 2001. *Outside the Fold: Conversion, Modernity, and Belief*. New Delhi: Oxford University Press.

———. 2002. *Masks of Conquest: Literary Study and British Rule in India*. New Delhi: Oxford University Press.

Wadud, Amina. 1999. *Qur'an and Woman: Rereading the Sacred Text from a Woman's Perspective*. New York: Oxford University Press.

Wadud, Amina. 2007. *Inside the Gender Jihad: Women's Reform in Islam.* Oxford: Oneworld.

Wiertsema, Wiert. 1984. 'The Caste System and the Hindus and Muslims of Kerala'. *Journal of Kerala Studies* 11 (1–4), 81–99.

Women Make Movies (WMM). 2011. *Invoking Justice,* A documentary by Deepa Danraj.

Wollstonecraft, Mary. 1996. *Vindication of the Rights of Woman.* New York: Dover.

Yesudasan, T. M. 2010. *Baliyadukalude Vamsavali (Genealogy of the Scapegoats).* Thiruvananthapuram: Prabhat.

Zacharia, Scaria. 1992. 'Amukha Padanam' ('Critical Introduction'). In Hermann Gundert (ed.), *Keralolpathiyum Mattum,* xiii–lxvii. Kottayam: DC.

Zaidi, Syed M. H. 1937. *The Muslim Womanhood in Revolution.* Calcutta: Syed.

Zainuddin Makhdum, Shaykh. 2006. *Tuhfat al-Mujahidin: A Historical Epic of the Sixteenth Century,* S. Muhammad Husayan Nainar (trans.). Kuala Lumpur: Islamic Book Trust.

Index